BARBARA MAILER WASSERMAN

Love Of My Life

ARBITRARY PRESS
New York

First published by Arbitrary Press 2021

Copyright © 2021 by Barbara Mailer Wasserman

Barbara Mailer Wasserman asserts the moral right to be identified as the author of this work.

First edition

ISBN: 978-1-73-473413-3

This book was professionally typeset on Reedsy.
Find out more at reedsy.com

To Eden

Contents

Preface

This book is not an autobiography. It is a book of stories about people and places in my life, each story usually triggered, if not by Proust's madeleine, at least by something heard or seen. Since some of the memoirs cover many years, or more than one period in my life, I present them not chronologically, but more or less in the order in which they were written.

My friend Barbara Probst Solomon once wrote of me that I had the air of someone who thought everything was going to turn out all right. Although I've had my share of miseries, disappointments and regrets, I think, for the most part, she was right. Most of the time I do feel like that.

There is a theory put forth by Otto Rank, the early 20th-century psychoanalyst, that our natures are much determined by the birth trauma, and that the difficulty or ease of one's birth has a profound effect on our temperament. My mother always said that my birth was easy, that I just popped out (in contrast to my brother, who was a breach case and whose birth was agonizing).

As an adult, I've sometimes had dreams of falling through the air, which is probably a replay of my birth. They're a bit frightening until either I land or the fall stops and I am all right. Mother liked to tell a story of coming into my room when I was still an infant and discovering that the bottom of my crib had dropped to the floor. Finding me fully awake but utterly calm and peaceful, she was astonished that I hadn't cried. But why cry when I had landed safely and was unharmed? Perhaps that is why even when I haven't been happy, I have always enjoyed being alive.

While all of the stories here are about events in my life, much of what I've experienced is not in these pages. Some of the people most important to me, particularly my son and his family, my stepchildren and step-grandchildren, my nieces and nephews, my best and oldest friends, appear only peripherally, or not at all. If there is a connecting thread in these pages, it is not one that ties together the entirety of my existence but rather one that gives a sense, however incomplete, of some of the people I have loved, places I have gone, and things I have done.

Barbara Mailer Wasserman, May, 2021

Spain, 1948

T he screening ends, the lights go on, the theatre empties. I want to join the exodus but I am trapped in my seat. By questions. The women sitting beside me want to know more. The film we have just seen is Barbara Probst Solomon's *When The War Was Over*, an autobiographical meditation in which the pivotal point is a trip to Spain that she and I made together in 1948, a trip that might be quaintly described as a derring-do adventure.

My friends want details. Who were the guys? How did we get them out of prison? Did our parents know what we were up to? And most of all, how did we have the guts to do what we did? It is hard to respond to an accusation of heroism. I am tempted to say that we were just dumb. This is clearly insufficient, so I try to explain that what I most remember half a century later is not any fear I may have felt, but that I was too preoccupied with a bout of the *turistas* to worry much about getting caught. They think I am being flippant and are more exasperated than amused.

They let me go at last. But in my mind, the conversation continues. It has been a long while since I have given much thought to that time. The years have layered over the event until it is deep in a substratum of my personal history. Now bits of memory begin to surface, shards

1

and snippets of images I didn't know were still there. Before I realize what is happening, I am digging down. I am excavating my past.

In the spring of 1948, I sailed to Europe for the first time. My father, an accountant, was in Paris, working for the Joint Distribution Committee, an organization involved in the resettlement of people displaced by the war. My mother was going over to join him. My brother, Norman, and his wife, Bea, had been there since the previous fall, studying at the Sorbonne on the GI Bill.

It was taken for granted by all of us that I, too, would go to Paris. Having graduated from Radcliffe the year before, I was living in my parents' home in Brooklyn, since my mother considered it highly improper for me to live anywhere else. I chafed at this. I wanted to be on my own. But to go to Europe would be the realization of a dream that, as a child of the Depression, I had had no large expectation of fulfilling. It never occurred to me to stay behind. Indeed, I even agreed to go first-class, much as that offended my social conscience. Mother's passage, however, was being paid by my father's employer and she was not about to renounce her first opportunity to travel in style.

In Paris, Mother found an apartment in an *haute bourgeois* building on the Right Bank. Because Parisian rents had been frozen at prewar levels, the chic woman who owned the building could only make ends meet by renting her own apartment to Americans, although what we paid was no more than our modest rent in Brooklyn. She moved in with a friend and we moved into Louis XV elegance. There was no refrigerator. Perishables were maintained for a day or two in an open-air closet built into the kitchen wall. And we were advised to run our hot water tank only at night and bathe only once a week if we did not want exorbitant electric bills. We compromised and took only half as many baths as we were used to. I found the lack of customary amenities part of the charm. In fact, the hot baths and the relative luxury in which we were living made me feel somewhat deprived. I hankered for the public baths where Norman and Bea went once a week because, like most of their friends, they had no hot water at all.

But that was a standard living condition, and even on the GI Bill, Americans were better off than most of the French. Indeed, it was extraordinary to be an American in Europe in those early post-war years when we were still looked upon as saviors. It was possibly the only time in history when one could be both rich and loved. Even the French treated us with a modicum of affection.

I soon gravitated to the Left Bank and the friends Norman and Bea had made in their six months in Paris. Among them were a group of anti-Franco Spanish students, exiles, and refugees. Some of them had fled Spain to avoid arrest for political activity. Others were the children of defeated Spanish Republican leaders who had died or escaped to South America ten years earlier. Some hardly remembered Spain, but they all wanted to return. Frustrated in this basic desire, and eager for even a tenuous sense of connection with their homeland, they were still talking about the car trip to Spain that Norman and Bea had made before I arrived.

Ah, the car! Desperate for dollars, the French were selling almost all the automobiles they produced to any foreigner who could fork over a thousand dollars. The only model available—the *quatre chevaux* Peugeot—was a small vehicle with cross-eyed headlights and a rear-wheel contour that intruded so far into the frame that in the back seat you had to sit with one haunch high. And as I was to learn, four horses is not a lot of power. However, the Peugeot presented one advantage. One could at any time sell it to a Frenchman for more than one had paid. So, Norman bought a car.

The Spaniards talked to him about pulling off a coup. They wanted to spring some of their friends in Spain who had been imprisoned for political activity. They hoped to get them out of the country. An American-owned car could be a formidable weapon.

3

Particularly persuasive was Paco Benet Goitia. A bright 21-year-old, very intellectual and passionately anti-Franco, he was the only one of the Spanish students who was not a refugee and could therefore travel back and forth. He also had a network of contacts in the small world of anti-Franco resistance that still simmered inside Spain. He would accompany Norman and Bea. They decided to go.

They smuggled in some anti-Franco leaflets, stashed inside the springs of the back seat and in the deflated spare tire. The literature was handed over to some of Paco's friends in Barcelona, but when they got to Madrid, Paco found that circumstances were not propitious for the escape. Norman and Bea stayed a few days, went to a bullfight, and returned to Paris with their mission unaccomplished.

I arrived shortly after, and in May and June, Beatrice, Norman, and I took to the road—a trip to Mont St. Michel, Brittany, the Loire Valley; then Switzerland and Italy, and back through the south of France. In late June we stopped at the American Express office in Nice and found a mountain of mail that had been forwarded from Paris by our parents. Norman's first novel having been published in May, the reviews were just beginning to reach us. We could hardly believe they were so uniformly favorable. *Time* magazine compared *The Naked and the Dead* to *War and Peace*. Letters from our friends in the States were exultant. We sat in the car, mail on the floor, on the seats, in our laps, reading distractedly as we traded choice items and passed the pieces of paper around. Until Norman offered up still another newspaper clipping. "Gee," he said in a small boy's voice, "I'm first on the *Times* bestseller list." Suddenly we were shrieking with laughter. There we were, tired and grubby from a long day's drive, the little car a mess, and my brother was creating this stir three thousand miles away. It seemed so remote as to be absurd.

By the time we got back to Paris, however, the reality had reached him, and he decided it was time to return to the States.

4

While he and Bea were preparing to leave, Paco learned that the conditions for an escape operation had now improved. Flush with success, Norman decided to donate the Peugeot to the Spanish resistance. However, there was no way the Spaniards could use the car themselves since most of them couldn't go to Spain and Paco didn't drive.

Norman asked me if I would like to go.

He knew I would be thrilled. While I didn't know very much about Spain, I did know that the Spanish Civil War—won by the bad guys—had been one of the catastrophes of our time. Like many other people, I had assumed that once the fascists had been defeated in Germany and Italy, Franco would also be disposed of. However, three years after the war, he remained in power and Spanish refugees were unable to return. Instead of opposing Franco's regime, our government seemed to be supporting it—in the service of the Cold War.

My politics were less militant than romantic. I would have liked to be a nineteenth-century revolutionary. In lieu of that, I had been working for the Progressive Party. And before we left for Europe, I had started an affair with an 'older man' of 38, a journalist and Marxist. For a bon voyage gift, he took me to the left-wing bookstore on Fourth Avenue and bought me a bunch of tracts—Lenin, Stalin, Bukharin, Clara Thompson. I dutifully toted them along to Paris, where, under the prevailing 15-watt bulbs, struggling to keep my eyes open, I even more dutifully read them, all the while resolutely squelching the complaint, even to myself, that it was the most mind-numbing prose I had ever encountered.

In fact, I had found grassroots political activity not much more congenial. But the proposed mission to Spain evoked an entirely different model—the heroism of the resistance movement in France during the Nazi occupation. Just as the Maquis had struggled against the Vichy regime, I would be redressing my government's support

5

of Franco. (Which did not prevent me from believing that my government would bail me out should I get into trouble.)

It seemed there was only one difficulty. Like Paco, I didn't know how to drive. Norman said it was no problem. He would teach me. I should also take along another driver — he suggested Barbara Probst.

At the time Barbara and I hardly knew each other. We had met in April sailing to Europe on the S.S. America, Barbara traveling with her mother, as I was with mine. Our mothers met and liked each other, but I didn't pay a great deal of attention to Barbara because for most of the trip I was deeply involved in a shipboard flirtation. Since Barbara was two years younger than I, had not yet gone to college, and was still a virgin, I suspect I saw her as not quite my peer. In Paris, however, we began to see something of each other. What I did not recognize at the time was that this pretty, privileged nineteen-year-old, whose take on things sometimes seemed to me a bit fuzzy, had come to Europe possessed by an iron determination to engage the world. She was as eager to go to Spain as I was. And she had a driver's license.

As for learning to drive, I was less sanguine than Norman. I didn't tell him that a year earlier a friend had given me a couple of lessons which had been a total fiasco. I hadn't understood why I couldn't seem to turn a corner at less than thirty miles an hour, but after climbing a couple of curbs I had decided to call it quits. The residue was a year of bad dreams. The night before Norman's first lesson I had one last nightmare in which I was forced to drive a car.

He took me to a short empty stretch of road, explained a few things about the way a car worked, then made me practice starting and stopping until moving my foot from the gas to the brake was automatic. Only then did he begin on the intricacies of the clutch and how to shift gears without stalling. At last, I understood what my problem had been. My friend had been so intent on teaching me the gear shift, he had never really taught me how to stop.

After four lessons, Norman decided I needed a practice run, so I drove the family to Chartres. All went well and he dubbed me a driver.

The license, however, was another problem. My linguistic skill was hardly up to a French driving test. We decided to use Norman's international license. Substituting my picture for his, we clumsily erased his first name and wrote in mine. It was probably worse than useless.

Naturally, we did not tell our parents about the purpose of the trip to Spain. I'm astonished now that they asked no questions and expressed no concern about my ability to take a long road trip so soon after learning to drive. Of course, Mother, though a woman of great energy and competence, didn't drive at all. And Dad, always a bit baffled by the used Chevvies we had owned during the Depression, preferred to leave the driving to others. Perhaps they thought of driving as something young people just did. Or perhaps, for once, they were so deeply enmeshed in their own lives that they weren't paying a great deal of attention. We were all giddy with Europe. Since they were going off to the fjords of Norway, they may have thought it only fair that I too should be setting out to explore another country.

One task remained before Norman's departure—to change the ownership of the Peugeot. With three days left before his boat sailed, Norman and I entered the Kafkaesque world of French red tape. Nobody could believe that he was giving me the car. No bureaucrat wanted any part of it. They sent us from one office to another, and of course, the offices were always closing for lunch. At the end of three days, we were still on square one. As I remember, Norman gave me a letter signing over the car. Then Barbara and I spent the next week, all day, every day, trying in vain to get the registration changed.

One day Barbara was out with the car and got arrested for illegal parking. Since she didn't have a registration, the magistrate wanted to call me. Afraid I would be alarmed if she didn't call me herself, she refused to give him my number. Hearing the story afterward, I was greatly impressed—particularly since her French accent was as American as mine. But she didn't give a hoot about errors of pronunciation or grammar, an arrogance that had the effect of disarming French contempt. She said to the official, "*Vous ne m'aidez pas, je ne vous aide pas.*" (You don't help me, I don't help you.) He finally gave in or gave up. She called me and we got it sorted out. And found a bit of good fortune. Someone we met in the court that day, to whom we told the story of our troubles, suggested we contact an organization, a French equivalent of the American Automobile Association, that would, for a fee, arrange for the change of registration. I remember he said, "*C'est moins cher aussi.*" Indeed he was right—it was cheaper. And within 48 hours I was the official owner of the car.

At the end of July, Barbara, Paco, and I left for Spain.

In 1948, traveling through France by car was perpetual bliss. The sky was soft, the air fragrant, and the scenery, unlike any I had known before, changed constantly — through *allees* of trees into the narrow streets of old towns; from the geometric patterns of perfectly manicured farm fields to the kind of heart-stirring mountain ravines I had seen only in nineteenth-century landscape paintings. Everything from the thick stone walls to the black dresses of the women was wonderfully old. I believed it would stay like that forever. The main routes were two-lane roads that meandered through the countryside from town to village and never avoided a city. On the other hand, there were very few cars on the road, so no traffic jams—unless one got caught behind a farmer in a horse-drawn wagon.

The quatre chevaux Peugeot was well suited to all of this. Its cruising speed was no more than 50 miles an hour. But since the road signs and the maps and the speedometer were in kilometers, we were traveling at 80 on the European scale, and this seemed quite fast enough. The tough part was the mountains and the weather. At night we kept running into fog. And in the mountains, one never knew if our underpowered car would make it up and around the next hairpin turn. I often felt as if I were coaxing a balky pet, and the intimacy I developed with that car in the course of the next two weeks has made me ever since prefer small cars on back roads.

As I recall, we reached the south of France in a day and a night of driving. We had taken along a couple of friends—a penniless painter and his girlfriend. It was August, so like everyone in France, penniless or not, they were going on vacation. Since they could not afford even the cheapest hotel, we all went without a bed. Instead, we traveled through the night. I still have a vivid image of hunching over the wheel while I peered into a mist so thick that the car lights could penetrate but a few feet and a ghostly hint of trees was my only clue to the shoulder of the road.

We dropped our friends off in Hendaye and proceeded to the border. The contraband leaflets stuffed into the back seat of the car made us a bit nervous as we approached the Spanish side, and we probably overdid our nonchalance during the few anxious minutes it took to stamp our passports. No sooner were we into Spain than Paco informed us that we were going to visit his mother who was vacationing near St. Sebastian.

Given the purpose of our trip, it seemed to me unfitting to visit one's mother. I realize now he probably wanted to pick up the key to her Madrid apartment. Besides, he hadn't seen her for some months. Indeed, as I looked at the ocean from the lovely promenade along the beach in San Sebastian, I was struck for the first time by the double-edged reality I was inhabiting. I knew I looked just like any other tourist. And I loved the ocean. But given my sense of mission, I had no desire to join the swimmers on the beach.

For a couple of hours, we sat in an arbored garden with Paco's mother and his brother, Juan. Their mother was a beautiful woman of much

9

presence. Juan seemed dark and brooding and not nearly as good-looking as Paco. Because I was told Juan was nineteen, I thought of him as still a kid (after all, he was half the age of my lover in New York). Meeting him again after he had become a major Spanish novelist and a stunning 50-year-old man, I was startled to discover that he had been very taken with me those thirty years earlier, when, with the heedlessness of a 21-year-old, I had so blithely ignored him.

Of course, no conversation was easy. Barbara and I spoke no Spanish. Neither Paco nor anyone else we met in Spain spoke English. All communication, except between Barbara and myself, was in French. Paco's French was fluent, and since he loved to spin out convoluted theories, I seldom understood what he was talking about. At the time I thought it was due to the language barrier, but a few years later when he came to America and learned English, I was still never sure we were speaking the same language. All the same, he was very attractive. Fair and downy-cheeked, his boyish good looks were spiced by the manly slash of dark bushy eyebrows that ran across his forehead. I always liked him, but we were on different wavelengths. As later events would prove, Barbara didn't have this problem.

For me, that was one of the strangest things about the trip. I felt enormously involved with the people I traveled with, but never felt any real rapport. Even Barbara and I did not begin to become close friends until twenty years later. To some extent this was no doubt due to the mental blinders I wore at the time. There were only two things that seemed really important to me—falling in love and saving the world. And since I didn't fall in love with Paco, I concentrated only on the job at hand—getting the guys—*les types*, as we soon began to call them—out of jail and out of Spain. What astonishes me now is the total confidence I had that Paco and his friends could handle the details. I knew that things might not work out because of forces beyond our control, but it never occurred to me that somebody might screw up.

After leaving Paco's mother we drove to Madrid, arriving so late that Paco put us up in his mother's apartment, where he would be staying. We took the car seat in too, so we could empty out the "literature". Barbara and I slept on sofas in the living room, and I remember waking the next morning to the sight of sheet-shrouded furniture and an El Greco on the wall above me. Clearly, Paco's family was not poverty-stricken. In fact, it turned out that we were in the neighborhood of the Prado and the Ritz, and later that day Barbara and I moved across the plaza into the Palace Hotel which was then considered the best hotel in the city (the Ritz was closed). The Palace was being renovated and was almost as empty of guests as the roads were of cars. We paid the enormous sum of four dollars a night for the room.

The prospect of having a bed and a bath was delicious. While I luxuriated on the bed, Barbara went to run a bath in the huge tub. A minute later she came out, laughing with dismay and holding the cold water handle. It had come off in her hand and she couldn't stop the flow of water. We called the desk, where English supposedly was spoken and were told that someone would come. No one did. Meanwhile, the water was gushing fast, the tub was almost full. We called again, this time in French. Again no one arrived. By now the water was spilling over to the floor of the bathroom. When it began to flood the room, we waded out in bare feet and closed the door. Still, no one came and the water started seeping into the hall. I ran down the several flights of stairs to the front desk. My bare feet and English/French frenzy caused a slight ripple of shock in the management. They promised action. I ran back up the stairs to discover that the hall had become a lake. By the time a sweet little man with a wrench appeared, the water was creating havoc in other rooms, but he seemed hugely delighted by us and the mess. *"Mucha agua fresca,"* he kept saying as he opened a little hatch in the wall and turned the water off. He had no sooner

11

left than all kinds of help arrived and we were moved to another floor. I no longer remember whether either of us dared to take a bath that day.

Indeed, I remember surprisingly little about the week we spent in Madrid. We arrived on Sunday and left the following Sunday, thus frustrating Paco's wish to take us to a bullfight—the *corridas* were held only on Sundays. I would have liked to see a bullfight (having read all of Hemingway and not yet forgotten the movie Blood and Sand, seen ten years before when I had a schoolgirl crush on Tyrone Power). But it hardly seemed important. Given the purpose of our trip, I tended to regard Paco's eagerness to expose us to Spanish culture as touchingly superfluous. Most of the time there wasn't much else for us to do, and I realized when he took us to the Prado that he had a point. I was mesmerized by the Goyas.

I also realized that I liked the Spanish people. Although I had arrived in Europe with an early case of political correctness which considered the stereotyping of any ethnic group an act of bigotry, I soon discovered that 'national character' was not entirely a myth. Unlike the French, the Spanish were friendly, and unlike the Italians, they seemed more dignified in their poverty. I sensed in them a reserve and pride that made me feel they acted out of genuine curiosity and goodwill rather than in the hope of currying goods or favor. In a time when the other countries of Western Europe were struggling back to a semblance of past position and future affluence, Spain was out of the loop. For most Spaniards, life was probably not much different from what it had been fifty or a hundred years earlier. Barbara and I must have looked to them like apparitions from another planet. Two young women—girls rather, wearing clothes (light summer skirts and off-the-shoulder peasant blouses) that looked like nobody else's, and roaming around unchaperoned, going to nightclubs where men took only their mistresses. Paco explained that what we called dating was still not done in Spain. No doubt a number of people viewed us disapprovingly, but most seemed puzzled, even delighted. Paco, having lived in Paris, was fairly sophisticated, but I remember a friend of his—another young man from a well-to-do family — who often joined us. When we went to a nightclub his eyes sparkled wickedly and he kept saying that he was going to "rrropp" me. He had a few words of English, most of which were unintelligible, and it wasn't until years later that it finally dawned on me that he'd meant "rape." I suspect he didn't quite understand the meaning of the word since his behavior was otherwise "perfectly proper."

One day Paco took us to meet some people who were too poor to afford any regular housing and lived in caves on the outskirts of the city. It was a hot, barren place, devoid of grass or trees. While Paco went inside a cave to confer, the two American girls waiting outside were objects of curiosity to the children who milled around. I was filled with pity for a life I could not quite imagine, and with shame for feeling grateful that it wasn't mine. It was the first time I experienced that dichotomous sentiment, which now often gets evoked on the streets of New York.

The family living in the cave was harboring a man who had just broken out of prison and, as I later learned, Paco's purpose in going there was to propose that he join our escape party. He refused. Sick and skeptical, he didn't believe we'd make it. He was caught soon after and died in prison.

When he wasn't shepherding us around, Paco was making arrangements through his contacts. We did not inquire closely into the details. It was agreed that the less Barbara and I knew, the better. In case things went wrong. Toward the end of the week, we learned that the plan was a "Go". We would leave on Sunday.

The guys we were going to free were in a forced labor camp about 30 miles northwest of Madrid. The camp's inmates, many of whom were

13

there for their anti-Franco activities, were being used to construct the monument in the Valley of the Fallen that was to be both Franco's future tomb and a memorial to his soldiers who had died in the Civil War. While their politics were being thus punished and their bodies exploited, this was a Catholic country and the prisoners were encouraged to save their souls. On Sunday, they would be going to noon Mass at the Escorial, just a few miles from the labor camp. I wondered but did not ask how we were going to hook up with them.

Sunday morning arrived. Barbara and I checked out of the hotel. Paco put our bags in the trunk of the car and threw into the back seat a package containing two sets of men's clothing. He was also carrying two sets of false papers.

We reached the Escorial well before noon. As we wandered through corridors and rooms and gazed at paintings, Paco would occasionally disappear to case the situation, and I believe he cached the packet of clothes in a bathroom. But most of the time he spent giving us a guided tour of the art, architecture and history of the Escorial, an enormous palace complex built in the sixteenth century by Philip II to house not only the royal quarters, but a museum, a library, a mausoleum, a monastery, and a very large chapel. Perhaps Paco's purpose was to make us look like tourists for the benefit of anyone who might see us. But as always, with regard to things Spanish, his lecture was genuinely enthusiastic. I absorbed none of it.

At last, he told us to go back to the car and wait. Barbara sat in front, I sat in back, as Paco had instructed. The sun was hot. The air was dry. The oppressive bulk of the Escorial stretched endlessly along the empty street. Not a soul. Silence. I was beginning to think it just possible we might never see Paco again when he emerged through the entrance door with *les types*. Whatever we might have been expecting, it was a shock to see three college boys sauntering down the steps looking like—three college boys.

Les types, Nicolas and Manolo, jammed into the back with me. Just how they separated themselves from the other prisoners I'm not sure. Presumably, they got permission to go to the bathroom, where they changed into the clothes Paco had left for them. Paco jumped into the front seat. "*Vite, vite, vite,*" he said, and we were off, laughing a little hysterically. It all seemed so simple, so unremarkable. Not unlike a jaunt to the beach.

Les types and I looked at each other, smiling with the helpless amiability of strangers who have no language in common. They knew no English or French. Conversation had to be mediated through Paco, which made every question or comment weightier than one may have intended. And though I wasn't aware of it then, it was my first experience of how difficult it can be to talk to people with whom you have in common no friends, no work, no past.

Perhaps for that reason, I was acutely conscious of sitting thigh to thigh with two young men who had just spent a couple of years in prison and for whom this must be the first physical contact with a woman since they had been arrested. I felt they were as uncomfortable as I was.

Although Paco did not speak English, he did know a couple of words, which he kept using incorrectly. He always said, "Right," when he meant straight ahead, and "*Stret* ahead," when he wanted us to turn right. So we had to keep double-checking his directions. Or ignoring him when he would cry out, "*Vite, vite, vite,*" every time we saw a Guardia Civil. We knew it would have looked suspicious if we had speeded up, even if we could have, which usually we couldn't because we were already going as fast as four horsepower could carry five people.

We were stopped a few times, but the false papers worked. The guards seemed to find us curious, yet not suspicious. Whether this was because Barbara and I were American, or because we looked like a

15

bunch of rich kids, I do not know. After we passed Madrid there were few checkpoints. And almost as few cars.

We began to talk about lunch. Paco suggested an excellent restaurant that we would soon be approaching. It was a few miles off the road, but it had, he promised, a spectacular view. We were hungry and it seemed like a good idea to hide in an elegant establishment where no one back at the prison would think to look.

Then the accident happened.

Barbara was still driving. We were in the mountains, the road climbing, dipping, curving. Suddenly we went into a skid, careened a bit, and ended up, fortunately, sliding into the mountain rather than off it. The car jumped a small rock and stopped.

We were pretty shaken up, particularly when we looked at the sheer drop at the other side of the road. But we weren't hurt. We lifted the car back onto the road and to our relief, the motor started. But we soon realized something was seriously wrong. The tires squealed continuously, even on straightaways, as if the car were in a never-ending curve that it was taking too fast. Since it was still hundreds of miles to Barcelona, we decided we better find out what the problem was. We stopped at the first town that had a service station. They only sold gas but told us there was a good mechanic in a village a couple of miles up the mountain. We turned off the road. The car wheezed and shrieked up a rutted and rock-strewn dirt path. Less than a half-mile into it, I felt as far from civilization as the moon, and the village we finally arrived at looked as if it had grown from a landscape as barren. The mechanic, it turned out, was the local expert on oxcart repairs. Our arrival was possibly the most exciting event of the year.

My urban middle-class prejudices and assumptions surfaced quickly. I was more appalled than impressed by the way they raised the car and diagnosed the damage. With only one jack, they hoisted up each wheel, then piled stones under it so they could free the jack to raise another.

16

A couple of times the stones slipped and the hubs came down with an ominous clang, but eventually, the whole car was raised and all the tires removed. By now the entire village population was circling the car, and someone pointed out the problem. One of the connecting rods between the axle and a wheel had been bent into a right angle. After a little discussion, none of which I could understand, the "mechanic" got an iron mallet and began to hammer the part back into shape. I could hardly believe what was happening. And I couldn't bear the sound. It was a little like watching a friend get his leg sawed off. I walked away with my hands over my ears, sure the axle would break and we would be stranded.

I was wrong. Primitive surgery worked. *La direction*, as the wheel alignment was called, was hammered pretty much into place, and we set off. But having lost a couple of hours, we gave up on the elegant lunch. I don't remember what, where, or if we ate, but my stomach, which had been suffering from occasional *turistas* all week, began to kick up again. For the rest of the drive to Barcelona, I worried not about the Guardia Civil so much as I lived in fear that I would be humiliated by my own gut. It was long after dark when we stopped for dinner at a local cantina in a small town. I tried using the privy in back but was routed by the dirt and the smell. At some point that night I think I simply took the only remaining option and squatted in a field.

Driving was infinitely preferable to sitting three in back, and Barbara and I took turns. As the night wore on, I tried to sleep while she drove, but only managed to nod off for a few minutes at a time. Therefore, at three in the morning, when Barbara turned the wheel over to me again, I was bleary. Not quite awake, I drove. And drove. I don't know which was more agonizing—trying to keep my eyes open or trying to control my sphincter. Comparing notes thirty-nine years later, when Barbara and I were once again traveling together through

17

Spain, she discovered for the first time that I had been more afraid of embarrassing myself than of landing in a Spanish jail, and I learned that she had been in a lowgrade state of terror through all the hours in the mountains because she was afraid of heights.

Everyone else fell asleep and the car was deathly quiet. However, I managed to open my eyes often enough to stay on the road until daybreak, when I had the sense to tell Barbara to take over again. Paco, who was getting a little nervous about how far a police alert would have reached by this time, decided we should turn south on a back road and enter Barcelona by way of Tarragona. This route was barely distinguishable from a cross-country trail, and as the car bumped along those last couple of hours, I lapsed into a miasma of half-sleep, waiting for the next sick spasm, and only vaguely aware that Paco was helping another very sleepy Barbara to steer.

We reached Barcelona around mid-morning. I remember waiting on a little beach while Paco went to look for a safe house. He found something for the guys and himself. Barbara and I went to a hotel on the Ramblas. It was sheer happiness to find myself in a room with a private bath.

The next day Paco took us all up to the unfinished Gaudi cathedral. He was very proud of it and expounded for a while on its architectural significance. Contemptuous as I was then of any esthetic of modern architecture which did not adhere to the Bauhaus, I'm afraid I didn't appreciate the building. I did like the setting—a lovely wild hillside. I seem to remember that we brought along a picnic lunch which we ate while we studied the map on which Paco had outlined the escape route. While he remained in Barcelona, the rest of us would leave later that afternoon and travel north. About 30 miles before the French border we would come to the first of four checkpoints. They would look at our passports and I.D.s, list all our names on an official form which we would have to show at each checkpoint, and which would be collected from us at the last one, just before we reached the Spanish border town of Puigcerda. Between the third and fourth checkpoints—Paco gave us the exact mileage — the road ran for a bit along the border. At that point, all that separated Spain from France was a high hill. Nicolas and Manolo were to get off there (by this time it would be well past dark), go over the hill, and, *voila*, they would be free. Barbara and I were to stay the night in Puigcerda, then cross in the morning to Bourg-Madame on the French side. From there a back road in the mountains would take us to the village of Osseja, which, as the crow flies, was not more than five kilometers from where the guys would have left the car. With any luck, they would be there waiting for us by the time we arrived. Then we would all drive to Paris.

Amazingly, it almost worked. We said goodbye to Paco and started out. At the first checkpoint, we held our breaths but had no trouble getting the necessary piece of paper. We even had a giggle when we discovered that they had listed Barbara as Great Marsh, the name of her family's home in Westport. Near midnight we reached the stretch of road at which to debark. We slowed the car. To the right, the hill loomed but did not look impassable. We turned off the headlights, stopping for a moment. Goodbyes were hurried. The guys got out and for a brief moment before they disappeared I saw them scurrying up through the brush.

Barbara and I continued, driving very slowly, wanting to give them as much time as possible before our arrival at the last checkpoint set off an alarm. We were to say we hadn't known the guys, had simply given them a lift and they had wanted to get off.

Barbara said thoughtfully, "Let's try not to give them the paper. Let's pretend we don't understand."

The checkpoint was manned by two young soldiers. They may have been even younger than we were. We just kept speaking English and shrugging our shoulders. They began to laugh. Two girls. In the middle of the night! Driving a car! Americans! We laughed too. And finally, as if we understood what they were asking for, we handed them a partially used pack of cigarettes that we had. At that moment my admiration for the Spanish went up another notch. Instead of taking the whole pack, as we had meant and expected, they each took one cigarette, handed back the pack, and waved us on. I've sometimes thought of those two boys and hoped they did not get into trouble because they did not obtain that official piece of paper.

We drove into Puigcerda giddy with relief. And with exhaustion setting in. Driving slowly through the deserted streets, we searched vainly for a hotel. At last, we saw one lone soul and stopped to inquire. He took a look at us and his eyes lit up with that by now familiar gleam of curiosity and goodwill. He must have spoken French since we were able to communicate. It would be difficult, he said, because at this time of year the few hotels were crowded, but he would help. Dismissing our invitation to get into the car, he hopped onto the side, and canted out like a figurehead, he waved his free arm to direct us from one hotel to another. It was nice to see him enjoy himself so much, but indeed all the hotels were full. When he had no more suggestions and we were contemplating sleeping in the car once again, we noticed another Hotel sign down the street. What about that one?

He looked unhappy. They'd probably have room, but we really didn't want to stay there, he said. We said anything would do. Reluctantly, he went in to inquire and came back with the news that yes, we could have a room—pay in advance.

The hotel was seedy. As we climbed the stairs we heard voices and squeals, doors opening and closing. "A whorehouse," Barbara said. Which made us giggle. Until we saw that the sheets on the bed were filthy with the remnants of numerous couplings as well as a few squashed bugs. I couldn't care. I lay down and my eyes closed. Barbara tried to wake me, saying, "How can you sleep on this?" But she too finally fell off.

It was not hard to get out early the next morning, and we arrived at the border office as soon as it opened. Here we were told by the customs official that we hadn't changed enough dollars and would not be permitted to leave until we did. Spain's monetary policy at the time required foreign tourists to change something like ten dollars at the official rate for each day spent in the country. Since the official rate was a fraction of the black market rate, and we had been told that the rule was generally not enforced, we had bought only a couple of days worth when we arrived. We tried to plead ignorance, said we'd stayed with friends and hadn't needed much money, and how could we use pesetas now that we were leaving Spain. He knew we were lying and was adamant. We considered going to another border town where we might find a more lenient official, but we didn't want to keep the guys waiting. Already we felt we had wasted too much time. So we changed the money—probably fifty or sixty dollars apiece, a goodly sum at the time. I can't remember what we did with the pesetas.

Then we crossed to Bourg-Madame, and drove on to Osseja.

They weren't there.

It was hard to believe it could take so long to walk a few miles, even in mountainous terrain. A small bud of dread sprouted in my belly.

Thus began the two longest days of my life. I read once that the most difficult part of partisan resistance was not fighting, but waiting. Indeed, the minutes were longer than any I'd ever known. There was nothing to do but wait. Impossible to read. We didn't even talk much. What, after all, was there to talk about when everything else in our lives seemed insignificant? With each hour, I sank a little further into the realization that we might not be living charmed lives. For the first time in my life, I began to recognize that my actions could have enormous consequences not only for myself but for others. Nicolas and Manolo had probably been caught. They might even be dead.

When the waiting became unbearable, we took to the car. We would drive the couple of miles from Osseja to Bourg-Madame, then double back through Osseja and on another couple of miles to the village of Valcebollere, where the road ended. Driving slowly, the whole route took maybe twenty minutes, but it gave us a small sense of action. Most of all, it allowed us the ever-dimming hope that if we did not find the guys on the road, we might find them in Osseja upon our return.

The second day was worse. We decided to call the telephone number in Paris we had been told to contact in case of a problem. We reached Carlos, one of the Spanish refugee students. The connection was terrible, as was usual in Europe in 1948. Finally, we eked out a few instructions. If the guys did not show up, we were to go to an address in Perpignan and say that Juan had sent us. The people there would tell us what to do next. Static surged on what might have been Juan's last name.

Soon after the phone call, Barbara became unaccountably obsessed with a house in Osseja called "Beau Soleil." She kept repeating it over and over and saying, "There's something about that name." I thought she was being a bit peculiar.

On the third day, we gave up waiting and drove to Perpignan. Awful as we felt, it was a relief to be on the road again.

It was dusk when we arrived at the Perpignan address. "Juan" didn't work. The young woman at the door said, "There are lots of Juans." Dismayed, we went off to get some dinner, and as we sat discussing what to do next, Barbara suddenly said, "That house. That's it. I think Carlos said Juan's name is Bellesoleil." Thus armed, we returned to the house, were taken in, and told we must make contact with still another person in another place—Pallach in Collioure, some 20 miles or so down the coast. We set out right away.

I'll never forget the drive to Collioure. There was the intoxicating smell of the sea, and a warm, wild wind blowing through the trees. I would have been euphoric had I not been feeling so wretched. The dichotomy intensified when we reached Collioure. It was a beautiful old walled town, a festival was going on, and it seemed as if the entire population was dancing in the central plaza. What made it particularly poignant was that the band was playing what I thought of as the theme song of that summer in Europe. It was a marvelous bouncy samba that I had heard for the first time on the ocean crossing. We heard it all the time in Paris, and everywhere else we went. I loved it, and despite a dismal musical memory—I may forget the theme of a Mozart sonata I was playing last week—I can still sing Ay Yai Yai Maria.

We soon found our address. I have a memory of climbing several flights of ancient stone stairs to an apartment that seemed dark and bare—in France that year no one but Americans used electricity freely. A pretty but cautious young woman told us that Pallach was out and not expected back for some time. So we wandered aimlessly in the Square, feeling remote from the holiday frenzy around us. To our surprise, Pallach found us — not very many minutes later. It amuses me now to realize how easy it was to spot us in the midst of that throng.

Pallach was somewhat older than we were, and he had a sweet comforting presence. He said there was a good chance the guys had been taken by the French border police, which would mean that they were alive and safe. In the morning he would check through a contact he had, and get word to us. As we drove back to Perpignan we were somewhat more sanguine.

But the news in the morning was not good. Nicolas and Manolo were not in the French internment camp. It was agreed that there was nothing left for us to do. Convinced that the guys had been captured by the Spanish, we drove back to Paris in a blue funk. I remember nothing of the trip, or how long it took, probably no more than a couple of days. I do remember driving into Paris on August 15th or

23

16th, to find the city empty and morgue-like, hushed and melancholy enough to mirror our mood. In the late afternoon, in the late summer light, it was also more beautiful than ever. We had returned on the one weekend of the year when every Parisian leaves town.

Some days later the news came that Nicolas and Manolo were safe in France. Without a compass, they had lost their bearings almost as soon as they left the car. Afraid to travel during the day, they had wandered by night, for all of that week, and probably back and forth across the border. Weak and famished, they finally stumbled onto a road where the signs were in French and they gladly followed it into the arms of the French police. The next few weeks they spent in an internment camp.

Paco, too, had trouble getting out of Spain. The authorities soon traced the escape to him and put out a warrant for his arrest. His mother warned him not to come back to visit her, and, awesome woman that she was, arranged for a small fishing boat to take him back to France.

By the time Paco and Nicolas and Manolo reached Paris, I had returned to New York—to my unfinished romance and to work for the Progressive Party and Henry Wallace's presidential campaign. Eventually, Nicolas went to Argentina to join his father, the President of the Spanish Republic in Exile, and Manolo went to England for a while before he too left for South America.

Barbara remained in Europe for a couple of years. She and Paco became lovers and put out a Spanish exile magazine, Peninsula. Almost twenty-five years later she would write about that time in her memoir, *Arriving Where We Started*.

I never again saw Manolo. Recently, I learned that he had died. And it was twenty years before I met Nicolas again. Barbara called one day and asked if I were free that evening. Nicolas had arrived in New York for the first time and very much wanted me to join them for dinner.

Naturally, I was eager to see him, but having a date for that evening with the man I would soon marry, I suggested the next day. Barbara was most insistent that it could not wait, so I persuaded Al to come along. Nicolas had been married and divorced and was traveling with a "fiancee."

That first meeting was strange. In a way, almost comic. We met at a small Spanish restaurant on Houston Street. Nicolas now spoke English, his lady knew none, and she was, for some reason, furious. I don't think she said a single word throughout the meal, but she was completely successful in throwing up a stone wall between the men and the women. Barbara and I talked nervously to each other—I now understood why she had so badly wanted me to be there—while Nicolas talked to Al the entire time. Al marveled afterward at how odd it was that he, not I, had been the one to spend the evening with Nicolas.

Nicolas eventually married someone else, moved to New York to teach at NYU, and sometime after Franco died went back to Spain. While he lived in New York we would occasionally see each other at parties, but we were never easy with each other and I never asked if he has any regrets about the way he has spent his life. But something Barbara told me has made me wonder. She said there had been a third man in the prison whom Paco had wanted to free, but who had decided not to come with us. He was released a couple of years later and continued to live in Spain. Which of course was what they all wanted — to live in Spain. Instead, Nicolas and Manolo, who had probably expected that they would soon be able to return, spent the next thirty years as exiles. And Paco, who died in an automobile accident in 1966, was never able to go back. So I cannot help but wonder if their lives might have been better if we had not been there to help the guys escape.

The passing of the years has developed my taste for irony, and so

I am not exactly surprised to realize now that this one act in my life about which I have always felt so virtuous, is still subject to a most basic lesson—that one's deeds, no matter one's intentions, almost never result in unambiguous returns. I'm grateful, however, I did not know this fifty years ago. I only knew that given the chance to rescue a couple of political prisoners, I had to go to Spain.

My Date with Randolph Churchill

Recently I read Shirley Hazzard's fine memoir of Graham Greene on Capri. I have always admired Greene as a writer. Hazzard not only admired him but was obviously fond of him as well. However, her honesty about the more unpleasant aspects of his character made me feel that I probably would not have liked him. He had that quintessential rudeness of the upper-class English that always arouses my ire, and it reminded me of an incident squirreled away in my past.

In 1961 or 1962, when my brother, Norman, and Lady Jeanne Campbell had been together for a few months, early one evening I got a phone call. Norman said, "Randolph Churchill's here and we're going out to dinner. Come and join us."

Winston Churchill's son. That was exciting. So I threw myself together and taxied up to East 94th Street where Jeanie was then living.

He was a big man and looked exactly like his father. He was probably in his 50's, possibly older, and by the time I arrived, he'd been drinking for hours. Jeanie, as a correspondent for the London Evening Standard, was saying she really shouldn't go out as a piece was due the next morning. Norman and Randolph said they'd write it for her, and pacing around the room, took turns spouting paragraphs of over-the-top prose.

It didn't occur to me that there might be a macho contest going on. From my seat on a very low divan, no doubt believing I was entering into the spirit of the thing, I injected a few words. What I said may not have been particularly bright. Or perhaps it was, and that was the problem. Randolph stopped talking and walked over to where I was sitting. He loomed over me. So close to the floor, I felt a bit like the camera looking up at Orson Welles as Citizen Kane. If he had wanted to win my heart it was the perfect time to say something gallant. But it's no accident that the concept of *noblesse oblige* comes, not from the English but the French. In his very British accent and biting British contempt, Randolph said, "SHUT. UP."

It was breathtaking. I was indeed struck speechless. However, my rage was evident, because Norman came up to me a few minutes later and said softly, "You're mad, aren't you?"

"I'm not only mad," I muttered back, "I'm going to get even."

Which surprised me, since I had no idea of how I might.

Despite her unwritten piece, Jeanie finally acquiesced to dinner, and off we went to the Stork Club, Randolph's choice, and a pretty tacky one, I thought. I'd been hoping for an elegant French restaurant. When we arrived, I immediately understood: they knew him well and he was much fawned over. Which dropped him another notch in my estimation.

We all drank through dinner but Randolph and I never cozied up enough to talk to each other. After coffee, I excused myself for the ladies' room, and once there felt no compelling desire to return. The telephone looked comfortable, so I called my (somewhat problematic) lover of the time. Not above wishing to give him something to mull, I told him where I was and with whom. He was reluctant to get off the phone and we chatted for half an hour.

When I got back to the table, I was met by two pairs of reproachful eyes. Randolph Churchill had left. In a huff.

"Well," I said, "I guess I did get even."

Jeanie said, "But he's really a pussycat when he's not drunk."

We got up to leave. At the check room a very delighted South American playboy was on the phone, telling a friend, "Randolph Churchill, Randolph Churchill has taken my vicuna coat."

I must explain that vicuna coats, made from the wool of the Andean vicuna, cousin to the llama, were a status symbol of the time. Indeed, just a couple of years before, Sherman Adams, Eisenhower's chief of staff, had been forced to resign because he had accepted one as a gift. Now it seemed that Randolph, too drunk, too angry, or too arrogant to dig his check out of his pocket, had walked off with a new and expensive coat in place of his own ratty old camel hair. And this young man seemed too delighted to care.

I giggled inside, not sure which of them I found more contemptible. But Jeanie was mortified and kept assuring him that she would get his coat back.

I must ask her someday how she arranged for the exchange. And if she turned her article in on time.

Postscript: Recalling this episode after forty years, I'm struck by my own brand of snottiness. It must not have been easy to be Winston Churchill's son, and perhaps if I had met Randolph later in my life, I might have felt a modicum of compassion. So perhaps, after all, like Shirley Hazzard, I might have liked Graham Greene despite his English bloody-mindedness.

Aftermath: I showed this brief tale to half a dozen friends and relatives, all of whom expressed moderate to enthusiastic appreciation. Indeed a couple of them were regretful that Randolph hadn't received more of a comeuppance. I thought the story would amuse Norman as well, and I was curious to see whether his memory of the incident would differ enough to give me a Rashomon-like perspective on it. I sent him a copy. And heard nothing. Finally, I called and asked him if he'd read it. I hadn't heard from him because he hadn't much liked it, though, to my surprise, he said I'd gotten all of the details right. He had no quarrel with that. But he had been fond of Randolph and he thought the tone was wrong, that I was still too angry. He then described to me how visibly Randolph seemed to shrivel as he became convinced that I had left the restaurant, as if he had sunk so low that even a snip of a girl could snub him.

It did not much please me now to discover that my revenge was greater than I had thought. Norman also said that he felt a bit guilty. Perhaps he should in some way have come to my defense. It never occurred to me either then or now that there was anything he could have done. He probably felt as speechless as I did. At the time I was just glad that he recognized my anger. But it set me to thinking about what I might have done myself at the moment of the insult, instead of going into a paralytic rage. The curse of my life—when people are mean to me I'm so shocked I'm frozen. Mother's fault? She loved us so much that as Norman once said, she never taught us how to deal with people who don't. But why have I never learned? There were certainly other options that day. I could have walked out. Or better, I could have retorted right away. In what may be the longest hiatus in the department of "If only I'd said...." I suddenly remember now, 40 years later, a line I'd heard many years before I met Randolph, given by someone else in a similarly outrageous situation. If I'd had the wit to use that line and Randolph had the wit to appreciate it, perhaps the whole tenor of the evening would have changed.

But I'll save the line for the next story—the story of Mr. Yardeny and Mr. Bodkin.

30

Mr. Yardeny and Mr. Bodkin

I n the Spring of 1949, I decided that the only way I could leave my parents' home in Brooklyn, was to leave New York. Under the guise of visiting my friend Adeline in Chicago, I took the overnight train. Coach, naturally. I stayed for several months, working odd jobs—waitress and housing interviewer for the Bureau of Labor Statistics—while writing the first draft of a novel.

The waitress job was in the drug and grill of a midtown hotel, and I think the only reason I was hired since I probably oozed a lack of experience, was because I was the only one to apply. The restaurant had a few booths, but it was primarily counter service, and I managed to make the short-order cook behind the open range immediately detest me because on my first order, in my best polite girl's school voice, I said, "Please, a bacon, lettuce and tomato sandwich on toast." He snarled, "That's a BLT down." I don't think he ever spoke to me again. The senior waitress on the job was nicer. She taught me how to carry two cups of coffee in one hand and said, "I'm going to make a waitress out of you yet." Adeline lived ten miles away from the room I had rented. I did not see her often and I made no other close friends, but I did meet a young woman who was studying sociology at the graduate school of the University of Chicago. She too had worked as a waitress, and she loaned me a book called *Social Relations in the Restaurant Industry*, with a chapter called "Why Waitresses Cry." It was so right on that I managed not to cry on a very bad day. That was the day that all the out-of-town non-tipping folk attending a convention, created such an overload at the counter that one of our waitresses did break down. It also made me realize how little I understood or liked about many Americans.

It was time to move on. Norman and Bea had moved to Los Angeles, so in August I boarded the train for the two-day trip to the West Coast, thinking I might even stay there. But once again I felt no great sense of rapport with any of the people I met. Since I also felt that I hadn't really had enough of Europe, and one could live there on less, I decided I might just as well go back to Paris to write my novel.

That would require some money. So in September, I returned to my parents' home in Brooklyn and immediately began to look for work—in *The New York Times* want ads, of course. I also practiced typing and honed my shorthand (in my senior year at Radcliffe I had been told that if I didn't want to teach I had better learn shorthand so I could get a secretarial job). The going rate for a secretary with a year or two of experience was then about forty or forty-five dollars a week. One ad, however, with no salary specified, called for a knowledge of French. Thinking that would enable me to ask for an extra five dollars, I responded.

To my surprise, I got the job and the fifty bucks. I was going to be the second, one might say the undersecretary, in a small firm that was manufacturing batteries. It was housed in a wonderful old building at the corner of Chambers and Church Streets. It was a loft building though I don't think I even knew the term then, and it had an ancient caged hydraulic elevator that inched its way up and down the five or six stories. The personnel of the company, which occupied the second floor, consisted of the owner, Mr. Yardeny, Mr. Karolkoff the bookkeeper, Martin Kagan, a chemist who ran the manufacturing operation beyond the offices, and a secretary who was leaving. She was a smart, tough, bleached blonde of about 40, gravel-voiced and New York savvy. One could bet that she would give as good as she got. She'd had the job for some time, and hinted at dark reasons for quitting. It seemed that two of us were required to take her place.

The business, in which I was totally uninterested, was the 1950's version of a dot com. Yardeny, who had probably emigrated from Europe during or shortly before the war, had discovered what he was sure was going to be a ground-breaking technological invention. Or rather, he had discovered the inventor—a sweet Frenchman with no worldly know-how, who had developed a lightweight battery using silver rather than zinc. The first use to which it was being applied was in hearing aids and Yardeny had just landed a contract with Maico, a major hearing aid company. Perhaps he thought he needed two secretaries because he expected the business to burgeon quickly. His welcoming oration included visions of revolutionizing the automobile industry with cars running on batteries instead of gas. In fact, he was so afraid that someone might steal the battery invention, that only he and Martin could go through the closed door to the factory without a safe-conduct.

The front offices consisted of Yardeny's large corner office and three good-sized cubicles that fed into each other like a railroad flat and were separated by a partial glass wall from the corridor that ran from the entry door to the stock and coat room at its end. So the two secretaries and the bookkeeper were each to have a space of their own, the first secretary next to his office, the bookkeeper at the end, and myself in the middle.

It was quickly apparent that this was more than was needed. Mr. Yardeny was impossible. By the end of the first week, not only was his departing top secretary gone, but two replacements had left. After another week or so of secretaries, none of whom lasted more than two days (one left the same afternoon), he gave up. For one thing, a glitch in the battery had surfaced, endangering the contract with Maico, so he undoubtedly wanted to save money. It was also evident that I could handle the workload. Up to this point, I had been somewhat insulated by my underling status. Now I was thrust into the first secretary's office next to his, and for the first time in my life began to experience what it is like to work for a bully. He was manipulative, impatient, irrational, abusive, given to apoplectic explosions, and even on occasion, unexpectedly charming. Most days he kept me working late in unpaid overtime. Once, he kept me so long that a date who had come to pick me up, fell asleep in the small waiting area where I had parked him. Yardeny, wandering around while I typed, found him there, and rushed in to accuse me of having neglected to tell him that a customer was waiting. Since it was hardly the kind of business in which customers wandered in off the street, the double absurdity of it was just too much. I laughed in his face.

Then there was the time he barked out an order which was the exact opposite of something he had demanded two minutes before. Puzzled, I said, "But you said..."

He didn't let me finish. "Don't tell me what I said. Just do as I say," and turning on his heel stalked back to his office. Indeed, he had a habit of striding the premises with the forward lean of Groucho Marx. But I will give him this. He always knew when to disappear.

And that was my problem. It seemed as if I could never find the right moment to quit. He would enrage me at the end of the day, then disappear before I could react. Or I would be so hurt I was unable to open my mouth for fear of bursting into tears. I would come in the next morning swearing to myself that I would tell him I was leaving. And he wouldn't be there, or he'd be so mild, my resolve would waver.

My inertia was not totally uncalculated. It would be a bitch to find another job for just a couple of months. While I debated what to do, Yardeny announced that in a few weeks he would be going to Europe for a month. Great. I had already made plans to go to France in March. I would have a month free of Yardeny and give him notice when he got back. So I stayed.

Not wanting to take any chances, I wrote to him while he was gone to say I had decided to leave the job because I wanted to write a book. I softened it by saying that I would wait until he got back and give him a few weeks to find a replacement. To my surprise, he didn't blow his top. He said he was very sorry and that if I stayed I would have a big future in the company, but of course, I had to follow my heart's desire.

Very quickly, he decided that he would hire a young man who had once worked for him on a brief project and with whom he had been impressed. Mr. Bodkin, however, was living in California with his wife and two children. Negotiations followed and Herb Bodkin came to New York. He was to make $100 a week.

That my replacement was to get double my salary annoyed me only slightly since I took it for granted that a man would be better paid. I'm sure it bothered Yardeny more. However, he had great expectations for what Bodkin could do for him. He thought he was hiring a salesman/secretary. Herb started on a Monday, and on Tuesday or Wednesday Yardeny took him to New Jersey to a meeting with a prospective customer. I don't know what Yardeny expected his new employee to do, but since Bodkin was new to the business, he probably thought he was having a learning experience and didn't say very much. In any event, the meeting did not go well.

The next morning Yardeny called Herb into his office. With the advent of Bodkin, I had been displaced from the first cubicle and was once again occupying the second. So I was surprised when the murmur issuing from the corner office escalated to a recognizable sound. It very quickly became apparent that the two men were having an argument, and I soon realized that Mr. Yardeny was trying to fire his new assistant. I couldn't believe it. I said to myself, he can't be doing this. The man has come 3000 miles for this job, he has a three-month contract. I thought it was both morally appalling and legally impossible. I even said to myself, "I won't stand for it. If Herb leaves, so will I."

By this time the two men were shouting at each other. Suddenly there was silence. Bodkin came out of Yardeny's office and strode through the cubicles, Yardeny following close behind — through the first one, through mine. I watched the brief procession, noting the twitching of the back of Karolkoff's left shoulder as they approached and passed him, and went across the hall to the cloakroom. Bodkin picked up his coat and I could see his shadow through the translucent wall as he came back down the hall to the front door of the office, Yardeny on his tail all the way. At the door, Bodkin turned to him and in a ringing tone, said, "Mr. Yardeny, I'm speechless, or I'd have a great deal more to say." And he walked out.

I felt like cheering.

Predictably, the Yardeny/Bodkin saga did not end there. After Bodkin left, Yardeny went back into his office and telephoned his lawyer. I couldn't hear much but he was rather subdued when he emerged and came to sit down beside me. He must have sensed my disapproval because he came on softly and ingratiatingly.

Bodkin, he said, was too pushy. He didn't know the business, and he was already talking about getting a secretary. The complaints went on. And the invidious comparisons. (Obviously, I'd spoiled Yardeny.) "Now take Martin," he said. "He has a great deal to offer, but he's patient. He knows not to push when we're having problems. Someday Martin will be a big man in this company."

Finally, he came to the point. He would like me to call Bodkin and ask him to come back for a talk. I demurred a bit, suggesting Yardeny make the call himself, but he insisted until I agreed. To my horror, I realized that he intended to go on sitting beside me while I made the call. I remember thinking I shouldn't have to do this. I'm only 22.

Exactly what I said I don't remember. With Yardeny no more than a foot away, I couldn't very well tell Herb what I really thought. But I did feel afterward the glow of having managed it—something noncommittal, like it would be really helpful all around if he came back to talk. At the same time, I made my voice drip with fellow feeling. Yardeny couldn't complain about the words I used, but I was sure Bodkin knew I was on his side.

Martin Kagan came out of the backroom to tell Yardeny that in a break from his usual routine, he was planning to go out to lunch. Yardeny said fine, that he too was on his way out to lunch. He left, and I filled Martin in on what had just transpired.

"My God," he said, "this couldn't have happened on a worse day." Before he started working for Yardeny he had applied for a job with the city, and they had finally called him in for an interview. The pay was higher, it was more secure, and the hours would certainly be better. What should he do?

He looked genuinely troubled, but neither one of us could stop smiling.

We talked for a while. I thought he ought to take the job. But I did tell him what Yardeny had said about his one day becoming a big man in the company, to which I did not give much credence since I couldn't imagine how anyone who was sane and had other choices would last very long. But I guess Martin didn't get as much guff as I did because that really interested him. In any event, he went off to his interview still unsure of what he would do.

Before I took out the sandwich I had brought with me that morning, I lay my head down on the desk, astonished at my own mix of

37

emotions—glee at the thought of this crazy little world in which I'd landed going up in smoke, tempered by my congenital dismay at the prospect of any world falling apart, and under it all a sense of pride because everyone was coming to me for help, as well as a measure of astonishment because they all seemed to be under the impression that I was an adult. Indeed, I did feel as if I had matured a few years in the past few hours.

Herb Bodkin came back, and an uneasy truce was signed, which probably lasted no longer than his three-month contract. I was by then long gone. But Martin stayed on, and Yardeny kept faith, and as the firm prospered, made him vice president. Although I did not stay in touch for long, I did notice some years later that a sizeable building in lower Manhattan was emblazoned with the sign, YARDNEY ELECTRIC.

That too is now gone. But the beautiful old building where I worked for Mr. Yardeny, is still there on Chambers Street.

All these decades later, I suddenly wish I'd had the wit to summon up Bodkin's exit line when Randolph Churchill told me to shut up. Perhaps it would have changed the air of the evening if I had retorted, "I'm speechless, or I'd have a great deal more to say."

At the least, it would have made me feel better.

A Serious Man

April of 1963. Harry Jackson, the man I thought of then as the love of my life, had dumped me the summer before. The winter had been a financial struggle as few free-lance jobs had materialized. And I was catching my fifth cold in as many months. I had turned 36 the week before and the only people who remembered my birthday were my parents and my friend Phyllis's ex-husband whom I didn't particularly like. So I was in a foul humor, preparing dinner and banging pots on the stove when the phone rang.

"Hello," I snarled.

The voice at the other end said, "This is Al Wasserman."

"Oh hello," I said, my voice traveling up into surprised delight.

I'd first met Al in 1953 when we were both working on *The Search*, a television documentary series of 26 half-hour films about research projects at universities. *The Search* was the first series of its kind on television and a major effort on the part of CBS to satisfy its public service obligation. The series had been aborted by a bad start, and my boss, Irv Gitlin, whose secretary I had been for a year, was called in to salvage it. I became the researcher on the project and a whole lot of filmmakers were hired in a hurry. Al, having written an Oscar-winning short film, was called in. I still remember noticing him as he waited to go into Irv's office, thinking to myself, "What a nice face." He was obviously preparing himself for an interview and at the far end of a long room did not, I think, notice me at all.

In any event, he was not only hired but wrote and directed the three best films in the series. While I didn't see him much, if at all, during the run of the project, he was inadvertently responsible for my getting an undeserved kudo from my boss. One day Irv dropped on my desk the proposal that Al had written for one of the films he was doing. "I need a press release on this," Irv said. The proposal was so good I felt I couldn't improve on the writing, so I just lifted a few paragraphs from it and passed it back. Irv came out of his office to congratulate me. "This is the best damn press release I've ever seen," he said. While I was delighted to get the praise, I thought, doesn't he realize that all I've done is plagiarize.

A couple of years later I did some research for what was possibly Al's best-known documentary, *Out Of Darkness.* He was in California shooting the film and I don't remember having any contact with him. When the film was aired in 1956, I was enormously impressed with it. It was unlike anything that had been done before on television.

Fast forward to the spring of 1961. My husband, Larry Alson, and I were getting a divorce and I needed to earn a living. However, I didn't want anything full-time as our son, Peter, was only 6 years old and I didn't want to be away from him that much or have the pressure of a nine-to-five job. Instead, having landed a part-time job with the photographer, Jerry Cooke, I needed to supplement it with freelance work. Irv and Al had recently moved from CBS to NBC, Irv to head up a special projects unit, and Al to start the NBC White Paper series. I don't know why I didn't contact Irv, whom I knew better. Perhaps I tried and he was away, or ill. Since, from the little contact that we'd had, I felt that Al was approachable and sympathetic, and because I so admired his films, I thought it would be interesting to work with him,

I called him up and made an appointment.

We had a nice talk. I explained my situation, and he said he and his wife had been going through some personal turmoil, but he felt they had worked things out. He _was_ sympathetic, but he had no work for me.

So when his phone call came two years later, my first thought was, "Oh goody, he's going to offer me a job," and that was why I started smiling.

Instead, he said, "Are you still single?"

In the parlance of the time, you could have knocked me over with a feather. Of the men I had known at CBS, he and Irv were the only ones who had never in any way come on to me. I guess I stammered, "Well, yes. Why?"

He said, "Because I'm about to be."

We made a date, but I didn't know which situation I would have preferred. I really needed work. On the other hand, having in the past six months in the memorable words of Marlon Brando describing his roles, dated half the creeps, crumbs, and kreplachs in New York, I also thought, "At last, a mensch." In the interim before we saw each other, I began to fantasize about falling in love again.

For me, the date was a total bust.

We had agreed to see the Antonioni film, _La Notte_. I hadn't yet seen it but had admired _L'Avventura_. Al had seen it but wanted to see it again as he felt it resonated with his own troubles. When he arrived to pick me up, I sat him down with a glass of Scotch. He was not much of a drinker and by the time we left my apartment, he was weaving a little. The movie was on 42nd Street and we had just enough time to get a quick bite at the now long gone Crossroads Restaurant in Times Square. I do remember that I liked the protective way he put his arm around my waist to guide me through the traffic on Broadway. After the movie, we went to another restaurant and I guess that's when we began to talk. Or rather, he talked. The cold I had been catching when he called, had turned into laryngitis and I couldn't speak above a whisper, and that with difficulty.

His story was that he was breaking up his marriage because he had been cuckolded. And he was feeling terribly sorry for himself.

It was a turnoff. It sounded to me as if the marriage had never been all that happy or, for him, that desirable, so I couldn't see why he was so done in. They had married at a very young age, Al at 22 or 23, and Della even younger. He hadn't really been ready to get married, but since she wanted to, and he felt guilty, or at least responsible for having taken her to bed, and also, no doubt because, as for so many of us at the time, getting married was the only way to shack up without sneaking around, he'd proposed.

Della was a dancer and had been in a Broadway musical. But she'd had to give up dancing professionally after she tore her Achilles tendon. As a mother with two children, she had struggled to find another *metier*, and also began to exhibit some very neurotic symptoms, often feeling that she was ill or dying. There was a period when she was afraid to leave the house. To me, it was clear that she wanted desperately to bust out of her domestic cocoon but was terrified of what she'd do if she actually went out into the world. So in a way, it made total sense that when she did, she would have an affair. What was the big deal? Al was particularly enraged because Della had been so jealous that in twenty years of marriage he had been afraid even to look at another woman in her presence, much less be unfaithful to her. So again I thought, Aha! She was projecting onto him her own desire to stray. I could well understand that—the frustrated housewife eager for experience beyond her domestic role, her boredom probably exacerbated by the fact that Al was sometimes away on location and often spent long days and sometimes nights in the cutting room. An affair made sense. But the psychosomatic histrionics floored me. How could he have endured that?

None of this did I say. It was too hard to talk. Mostly, I just listened. But I was not very sympathetic. At one point I did manage to whisper that since she was so demanding and he didn't think he was any longer much in love with her, her infidelity was probably the biggest favor she'd ever done him.

I don't think that went over very well. He took me home and we said a polite goodnight. I was very disappointed and fully expected never to hear from him again.

But a few weeks later he called and asked me to dinner and a play—an Off-Broadway production of Pirandello's *Six Characters in Search of an Author.*

Well, why not? However, I had an invitation to a cocktail party the same evening so I suggested we attend that first, and since it was on the Upper East Side, I said that I would pick him up at his office. The party was in honor of Bianca Rosoff whom I had met through my sister-in-law Jeanne Campbell. Bianca was a countess, a character, and an artist, and I had no idea of who the host was, so taking a quick look at the invitation, I threw it into my bag as I left the house. I didn't bother to look at it again and gave Al the address as we drove over there.

One-Sixty-Three East 63rd Street (I've never forgotten the address) proved to be a very wide townhouse with one bell on the outside. A butler came to the door, took our coats, and asked what we would like to drink. Another butler appeared and ushered us up a very grand staircase that opened into a living room that was probably forty feet long. It looked like a hundred. At the far end, sitting around the fireplace were eight or ten people in evening dress. Al always looked elegant, and I was wearing the most expensive suit I'd ever owned, but I realized with some confused dismay that we were underdressed—what had that invitation said?

A beautiful woman in a fabulous cocktail gown started toward us. Slowly, sedately, we approached each other. It began to feel a little like the foes in the movie *High Noon,* marching toward each other. Halfway down that long, long room, we met. She looked at us inquiringly. I flubbed it. Instead of saying, Has the countess arrived, I stammered, "Is Bianca here?"

Very coolly, she said, "What address did you want?"

I took the invitation from my bag. It fluttered to the floor. Al retrieved it. I looked at it. "Oops," I said, "168 East 63rd Street."

More icily, she said, "That's the apartment house across the street."

Her hauteur mortified me. But Al did something which should have immediately made me fall in love with him. As we turned to leave, he said to her, "If it's no fun over there, we'll come back."

After we left we agreed that uninvited guests were a hazard of having a butler answer your doorbell, but she should at least have invited us to stay for the drinks we'd ordered. What did they do with our drinks? Did the kitchen celebrate?

By the time we left Bianca's party, there was no time for dinner so we didn't talk much until after the play when we went to get some coffee and dessert. I had my voice back but I was still mostly listening and Al was still feeling sorry for himself. He'd been living in a hotel, but his lawyer had told him that was risky as his wife could claim abandonment, so he had moved back to his home in Ardsley. I thought maybe the separation was not so final after all.

Another few weeks went by and he called again. He said it had proved too painful to be living in the same house with his wife, so he'd moved out again and was now ensconced in a sublet in the city. We made another date.

This time, we had dinner and went to see a performance of *The Second City,* and I found myself doing most of the talking. Maybe I wanted him to stop obsessing about his marital problems. Perhaps, without conscious intent, I was just trying to be entertaining. I also behaved in a way that startled me. I kept dropping things or leaving them behind, a scarf, my glasses, whatever. He kept retrieving everything for me. I asked myself, why am I doing this? Was I trying to make him feel protective and necessary? My fecklessness seemed compounded when, at midnight, we got to my door and I realized that I had left my keys at home.

I rang the bell—and rang and rang. But the young woman who was my live-in babysitter was fast asleep and nothing could wake her.

Al gallantly offered me the second bedroom in his apartment.

"No, no," I said. "I've got to be here in the morning."

I had deposited a key with an ex-sister-in-law who was living around the corner on Perry Street. We walked over, rang her bell, which at that hour scared her half to death. But I got the key.

I could hardly do less than offer Al coffee, so he came upstairs with me. Over the coffee, I kept talking. And talking. The only thing I remember was telling him about my few ESP experiences. He seemed fascinated but totally skeptical. About two a.m. I said he really had to leave because I had to get up in the morning to get Peter ready for school and myself off to work. At the door, he said what a nice evening he'd had, and his arms went around me and we were kissing for the first time.

It was a long lovely kiss. Forty years later Al still talked about it.

At the time, he said, "Now I don't want to leave."

"It's late. You must."

So he did.

The next morning, before I left the house, the telephone rang. It was Al, wanting to make another date.

As I hung up the phone, I thought, "I'm going to be courted." And then in what I can only think of as the greatest understatement of my life, I said to myself, "I better decide what I want to do, because this one isn't going to be casual."

We were both busy, so our next date did not take place for another week. In the interim, as I was still trying to decide whether I wanted to have an affair with Al, my good friend, Paul Jacobs, who lived in San Francisco, breezed into New York. Oddly enough, some months before I had first heard from Al, Paul and I had discovered that we both knew him. Paul had been both a consultant and on-camera interviewer in Al's documentary about Jimmy Hoffa, and we had talked about how much we admired him professionally. So when Paul called to invite me to lunch, the first thing I said to him was, "You'll never guess whom I've been seeing."

At lunch a couple of days later, Paul told me he'd gone to see Al at his office. Paul shook his head sadly and said, "He seems so emasculated."

I felt a sudden surprising rush of anger. Not at Paul specifically, but at everyone, including myself. We so easily write people off, I thought. And in the next maybe half a minute, while talking to Paul about other things, I had a series of memories and thoughts.

I remembered a conversation I had with Harry. Like many charismatic people, Harry suffered from the desire of those he had charmed for more of his company than he was willing to provide. So it was that he was complaining to me about some people who kept plying him with invitations he did not wish to accept. I laughed, and said, "Well you know, Harry, the Chinese say that if you save a man's life, you're responsible for him for the rest of yours."

This had made him angry. He said, "The hell with that. If I pull you out of a hole, I shouldn't have to go on pulling you out of holes. You should go and pull somebody else out of a hole."

Well, mad as I was at Harry for leaving me, I still felt he had pulled me out of a hole. Now I thought, "It's time I pulled somebody else out of a hole." My next thought was, I could make Al feel like a man again. And with barely a beat, I said to myself, "By God, I just will."

It turned out to be much easier than I'd expected. Given his hangdog air and his lack of experience in 20 years of faithfulness to one woman, I thought that he was probably having sexual problems, and I would have to be very patient and understanding. How wrong I could be. Twenty years of faithfulness had given Al the enthusiasm and ardor of a teenage boy. From the beginning, in bed, we were always in love.

But I was still getting over Harry, and I had it in my head that I wanted a man whose presence was magical. Which may have prevented me from realizing how much I was enjoying Al. We dined and wined, went to movies and plays, went on vacations, and some of his working trips together. In later years we had a game we called restaurant time travel, in which we imagined going back to the restaurants we'd loved that no longer existed. One of our favorites was the Flower Drum, a Chinese restaurant on Second Avenue in the East 40's. The food was good, but what made it special was a particular table, surrounded by a lattice that made it look and feel like a lover's bower. Without our asking they always seated us there.

I guess we always looked as if we'd just gotten out of bed. At a party one evening, a man came up to me and said what pleasure it gave him to see two people who so obviously were in the first enjoyable throes of knowing each other. I couldn't resist confusing him by saying that Al and I had known each other for ten years, but I didn't mention how little we'd known each other until a few months before.

What was I thinking? Al was undeniably the mensch I'd expected him to be. I admired his talent and his work. He was intelligent, interesting, and witty. I enjoyed his company and I loved him in bed. I just didn't think that I was In Love.

I wanted to be brave and adventurous, and Al seemed too conventional, too careful, emotionally unsophisticated. One hot summer night on the Staten Island ferry, we got into a discussion of relationships, and Al said rather piously that he didn't want to use anyone. I said, "Oh for Chrissakes Al, use me. Just use me well."

He looked like he'd just received an epiphany. But he continued to be careful. He kept telling me that he didn't trust me so he wasn't going to fall in love with me. This both amused and irked me since it certainly felt like he was in love with me. We had a funny conversation once as he again protested his lack of love. I said, "I had a man who told me continually and in myriad different ways how much he loved me, but I never felt as if he cared. You keep telling me you don't love me, but I feel as if you care."

"Oh," he said, "I do care."

Perhaps, I thought, I had the best of all possible worlds, since I had all of the advantages of his being in love with me and none of the responsibilities.

So we played on for a year. Until one night as we were rolling around on the rug in front of my fireplace, Al got very romantic and began to talk about how he felt about me. He said, "When I walk into a room and you're there, the whole world lights up."

I was thrilled. And envious. That was exactly the way I had felt about Harry. But all I could say was, "And you think you're not in love with me?"

Never again did he say he wasn't.

For a while, the future was moot since he was in the process of getting a divorce, and it took a couple of years. At some point, he did broach the idea of marriage. I didn't even say no. I said, "I don't know." He was so angry he didn't talk to me for a couple of days. But then we went on as before until some time around the third year I decided that much as I enjoyed him, I would have to live more dangerously if I was ever to fall in love again.

So I told him that we must break up, and we stopped seeing each other.

We were both miserable. Once again I was going out with an assortment of men I had no interest in. Al would call occasionally and I would think, why am I doing this? Why am I dating jerks when I could have this lovely man?

I don't remember exactly how we fell back into seeing each other again. I think because Al was going to Vietnam for a month to do a documentary on the South Vietnamese election, we felt we had to say goodbye. So to say goodbye we ended up spending a couple of great weekends together. I gave up giving him up.

Still, I wasn't in love the way I wanted to be. Then one day I realized that probably never again was any man going to light up the world for me because if someone like Harry came along, I'd probably run in the other direction. Rather than giving relief, the thought devastated me. Would life no longer be an adventure? I began to cry. I cried and cried. I went to bed and couldn't sleep. In the middle of the night, I called Al. He offered to come over. But how could I tell him what was wrong? How could I tell my lover that I was weeping because of what he wasn't? I said I'd be all right.

In the morning, after I woke up, I cried again for an hour. I had just stopped and dried my eyes when Al called.

"Are you okay?"

I started to sob again.

Al began to say concerned and soothing things, and something in me snapped. "Al," I said, "I don't need sympathy. What I really need is a good swift kick in the ass."

And in his own sweet way, he proceeded to give it to me. "Oh no," he said. "You don't often feel sorry for yourself."

We hung up and I thought, "Sorry for myself? I thought I was in despair." And then I realized that he was right. and that it was absurd for me to feel sorry for myself just because I would never again have something I no longer even wanted when there were people in this

49

world who really had trouble.

By then we had been together nearly five years, and Al still made me feel as if I lit up the world for him. My friend Phyllis had once talked about how much she liked the aura of the man she was with, and said, "Wouldn't it be nice if one could feel one's own aura." At the time I hadn't quite understood what she meant, but now I did. I realized that Al had given me an enormous gift. He had enabled me to feel my own light. It seemed a bit stuck-up, but I felt that I no longer needed to bathe in the glow of someone else's incandescence. I could even forgive Harry and understand that he hadn't needed me because he'd always felt his own light.

In a mean moment, I thought that the trouble with marrying Al was that because he was so caring, it would be like living with my mother. But in the next moment, I thought that it wouldn't be so bad living with Mother if she had Al's sense of humor. Perhaps living dangerously was not my bent.

I knew then that if Al asked me to marry him I would say yes.

As with so much in New York City, it got settled by real estate. His lease was coming up for renewal. Did he want to go on living in his enormous Central Park West apartment? Very nervously, because I think we both knew that if I still said no, he had decided to split, he said he thought it was time we moved in together.

"I said, "Oh, of course."

He had barely stopped kissing me when the phone rang.

It was his agent.

In high elation, Al said to him, "Well you're the first to know that Barbara and I are getting married."

The reality hit me then and I went into a state of shock. Hard as it had been to be a single mother of a growing boy, running a household, often juggling three jobs, and leading a full social life, I had enjoyed being on my own, and I was used to it. As Barbara Alson, I felt as if I had an identity I had fashioned myself. For the next two days, I brooded over having to change my name again. If my maiden name hadn't been well-known I would have taken it back. But I had come to treasure my anonymity.

I didn't tell Al any of this. He was *so* happy, I couldn't spoil it for him.

In fact, he was so happy, I fell in love with him.

What an idiot I had been. When we'd first gotten together I had thought that maybe I could change Al into the kind of man that I could fall in love with. My hubris now appalled me — to have thought that I could do it without myself making a commitment.

Real estate also got me over my brief blue funk. Al said, "Your place or mine?" and I said, "Mine." I could give up my name, but I couldn't give up Greenwich Village.

The first five or six years of our marriage were like one long honeymoon, despite the fact that those years were the most difficult Al faced professionally. He had left the networks to start his own film company, with the intent of making feature films. But the two promising film projects that he was working on never came to fruition. While they were being developed, and heartbreakingly, falling apart, Al made several offbeat industrial films—for Bell Telephone, Ford, and Parke Davis. I worked with him on the Parke-Davis film, a half-hour documentary on the history of medicine. I had a ball doing the research, much of it at the rare book room of the Academy of Medicine Library, a Renaissance-like structure on upper Fifth Avenue. Working with him, I was even more awed by Al's talent, intelligence, creativity, and professionalism. As an example: I had written a voice-over for a sequence in the film. Al said it was good but too long for the sequence which had already been cut. I groaned and said I didn't know if it was possible to give the necessary information in a shorter form. "Well, let me noodle with it for a while," he said. A little later he presented me with his rewrite. Not only did it time exactly to the film, but it was pithier, more interesting and more elegant than what I had written.

Al really loved solving problems. At work, he was unflappable. And funny. I was so involved in the content of the film that at one point he said to me, "You've got to think visually." Trying to think visually I worked up a sequence with fountains and aqueducts. I felt rather proud of the idea and at dinner one night with the two film editors who were working on his films, I described the pictures we would show. Al looked a little dubious. "But what are you going to be saying over it?" he said.

I went up in smoke.

Al noticed that this agitated one of the editors, so he turned to him and said, "The reason we work together is so that we'll have something to fight about."

Which cracked me up, and we went back to having a pleasant dinner.

Indeed, in all the years we were together, Al must have given me a belly laugh at least once a day. Shortly after we married, I decided that while all the usual things one wants in a marriage were there—the sex, the rapport, the caring, the good times—the real secret of our marriage was that we made each other laugh. Al certainly made me laugh. I loved his wit, his sense of how absurd so much of life is. In fact, I used to say that if he hadn't been good-looking, he would have been Woody Allen. He never let me take myself too seriously. If I got a bit pretentious, he would very sweetly, but with perfect aim, puncture the balloon.

I miss that. Without him, life has a different texture. But at least one great thing he gave me seems to last. Unlike the Kundera title, it is a very bearable lightness of being.

Ultimately, I guess, he may have changed me more than I changed him.

Dinner at the Finletters

L
ate in life, my husband, Al, became increasingly deaf, which
wiped out much of the easy give and take we'd always had.
My soft high voice was a source of irritation to him, and
I could not comprehend his reluctance to use hearing aids, or why
he treated the matter as if the problem were mine rather than his.
Naturally, we were sometimes cranky with each other.

Thinking about all this one day, I had an apercu about another
couple—Thomas and Eileen Finletter.

I had met Eileen in Paris in 1948 when she was married to Stanley
Geist. At Harvard, Stanley had been a protege of F.O. Mathiessen,
whom all of us who majored in American History and Literature held
in awe. So it was rather eerie that when I returned to Paris in 1950
and was visiting Eileen, she received a phone call which informed her
that Matthiessen had committed suicide. She said, "Stanley will be so
upset." With less reason, perhaps, so was I. The Geists remained in
Europe, and not until twenty-five years later did I see Eileen again,
by which time she had divorced Stanley, come back to the States, and
married Thomas Finletter, a man twenty-five years her senior. His
name was familiar to me because he had held a number of government
posts under Roosevelt, and had been the Air Force Secretary in the

Truman administration.

At the time, I made the conventional assumption that he found her to be a sexy younger woman. But later, mulling the trouble Al and I were having because of my treble and his deafness, I remembered that Eileen had a deep, almost baritone voice. Aha, I thought. Give sex its due, but the real basis of their marriage was that Tom could hear her. Lucky couple.

On the evening of our reacquaintance, I was lucky enough to be innocent of such problems. It was 1975 and I had come to Maine for a week to visit Norman and his kids. Norman picked me up at the airport in Bangor, and as we drove the fifty miles to Mount Desert, he informed me that during the week I was to attend a dinner party at Eileen Finletter's home in Bar Harbor. She had invited Norman, but when he told her that both I, and Carol Stevens who would become his fifth wife, would be with him, she said, "I don't have room at the table for everybody. Send Barbara for dinner and you and Carol come later."

I was curious, but not entirely happy at the prospect of going to the dinner alone. Well, I thought, at least I brought a dress that I can wear.

It was a dress I had bought in San Francisco a year earlier. I had seen it in the window of a shop in Ghiradelli Square, a long, loose crinkly cotton (it was the era of the muu-muu). There was no shape to it, but it was the color of the sky on a glorious day, and I knew immediately that I had to have it. What instinct made me take it to Maine, I do not know.

The day of the dinner was also a day on the sailboat. Remaining true to Norman's daughter Danielle's description of us as the Polish Navy, we got becalmed and arrived home much later than planned. Realizing that the dress was soiled, I threw it into the washing machine, then the dryer, then on myself. I was still feeling a bit breathless when I arrived at the Finletter's — an old gracious New England home. I wasn't late, however, and the eight or ten people who had already arrived looked very old and very Wasp. My heart sank at the prospect of what I thought would be a dull, stiff evening.

After greeting me, Eileen introduced me to Tom, who led me to the bar to get a drink. As he poured we exchanged pleasantries. Or rather what passed as such since everything I said seemed to elicit a non sequitur. Not until he ushered me to a seat did I realize that he was quite deaf.

Sitting next to me was a pretty elderly lady with white hair and eyes the color of my dress. Neither one of us quite knew how to begin a conversation. We exchanged names. There was an awkward pause. Finally, she said with some genuine enthusiasm, "That's a beautiful dress you're wearing."

Following her eyes, I looked down at my dress. And a huge bubble of glee welled up in me. All the seams were showing. I was wearing it inside out.

What the hell, I thought, we're all nuts. Suddenly I felt perfectly happy and ready to have a good time.

Indeed, it turned into a memorable evening. More people arrived and we were ushered to dinner. In the small low ceilinged dining room, two tables had been set with twenty places of fine china, crystal, and silver. We filed in silently, searching for our place cards, but once we sat down and everyone began to talk, the sound ricocheted back and forth, up and down the room, creating a din to rival the trendiest of New York restaurants. It was an unseemly racket. Once again I had to stifle a giggle. And my mood went up another notch.

I turned to the man on my left. He was Bowden Broadwater, a former husband of Mary McCarthy, and a classmate of Norman's at Harvard where they had both been on the Advocate, the literary magazine. A small, fair-haired man, he had a gentle air and he spoke barely above a whisper. In the hubbub around us, I could distinguish only about one word in three. My responses to him may have seemed as bizarre as Tom Finletter's had seemed to me. But I did hear enough to garner the somewhat astonishing information that while he had an administrative position at an exclusive girl's school in Manhattan, he had arranged things so that he worked only half the year. This left him a great deal of time to do the two things he most enjoyed — namely, read, and be a house guest, preferably combining the two. He knew enough people in the Northeast to have cased the library in just about every small town in New England. I was much impressed.

However, given the strain of trying to hear what he was saying, it was rather a relief when midway through the meal, we all turned, British fashion, to our other dinner partner. Mine was Bruce Mazlish, a psychoanalyst who wrote psychobiographies, a genre about which I have doubts but considerable interest. Perhaps because we were two Jews in a den of Wasps, we got along famously, and, leaning back toward the windows behind us, we could hear each other quite well. He was about to have a book published by my employer, Simon & Schuster, and he was ticked off at his editor because she wanted to delay his publication date. But when he had finished complaining, and I had tried to offer him some sympathy, he said to me,

"Tell me, what was it like growing up with Norman?"

Now for many years after *The Naked and the Dead* was published, this had been the kind of question that raised my hackles. With time, however, I had realized that no one is an individual in a vacuum, and so had accepted that I could not escape the fact that Norman was part of my identity, and that people would always think of me as his sister. But when Bruce posed the question, for the first time I felt eager and happy to answer it.

"It was wonderful," I said and proceeded to tell him why. Norman always made the air bounce. He was always fun to be around. He loved to instruct me and was always encouraging. I particularly remember how happy I was to be included in the Monopoly games he played with his friends when I was only ten years old. And when, as a typical adolescent, I was feeling awkward and inadequate, he repeatedly told me that I was pretty and intelligent. Since I took everything Norman said as Gospel, I began to believe it.

A look of pain crossed Bruce's face. "Oh," he said, "I didn't do that for my sister."

A moment of epiphany. I thought, so brothers, let alone extraordinary brothers, don't always do that for their sisters. How fortunate I had been.

Perhaps that's why when late in life Norman too grew deaf and would snarl at me, "Project!" I would patiently attempt to lower the register of my voice.

Dolph

s on many another day, I was pushing my shopping cart to the Farmers Market in Union Square, jostled a bit by the usual crowds on Fourteenth Street as people hurried in and out of discount stores or stopped to look at the bargain prices of the chintzy goods in bins by the entrance. Passing the armory near Sixth Avenue, I looked at the large stolid facade and was transported back to a day I spent inside the building more than fifty years before—early 1948, to be precise.

Dolph Winebrenner. He was the reason I was there that day. A leftist journalist, former member of the Communist Party, in 1948 he was working for the PCA (Progressive Citizens of America), which was about to become the Progressive Party. Perhaps that was the purpose of the meeting being held in the armory. I have no memory of what went on. The picture in my head is of having a sandwich in a greasy spoon across the street, with Dolph and a colleague or two of his. No doubt they talked about what was happening at the meeting. I don't recall any of the substance, but I do remember feeling that I was a participant in momentous events. However, I was there only because Dolph and I were having an affair that had begun a month or so before.

The noise and dirt of Fourteenth Street was momentarily wiped out,

59

not so much by the fragmentary memory of a long-gone day in my life, as by the overwhelming sensation of how that time of my life had felt.

My mood in 1948, although I was not consciously aware of it then, was an amalgam—the vicissitudes of recent history (the world's and my own) filtered through the good fortune of having been well-loved and protected, the beneficiary of a privileged education, and the natural inclination at the age of twenty to believe that I was an adult, while at the same time I felt that my life stretched endlessly ahead. I thought I was world-weary because I had loved and lost, but in fact, I experienced most days with sensuous pleasure. I was very sure of my opinions and blissfully unaware of my innocence and confusion. As I had grown up during the Depression and Hitler and World War II, deprivation and peril seemed like the natural condition of the world. On the other hand, we had triumphed, we had *escaped*. Though the notion of a world at peace was short-lived (for myself it didn't last much longer than the hour of euphoria I experienced on V-J Day), and my expectations were still trimmed by the inbred fear of scarcity and evil, there was a lightness, a sensuosity, and a mystery to being. Clothes, food, the feel of the air—anything—could produce intense delight or fill me with a mood that remained forever after in my memory—the joy of buying a couple of hats with my own money and feeling that each one made me pretty in a different way; the bar lounge at the Franklin Arms in Brooklyn Heights where the combination of a dimly lit room, a beer, and a pianist playing pop songs seemed like the height of sophisticated funkiness.

I didn't know at the time how much I was enjoying it all. I was very serious. I wanted to be admirable, which, in practice meant behaving like an adult; so I got a job. I wanted to be politically responsible; so I joined the PCA. And I wanted to attract men. Of course, what I enjoyed most was the last. My job, writing letters and sending out educational materials from the Bureau for Intercultural Education, a benign do-gooder organization, was pretty routine. The people at the local PCA club in Brooklyn Heights were all older than me and seemed to be a rather dull group. (If in this small collection of ordinary people I sensed some jockeying for power and position, I chose to view it as a contemptible aberration instead of letting it teach me something about the way the world works.) And in that year between graduating from college and going to Europe, I was not meeting a great many men.

So I was bored much of the time. But below all the Weltschmerz and confusion and deadly seriousness of being twenty, I knew that something new and wonderful might happen that day or the next. And every once in a while, something did.

For instance. The way I met Dolph.

It had been the dreariest of days. The local PCA had asked me to attend as an alternate delegate the convention being held in Albany. I guess it seemed to me an adult thing to do and I was still too in awe of the adult world to ask why they needed alternate delegates for a meeting that was going to take less than a day. So dutifully, I found myself in Grand Central Station before 8 o'clock on a very cold Saturday morning in January. A train had been chartered to take the hundreds of us who were going up from New York City. We were supposed to arrive at noon. But a few miles before we reached Albany the train came to a halt. There seemed no better information than that the temperature was 20 degrees below zero and this was causing railroad problems. We sat for two hours in a state of mounting paranoid whispers and rumors until the train inched forward again.

So the Convention began hours late. And naturally went longer than expected. I don't remember any of the specifics. There were probably the usual familiar speeches and parliamentary ploys, and since I had no active role to play I very likely did not listen too carefully. While my loyalty to the cause didn't waver, it could not mask my boredom. I ached to get home.

Therefore, I was not a happy camper when we boarded the train about 9 o'clock and discovered that there were not enough cars to seat everyone. Again the rumors came and went and ultimately another car was added to the front of the train. It was old enough to be extraordinarily uncomfortable—the seats were the varnished cane of a previous era, hard and straight-backed, each two facing, so that I found myself knocking knees with three companions from Brooklyn. I knew them well enough to feel I was not interested in getting to know them better. And the train had not even started.

I said I felt like some exercise and that I'd see if perhaps there was some space we had missed in the more comfortable cars. I walked to the end of the train and was on my reluctant way back when a young woman I had met once or twice called to me from her seat. Gratefully, I chatted with her. After a bit, a tall lanky man coming down the aisle joined us. I was very impressed to learn that he was working in the national office of the organization in what seemed to me like a position of importance. He was on his way back to his seat a couple of cars down and when I said I was resigned to going back to my cattle car, he came with me. I noticed that he had a slight limp, which added a fillip of vulnerability to someone who otherwise seemed like an awesome elder.

When we reached his seat, it was empty. He said that his companion had gone to talk to some friends and had not yet returned, so why didn't I sit there until she did.

I was delighted. Very soon we were exchanging the stories of our lives. He had grown up somewhere in the Midwest and had spent a number of years in California as a working journalist. Slightly lame from a childhood bout of polio, he had been unable to serve in the war. Instead, he had worked as a reporter at the Los Angeles Daily

Worker. He had joined the Communist Party while still quite young, but somewhere along the way, he had become disillusioned—perhaps by the Hitler-Stalin pact. However, he was still a Marxist. "Marxism," he said, "is not a political movement, it is a way of understanding the world. It is a method of thought."

My brother used to say at that time that all one needed for an excellent education was to read the greatest one hundred novels ever written. And indeed, having undoubtedly spent thousands of hours of my young life reading novels, I tended to appreciate an experience more intensely if I could refer it back to a character or situation or even a mood that I had lived through in those glorious hours spent in a chair with a book. On the basis of Dolph's quick biography, he seemed to me as good as a character in Dos Passos' *USA*.

Since he was 37 years old, he had a lot more to tell than I did. After hearing the sad story of my love affair with Jack Maher, a classmate of Norman's I had met on a visit to Harvard, he finally asked me how old I was. At the beginning of 1948, I was not yet 21, and he was obviously unhappy to hear this. He said, "I thought you were probably twenty-five."

I was startled. I was often taken for five years younger than my age (to my great irritation). And until that moment I had assumed his interest in me to be only kind. I suppose I did not realize how enchanting he may have found my rapt attention. In any event, I suddenly realized that this sympathetic older man was not thinking of himself as a mentor or father confessor, but as a potential lover.

We continued to talk. At some point, his seat companion came back, but as I prepared to get up, she said no need, she had another place to sit. What luck, I thought, though I was grateful even to have had the respite I'd already had.

The train began to move around midnight. Dolph and I went on talking. I thought him exceptionally glamorous because he was a journalist. And I was proud of myself. I'd had an affair with a man of 32 the previous summer, and here was an even older man now interested in me.

As the train crawled back to New York, we talked and we dozed. But when my head fell to his shoulder, it only made me aware of how much of a stranger he still was.

By the time we pulled into Grand Central, daylight was dimly discernible. Since he lived uptown and I was going back to Brooklyn, we parted, but with the understanding that he would call. As I walked alone through the cold gray station, I was too excited to feel any weariness, elatedly aware of how completely different my mood was since I had trod this same floor almost 24 hours before. One day and something new and wonderful had happened. My life might be about to change.

We did wind up getting together, and I found him very attractive, though not handsome enough to make me nervous. He was quite tall, with the long face and the long upper lip of a Wasp. And so he continued to hold for me the fascination of a stranger. There was also the glamour of what he did, and whom he knew. We would meet after work at Costello's, a bar on Third Avenue in the 40's, the neighborhood still Depression seedy, gloomy and ugly under the El. Costello's was a hangout for journalists, most of whom worked at the Daily News nearby. The ambiance thrilled me. If Dolph was a character in *USA*, the bar, with its sawdust floors and fast-talking cynical newsmen, was straight out of a Ben Hecht novel.

A couple of Dolph's friends lived in the Village and that was also an exciting new scene for me. One of them lived in the wonderful old Rhinelander houses on 11th Street, later alas torn down in order to put up P.S. 41. Another lived in a brownstone on 13th Street, practically next door to City & Country, the progressive school my son would later attend. This friend invited us to dinner and served artichokes.

That wowed me. I don't think I'd ever before met a man who cooked, and certainly, I had never before encountered an artichoke.

Dolph himself lived all the way uptown in Spanish Harlem. I'm not sure if it was by choice or because the rent was cheap. At any rate, we soon became lovers and, because I was living at home, I often visited him there, sometimes walking from the 125th Street subway station by myself. It didn't seem a dangerous thing to do then. Only once did I ever get frightened. On a dark night, Third Avenue was almost deserted, and a black police car screeching by gave me a frisson of anxiety which turned into real fear the next minute as I saw a policeman suddenly make a broken run in front of me to hustle a couple of women into the shelter of a doorway. I dove into the next doorway myself, expecting to hear gunshots ring out. All I heard was the sound of laughter. I peeked around the edge of the building and saw that indeed the three of them were laughing. At me, I supposed. Sheepishly, I walked on.

Just what Dolph saw in me I'm not sure. I was pretty, I was intelligent, and I was ignorant. I suppose he enjoyed instructing me—in sex and in Marxism. And while I was trying so hard to be sophisticated that I seldom admitted how excited I was by everything new, I suspect that I reeked with enthusiasm.

Still, I never fell in love with him, and I don't know how much he really cared for me. He probably didn't want to fall in love since I was leaving for Europe in a few months. And he probably felt, quite rightly, that I was too young to trust.

I thought about him while I was in Europe, but I didn't exactly miss him. He *was* part of why I returned in the fall; the other reason was to work for the Wallace presidential campaign. Since we were both working in the national headquarters, we saw a lot of each other through election day. Election night at headquarters remains vivid in my mind. Everyone had been expecting that Dewey would win, but we had been hoping that Wallace would get five million votes. As the returns came in and it looked like he would get no more than one million, our spirits sank lower and lower. To everyone's surprise, Truman was doing very well. About midnight, in an attempt to alleviate the pain, someone suggested that they might be even more depressed at Republican campaign headquarters, so a bunch of us traipsed over to the Biltmore, which indeed had the air of a morgue. We still couldn't believe that Truman was going to win, but the palpable unhappiness of Dewey's supporters made us feel a bit better.

After the election, Dolph fell on really hard times. His past association with the Communist Party combined with the witchhunt begun by the House Unamerican Activities Committee, made him unemployable by most of the news organizations. He scrounged for work here and there. I felt sorry for him, but I could not stem the cooling of my heart, as once again Dos Passos came to mind. So many of his characters were losers. I was young enough to think that Dolph was on the downhill side of his life and I did not care to contemplate that. As they say, we drifted apart. When I met another man a couple of months later, I lost contact with Dolph. I did hear a couple of years later that he had married one of my Radcliffe classmates. So perhaps despite his initial dismay, he really did like young women, particularly if they came from Ivy League colleges.

As for me, I ended up feeling less than proud of myself, because I knew full well that I had deserted him. And it pains me now that I made no effort to remain friends, now when I would like to know how the rest of his life turned out.

Medieval History

When my friend and classmate, Barbara Norwood, suggested that I write a memoir about Edmands House, the cooperative house where we both lived while at Radcliffe, and mentioned an incident I had almost forgotten, I at first dismissed the idea. Over the years I had not thought much about that time, nor had much contact with most of the girls who lived there with me. My most vivid memory was of the house itself. I believe it was the first time that I ever fell in love with a house. Indeed, it may be why ever since I have preferred living in houses rather than apartment buildings. Perhaps it has even been the source of the beautiful haunting dreams I've had over the years, the dreams I call architectural dreams, in which I wander through rooms and balconies unlike any I have ever known.

A couple of times over the years, incidental and utterly unlikely connections to Edmands House felt like visitations. In the mid-1970's I was working for the architect who had designed a new dormitory for Radcliffe called Currier House. To build it, Edmands House and several other old buildings were torn down. In an odd twist, while going through the company's picture files, I found a photograph my boss' daughter had taken through a window in the top floor room I had occupied in Edmands House my senior year—she, too, had gone to Radcliffe, though some years after me, and may even have lived in Edmands herself, perhaps even in the same room.

In 1997, at my fiftieth reunion, I once again roomed with Phyllis Silverman, who for two years had been my roommate in Edmands House. We were assigned a suite in Currier House, and as I looked out the window at the grounds of the Observatory across Garden Street, I realized that the room I was in was just where my room in Edmands House had been. Currier was very large and only two or three of its rooms could have had that same view. The feeling was very different. Boxy, brick and concrete, Currier had none of the warmth and charm and beauty of the rambling wood structure it had replaced.

Set on a plot of green lawn shaded in part by a large tree, Edmands had been a Victorian family home. On the first floor was a very large kitchen and pantry; adjacent was a dining room large enough to seat at one table the sixteen or so of us who lived there. The living room, as I remember, was just big enough for a sofa, a couple of chairs, and an old upright piano. We sat on the floor a lot. Mice often inhabited the piano, providing an eerie concert to anyone who decided to study in the room late at night.

There was also another room on the first floor, the purview of the House Mother, which I don't think I ever saw. The large dormitories on campus had mature and professional overseers, but since we were a pretty small operation, our house mother was a graduate student not much older than us, and either she didn't know or didn't care about the parietal rules. For instance, we weren't supposed to have boys in the house after a certain hour—probably ten o'clock. However, when we came home with our dates, we generally spent a lot of time necking in the vestibule. Mild stuff, but it felt momentous at the time.

Ah yes, that time. How different things were seventy years ago. It's perhaps too easy to sentimentalize the innocence and the simplicity and the straightened circumstances of that time. Most people still felt the shadow of the Depression. We were in the middle of a War. Gas was rationed, (although few students had cars). Sugar was rationed so we were sweet-deprived. And the only technological gadget any of us owned was a typewriter. Housed in the living room was a phonograph. Although it belonged to one of our housemates, it was used communally by all of us, as were the two albums of classical music, The Schubert Trout Quintet and the Mozart Hunt Quartet.

From the first floor, a central staircase climbed past cupboards built into the wall. The stairs had a half landing with a window fronted by a soft bench. The second floor had five or six large bedrooms, which we shared, two or three to a room. And there were two bathrooms, one at each end of the house. I loved the room that Phyllis and I shared—an L-shaped room with a green-tiled fireplace which we never used, and a bay window and door that led to a semi-circular porch. It didn't occur to us to use this deck since it had no furniture and most of the school year was too cold to consider sunbathing. But together with the fireplace, it made the room feel very elegant.

The bathroom for our end of the floor had a zinc bathtub set in a wood frame, and in the wall beside it, a speaking tube which went down to the kitchen, a nicety from an era before the house had hot running water. Of course, we played with it, spooking out whoever happened to be in the kitchen.

I believe 'consumption' was not yet a term we applied to our national habits. When it came to clothes, most of us, children of the Depression, had just a couple of sweaters and skirts and a dress for dates. It was a major economic decision when I abandoned my saddle shoes for a pair of trendy penny loafers. We also considered it high chic to wear a man's shirt cadged from a brother or a boyfriend. I don't know that we thought at the time that it might be an expression of incipient feminism, but we aped the boys in other ways as well, sometimes calling each other by our last names. We didn't care about variety. If we had an outfit that we loved, we wore it all the time. One year I had a periwinkle blue sloppy Joe sweater and Phyllis owned a pastel plaid skirt. We both felt they went well together, so for months one or the other of us wore that outfit every day.

As a cooperative house, we paid the college for our rooms, but the cost and preparation of food was our responsibility. The sixteen of us broke nicely into eight pairs. On a rotating basis, one pair would be assigned to prepare breakfast for a week, and the other seven pairs would each do one dinner during the week. We each chipped in five dollars a month for staples and breakfast. Lunch we each did on our own. For dinners, we kept a strict account of what we spent and at the end of the week had a reckoning. For dinner, the per-person cost per week came to between $2.50 and $4.00. The food was generally better than in the dorms and we each saved about one hundred fifty dollars over the course of the school year. These sums seem so minuscule by today's standards that it makes those years feel as remote as the Middle Ages when a penny had great value.

Since we cooked in teams of two, I cooked with Phyllis, who had some experience. I had none. On our first night, while Phyllis prepared most of the meal, I opened up the Joy of Cooking to find a dessert recipe. I guess because it seemed exotic to me, and cheap, and did not require much sugar, I decided to make bread pudding and hard sauce. It was okay but didn't seem worth making again. So the next time, I made a jelly roll. The taste was good, but it didn't roll and looked more like a layer cake. Challenged, I kept making it every week until I did get it to roll. I've never made one since.

Eventually, I got around to the main dishes and vegetables. Because we were cooking for sixteen or more, and because we pooled our ration tickets, we tended to make roasts and stews, and maybe fish on Friday. We shared recipes. When someone discovered a cake that didn't use much sugar and which we all liked, it ended up on the menu several times a week. We were remarkably good-humored and tolerant when a dish bombed. The standard comment was, "Well, this is interesting."

What I didn't quite realize at the time was that learning I loved to cook was not the least valuable lesson I got from my Radcliffe education.

In my last semester at Edmands House, I lived alone on the top floor, originally the servants' quarters. It had three small rooms. My room had two closets, in one of which the mice had taken over. Since I didn't have enough clothes to fill even one closet, the mice only bothered me when they got into a box of cookies I had left on the dresser.

I don't remember all the girls who lived at Edmands while I was there. Apart from Phyllis, my best friends in the house were Joan Raphael and Kathy Safford. Joan, from New York, was a highly intelligent political science major, and Kathy, a New England Wasp with red hair, who delighted me with the contrast between her chirpy voice and the considered way she approached all matters, was majoring in experimental psychology. Though both of them wound up in New York after college, my friendships with them faded, perhaps because our post-college interests led us into different social circles.

Besides Barbara and her roommate, Ruth Tuck, there was Gaby Fischer, the daughter of the German publisher who had escaped Hitler Germany, and another refugee, Sophie Freud, granddaughter of Sigmund, who was very involved with the man she would soon marry and wasn't around much. And then there was Kate Casale, whose serious Catholicism astonished me. Immediately after graduation she married a somewhat traditionally domineering man and had nine children. It was only at our 25th reunion that I came to appreciate her, remembering how hardworking and energetic and good-humored she'd been. She still was, even after nine children, and perhaps more remarkably, still looked the same.

The honey-haired house beauty was Jane Styne. She was tall and slim, pale and patrician. She had a reputation for high intelligence and great intellect. But ordinary conversation seemed to cause her so much pain that she hardly ever talked. When absolutely necessary, she would eke out a few slow words. The only exchange I remember having with her was when she insisted I take over a date she'd made with a man she obviously couldn't stand. Because I was so in awe of her, I agreed. He turned out to be a compulsive talker. I was sure I never said a word all evening, and I certainly didn't think he had any interest in me. So when at the end of the date he said he'd like to see me again, that Jane was a very nice girl, but really she was inarticulate, I burst out laughing. How could he tell the difference?

Phyllis, bright, pretty, funny, and flamboyant, occasionally wowed or worried the rest of us. She was avid for experience. Sometimes she got into trouble. Once, some Harvard boys announced that they were going to hold a male beauty contest. Big joke. Barbara Norwood came up with the idea of dressing Phyllis as a boy, and we sent her like that to the event. She was somehow unmasked, news of which, amazingly, made it into *The Boston Globe*. That got Dean Sherman so upset that she was reported to have said, "There are too many of the same kind · in that house." It seemed clear to us that she meant Jews, maybe New York leftist Jews. Astonishing to me now is that in the middle of World War II, our rather mild college high jinks should have hit the news, or that it could have upset anyone. Less shocking is the fact that none of us were surprised by Dean Sherman's expression of antisemitism which was, in reality, a total non sequitur.

On the other hand, I was wedded to my own prejudices, scorning anyone who was right of left, and frowning on Kate Casale because she believed a woman should remain a virgin until marriage.

Absorbed as I was in the quotidian details of courses, tests, writing, cooking, and boyfriends, I had no strong purchase on the future. But then I don't think any of us living in that house at that time could have imagined how much the world would change.

Postscript, 4/15/2015

A few days ago I mentioned this memoir to Peter's oldest friend, the biographer David Michaelis. He was curious about the history of the house, about which I had no knowledge. He said that I could probably find details in the Harvard Archive. I asked him to send me the website. Instead, two days later, having researched it himself, he emailed the following information:

The house was built in the mid-nineteenth century by J. Lincoln Edmands, a drug broker on the India Wharf in Boston. His last Edmands descendant, John Rayner Edmands, was a distinguished scientist and a member of MIT's first graduating class. Serving 25 years as the librarian at the Harvard Observatory, he had from his house a view of the Observatory grounds. Childless, he died in 1910 and willed the house to Radcliffe as a memorial to his late wife, Helen.

The house was first used in 1911 by seven Radcliffe freshwomen and sophomores who couldn't be accommodated in the dormitories, and the house 'mother' was a Radcliffe English instructor. Until it became a cooperative house, the residents took their meals at Bertram Hall on the Quad.

Manny

The other day I went to hear Norman's oldest daughter Sue, my niece, present a comment on a paper given by an analyst at the Relational Psychoanalysis Conference which Sue had come to New York to attend. Martin Frommer's paper was fascinating, as was Sue's extensive comment, both blessedly free of professional jargon. Afterward, as we were discussing the interactions between analyst and patient, and because their viewpoint reminded me of him, I asked if she had ever heard of Manny Ghent.

"Manny Ghent!" Sue said. "He was very important. He was revered." She began humorously bemoaning the fact that her very good friend Jessica, who had been analyzed by Ghent, was now living with the analyst Sue went to at one time. "I feel like I'm being triangulated," she said.

"Well," I said, "you can give them back some triangulation. You can tell them that your aunt was very good friends with Manny Ghent fifty years ago."

She loved that and said she would.

Manny. For years I hadn't thought about him much if at all—until I wrote about Harry and wondered if Manny had maintained contact with him. I googled Manny and discovered with a pang that he had died. When I reread my journal, I remembered how important he was to me in 1960 and how close we became.

That was months ago. But after talking to Sue, I realized that the intelligent, interesting and complicated 35-year-old man I had known, a psychoanalyst who, at the time, would have preferred to be a composer, had become a guru to a host of younger generation analysts. I began to obsess about an alternate life I might have lived if the timing had been different and I had met Manny before I met Harry. Might I have fallen in love with him instead? If I had and if it had ended in marriage, my life would have been very different. I would no doubt have had another child or two. And that would have been a plus. But on the other hand, I needed the years on my own that I had before I married Al. I needed the work and the people I might otherwise never have known. I needed the time to get over Harry. And most of all, it's hard to imagine that any other marriage would have been as happy as the one I had with Al.

I suppose what I wish for is not a substitute life but an additional life. Probably not an uncommon desire. Despite being so rooted in my actual life, when I think of Manny, I find myself wanting to cry, "Why? Why must I have only one life?" I liked him so much. And the irony is that I did actually meet him first. A week or so before I met Harry, I met Manny at a party, and though we talked only briefly, I liked him immediately. Months later he told me that he had thought of calling me but hadn't.

The other twist is that soon after my affair with Harry began, Harry told me that he had been Manny's patient but that after a while Manny had told him that he didn't want to be his analyst anymore, he preferred to be his friend. Given the psychoanalytic orthodoxy of the day, this cast Manny in an appealingly maverick light. Especially because Harry considered him his best friend.

Another party. This one given by a young man we hardly knew who had a great duplex in the Village. Like so many parties of the time, he probably invited 30 people and 75 or more showed up. We were typical—we brought our friends Jacques and Jillen Lowe. Larry hadn't wanted to go, but Harry had told me he might be coming and since I didn't want to miss a chance of seeing him, I insisted.

From my journal—February 15, 1960

He wasn't there when we arrived, and I felt a little depressed thinking he wouldn't come. There was hardly anyone we knew. Then Millie arrived with Manny Ghent. Manny is a psychoanalyst whom I met a couple of weeks ago at a cocktail party with Norm and Adele [Norman's second wife] . A wonderful, intelligent and sympathetic human being, whom I liked enormously and immediately when first meeting him, and even more Friday night. He's even attractive in a slight, funny-looking way. Appealing is more the word. But to really pique me is the knowledge that he's Harry's best friend and I thought just possibly he knew.

Anyway, I began to feel very gay, and Jill made me feel even gayer. She was drinking hard liquor since there was no beer, and she was immediately high and sexed, putting her head lovingly on the shoulder or against the cheek of any man who happened to be passing by, playing almost the 20's flapper. She set me off. I felt really good, excited, carefree, lovely, and perfectly high. I was both startled and not when, in an exchange with Manny, he said to me, "But you're never depressed."

Then Harry arrived. Larry, Jill, David Bernstein and I were talking in front of the fire, and near the door I saw Harry say hello to Manny, then whisper together for a moment, their arms

76

*around shoulders. It was really out of the corner of my eye that I
saw them. I knew I should call out hello, but I couldn't. I simply
pretended not to have seen him.*

*Then Jill said to me, "Who's that man over there?" "Who? "The
one who looks like Norm might with a beard." "Oh Jill," I said,
overwhelmed, "that's Harry Jackson."*

In truth, Harry really didn't look like Norman. But he had the same
stocky build and the same charismatic presence.

*Harry went upstairs. I talked for a while, trying not to be too
distracted, but the ants in my pants were too much. Jill and I
and Larry went up for drinks. There was such a press that there
was no clear view of Harry. I caught a glimpse of him a few feet
away, but suddenly I panicked at the thought of introducing him
to Larry. My heart was pounding, my chest constricted painfully,
and I decided suddenly that I couldn't make the introduction, so I
took Jacques' drink from Jill and said I'd bring it down to him.*

*A little later I did introduce them. Harry so embarrassed I could
have kicked him. Larry remote.*

*To my surprise, Norm and Adele arrived, entourage and all,
Roger, his girl, and Dick Devine, some Irish vice-squad chief.
Everyone began to say it was a dull party, but I was feeling good,
nervous but expectant, wandering around admiring the pad (it
was a great one) and finally I found my niche—I began to talk to
Manny about psychoanalysis and we sat down on a low round
coffee table under that two-story ceiling and there was lots of
room and light around us and nobody bothered us until Jacques
came over and said we were all going over to their house. I hated
to leave. I was so happy and contented and interested where I
was. Manny said he shouldn't go, he had to catch a plane in the*

morning, but he did come, and oddly enough we picked up again almost immediately, moving to the corner of the long settee in Jill's living room. Larry kept saying he was going home and he did about two o'clock. So did Millie, crocked. It was a good party, some weird African music on the phonograph or Jill playing the bongo drums, and Manny and I just kept talking (me wondering all the while if he knew about Harry and me) and then he said he really had to go home, and I said he'd probably regret in the morning having let himself be cajoled into staying. And he said no he wouldn't, and I realized that he didn't know because he liked me a little too much.

After he left Harry came over. I told him how much I liked Manny. He told me that Manny had told him earlier in the evening when he first arrived that he thought I was a wonderful girl. "Well," I laughed, "you may have to share me with your friend." "Oh, I'm queer for that," he said.

My love affair with Harry went up and down and on and off again for the next few months. There wasn't any mention of Manny in the Journal until June. It was during one off-Harry period when one day I ran into Manny on Charles Street where he lived.

From my journal—June 10, 1960

We talked for a while... He said the girl he'd just broken up with had been in an accident and that he'd been tied up with that, but that he had tried to call me once. At the party, we'd discussed playing piano and recorder duets, and he asked if I'd like to go ahead and do it. In the cold light of day, the tender interest with which he was looking at me made me feel both very good and rather nervous. And I had to laugh at myself because suddenly

78

life didn't seem quite so empty without Harry.

There's something both reassuring and challenging about Manny entering the picture at this point. Just by the way he looks at me makes it very obvious that he wants to take me into the sack with him. And I, I find him very appealing. I told Harry jokingly one day that he better never leave the two of us alone together and Harry said, "Like that's the one man in the world who could make me jealous. Because of the way I feel about you both." The trouble is, I like Manny too well to use him to make Harry jealous. Without knowing him at all, I have a strangely strong feeling of closeness to him. I had it right away even before I knew Harry, and of course, he being Harry's best friend, makes me want even more to make him my friend. Physically and emotionally I feel that it would be awfully easy to go to bed with him, and I also feel that it would be a terrible mistake. So the challenge is this. I've never been very adept at involving a man platonically. And yet that's exactly what I would like to do with Manny. It won't be easy. When I went to pick up some music a couple of days later, he was in the middle of a session, so we only spent a few minutes discussing the music. But the way he naturally, almost intimately put his arm around me as he ushered me in and out, and the solicitousness with which he asked me how I was, made me feel absolutely as flustered as a young inept girl.

Manny's obvious interest and the pleasure and excitement of connecting with someone new, no doubt imbued my mood, and when I saw Harry the next day, I was so relaxed and perhaps so eloquent, that he fell in love with me again.

From my journal—June 14, 1960

Manny came over yesterday afternoon to play duets. Harry had just told me on the phone an hour before that Manny knew about us — he had guessed. I felt much relieved, and easier with him than I would have if I'd been expecting him to make a pass. It's strange how close I feel to him. I told him so as he was leaving and he said, "I feel close too, and also somehow reserved."

All these years later I realize how gullible I was. There was no reason for Manny to have guessed. Undoubtedly Harry had told him. I can even imagine the conversation: Manny telling Harry that he was going to see me, and Harry saying, Manny, no one is supposed to know this, but Barbara and I....

Needless to say, things with Harry remained totally volatile, and I kept pulling my daisy petals.

Looking back I can't much blame Harry. He was alone and lonely. He envied me my family, and what he saw as my protected background, and without children himself, I don't think he realized how hellish it was for me to try to break up my marriage. Finally, he said that he would soon go back to Italy. Would I go with him? So finally I engineered a confession to Larry. At which point things got really complicated. Faced with losing me, Larry realized he really loved me, and our marriage got tender and interesting again. But since I was still in love with Harry, Larry thought I ought to go to Italy and find out if Harry was what I really wanted. However, at this point, Harry was going into a depression, and he didn't want me at all.

From my journal—July 4, 1960

Manny came over the other afternoon, and we talked for a couple of hours. He both excited and upset me. He talked about his divorce, how there was no good superficial reason for it (and

evidently his wife didn't want it), how shitty he felt after it, how
often he's felt that he gave up an awful lot, and for what? But that
he still feels as if it was right. I knew exactly what he meant. It is
better to live hard, to live lonely, with all the dreary mistakes one
makes that way, but at least to live with the possibility of trying
for something extraordinary, rather than live in the safe and
limited fashion that is so tempting. Later he said, "All of this talk
of failure, somehow it doesn't sit well. It gives me the feeling that
it's only an excuse for maintaining the status quo." I don't agree
with him. And I told him that for the first time he did give me the
feeling that he was pulling the analyst on me. Certainly he cannot
be without ulterior motive, both because of his own experience
and because of the attraction between us which was more than
evident that afternoon. But it gave me pause. It made me realize
again that to stay with Larry is a denial of myself. And Manny
makes me doubly aware of it, not only because of his own values,
but because of the feelings I have for him. I realized thinking
about it yesterday, that it isn't Harry who stops us. Indeed, what
is added because of him are the dangers and temptations of the
orgy, which I suspect both Manny and I have a yen for, and so we
are the more driven toward each other because this is the one way
in which we could indulge it. What really stops me is Larry...

At this point, I started seeing Manny a lot.

From my journal—July 8, 1960

Have seen Manny a couple of times this week. How much I like
him. Yet when he kissed me yesterday for the first time, I had
to try to open up and I couldn't. I felt like I was ten feet off and
watching. It's odd to feel so closed when I continually feel like

throwing myself into his arms. But then it's all so strange. How much of our desire is Harry and how much does he inhibit it? I feel rather sad about Manny now. It seems too bad that I couldn't have loved him, rather than Harry, because I feel that he too really wants to find someone. And it might just have happened. He told me yesterday that he had wanted to call me after the first time we met, going to the Rona Jaffe cocktail party. But somehow he hadn't, and then I met Harry and he guessed that Harry was interested in me. But it seems so impossible now. For one thing it's just the sort of thing that never happens just because one is so aware of its possibility. Manny told me yesterday too that I'm one of the few women with whom he's ever been able to envisage a permanent relationship.

Finally, I feel our sympathy comes from a very basic likeness. I remember I too had a fantasy about him shortly after we met. And we're both so much alike in our desire to let sex lead us where it will, but both too tight in our awareness to just let it roll. Harry is too much between us. And Larry too now. To carry on a clandestine affair is completely repellent to me now, in fact impossible. And to do it openly seems equally impossible so long as I'm living with Larry. And I feel too as if we're perhaps too much alike to be well-matched as lovers. I really don't want to get involved.

Larry, Peter and I went to Provincetown for several weeks. A letter to Manny which I wrote from there, was filled with my usual recognitions of a need to move on and my seeming inability to do so. I ended the letter by saying, "I doubt myself. Revelation always exalts me so that I stand about admiring it until the impulse toward action is gone."

Manny wrote back—a long letter, filled with his own complicated feelings and actions. He described meandering through a few days, excoriating himself for some prideful failings, trying to write a story about mistaken identity, and finally, he felt better because "Last few days I've gotten into scribbling music." The letter was typed, but at the end, he handwrote a critique of what he had written, and ended by scrawling, "You may not have realized it but I have lots to thank you for too. And what's more, I miss you."

Provincetown, as always, lightened my mood. Sea and sand and children wandering the beach. But back in New York, I was once again obsessing about Harry.

From my journal—August 31, 1960

I don't know why Manny is the only person I really want to talk to. Is it only the aura of Harry which by virtue of his being his friend, of seeing him, of talking to him, rubs off on Manny? I feel now as if I can't call Manny either, even though I desperately want to talk to him. I feel as if I'm using him, and I like him too well for that. It seems now as if we cannot be friends. We have reached an impasse, without sex it is even impossible to touch each other, perhaps even sex would be impossible now. He is too much man to my woman and yet not man enough to carry me away. He said the other day that he is afraid of me. Afraid of what? Of falling in love with me? Of my falling in love with him? Of neither one of us falling in love? Now really Manny, what is there to be afraid of? I ache so when you close up to me. It hurt the other day that you wanted to leave when you admitted to wishing you were somewhere else, away. I wanted to say, don't run, don't abandon me, and I also wanted to forget about my own aches, I wanted simply to put my arms around you, to cradle you, because out there where you were was so unbearably lonely. And I couldn't touch you. Even hugging you a little before you left,

I felt as if we weren't really touching each other. Manny, I fear now you are going to stay clear. In bad moments I feel that I have become a bore, and so quite naturally you don't want to see me anymore.

From my journal—September 7, 1960

Thursday, wandering the streets, 9/7/60 desperately looking for Harry, I ran into Manny at the corner of 4th and Charles. We went and had coffee together, and talked about how we felt about each other, and I talked about how I felt about Harry. At the end of it we felt close again and liking each other and Manny said to me, "I hope you do run into Harry, I'd like to see what would happen."

From my journal—September 9, 1960

Want to talk to Manny. Ran into him and Dina yesterday morning. Felt some strain. He called late in the afternoon and I was delighted that he did and that he sounded really concerned about how I was. But couldn't talk to him because Larry was home. In the morning I'd felt so frustrated because what I'd wanted to say was, how is Harry. I couldn't because Dina was there. And again when he called, what I wanted to say was how is Harry, and couldn't because I didn't want to ravage Larry's feelings. I think I'll call him today.

Later:

Spoke to Manny on the phone. I'm worried about Harry. He's still enormously depressed. Manny said that he doesn't like to see him leave in this state, that while he's left before when he's been depressed and pulled out of it once he got there, still he's never seen Harry quite so depressed as this.

From my journal—September 14, 1960

...I saw Manny yesterday for a couple of hours. I was feeling pretty down and when he finished with me I felt riddled with bullet holes, but much better. As I said to him, he made me feel good because he scattered me into pieces but still made me feel like he accepted me. He said, "I guess we all want to be broken up into little pieces and then put together again. I do too." "Are you ever?" I asked. "Only by the kookie ones. The kookier they are the better they can do it." A couple of things he said to me hit me rather hard. He said, "You talk so much about giving, you try too hard, maybe you'd give more by just being." Was he trying to tell me that I pull too hard at Harry by wanting too intensely to give? (I remember Harry saying to me at one point when I'd just cheerfully suggested a picnic that I didn't feel totally like doing, "you look like you're trying to keep a stiff upper lip.") And we had a funny exchange. I said that sometimes I feel so strong I feel as if I could hold up the whole world. Manny said, "That's a funny way to put it. Most people when they're feeling good feel like they're on top of the world." I laughed and said, "Well, I guess I'm afraid of heights." And maybe that's just about true. At the top I always know I'm going to come tumbling down.

From my journal—September 19, 1960

Manny. He said to me the other day (he had called to say he needed his manuscript and so I had run it over to him and since he had a patient, we stood for a few minutes talking in the hall; it was the day I felt so rotten, so confused, and I complained of how inert I felt, incapable of making up my mind even of so simple a thing as to whether or not to make a telephone call) he said, "Don't look for simple directives in the things I say to you, truly, I don't know either what you should do." And yet, it was in effect a directive, and a very wise one too, when he said to me the day before, "I know it often doesn't matter when you love and want someone whether they really do not love you or whether they simply have to move away from you from some deep necessity of their own. But sometimes, if you can, the best thing you can do is have the patience and the wisdom to wait and to be." I wasn't quite sure of what he meant then. Now it seems quite clear. What a funny, wonderful man he is. After two hours in which he made me into psychological mincemeat, he could put his arms around me, hold me and kiss me, not to make love to me but to comfort me (and himself), and then turn suddenly boyish and playful. When I made an arch remark, he grinned and said, "I feel as if all I have to do with you is push a button, only it's all over you," and pushing imaginary buttons on me he all of a sudden swung me upside down in the air. We giggled and shouted at ourselves and the whole goddam kaboodle of the world. And the next day, in the hall, talking about how beat and depressed I felt, he suddenly said, "My God your eyes are bright," and we were joking and laughing again and I felt in spite of myself full of life.

With nothing resolved between us, Harry finally left for Italy, late September or early October. In the journal, there are references to Manny calling occasionally, but after October 20th I stopped writing. I think I was too worried about Norman to write anything. However, Manny and I were still close enough so that I called him a month later when Norman stabbed Adele. I can't remember whether he offered or I asked him to talk to Norman. He tried. He went up to the apartment but Norman wouldn't even let him in. Later that day or the next, Manny came to the family conference with Mother and Dad, when I had to tell them what had happened. Mother got a strong stubborn look on her face—she was going to protect her son at all costs. Manny said to me afterward that she made him think of a Mafia mother. His disapproval was palpable. I felt that perhaps I too had become morally suspect.

I don't remember what, if any, we saw of each other in the months that followed. In January, Harry came back from Italy—for me, I suspect since he didn't plan to stay long. He asked me to go to Italy with him for a month. I did. And by the time I returned, Larry had found Libby and we separated.

I no longer kept the journal. As a single mother, earning a living, I was too busy. Harry came back to the States in the summer of 1961. I'm sure I had contact with Manny now and again. If nothing else we would run into each other on the street. And I do remember Manny and his girlfriend and Harry and I drove down to Philadelphia one day because Harry wanted to see an exhibit of Thomas Eakins paintings.

But by the time Harry and I broke up in the summer of 1962, I believe Manny had moved away. I was under the impression that he had married. Given the context and the intensity of our relations, and the unresolved nature of our attraction, I suppose it seemed unlikely that we could still be friends. I went on to another life. As did he. I wish I knew whether he and Harry stayed close. Or whether like me, Manny no longer wished to be broken into pieces.

The Dunes

Going through papers the other day I came across a number of letters from Charlotte Gilbertson, someone I hadn't seen or heard from in a long time, not since the mid- to late-1960's, now almost 50 years ago. She was a friend of Beverly, Norman's fourth wife, and what brought us together were the Peaked Hill sand dunes in Provincetown.

As a child, I was enthralled by a book about a girl who roamed the wild dunes near Barnegat Bay in New Jersey, and I had hankered ever since to have a similar experience. Years later as an adult, during summer vacations in Provincetown, one of the favorite activities of family and friends was to walk across the dunes from Route 6 to the ocean, where we would sometimes picnic or swim. On those walks, I'd see distant shacks, and pass by the remnants of the Coast Guard station that Eugene O'Neill had inhabited one summer in the early 1900s. I learned that residents or frequent visitors to Provincetown sometimes stayed in the shacks, some of which were owned, but in the years before the National Seashore took over, I think most were occupied by those who had established squatting rights. One such squatter was Hazel Hawthorne, whom I met in 1958. My first husband, Larry, and my son, Peter, and I had just arrived to spend a week or two at what was then called the Waterfront Apartments, run by Eldred and Mary Mowery. Immediately, we found ourselves invited to a cocktail party that was being held by one of our neighbors. It was certainly more fun than unpacking. While we were there some friends suggested that afterward, we go to dinner with them.

"But I don't have a babysitter," I said.

"Maybe Hazel Hawthorne could sit. She's a grandmother and she might like to make a few bucks." My friend pointed to a woman at the other end of the room—an athletic blond who didn't look nearly old enough to be a grandmother though, in fact, she was. Hazel had been spending her summers on the dunes for forty years. At first, she had stayed at the Coast Guard house, but over the years had somehow acquired squatting rights to two shacks, one called Euphoria, which she occupied herself, and one named Thalassa, which she rented out.

Hazel did wind up babysitting for Peter that night. And in the summers that followed, I would occasionally see her at parties or at the A&P when she came into town to refill her larder.

Six years later I bumped into Hazel at another summer party. By then it was 1964 and I had been divorced for several years. I found myself telling her how much I would like to try living on the dunes for a while, though the reality was that I couldn't leave my job for more than a week or two. Hazel told me that while she usually rented her second shack for the whole summer, a good friend of hers wanted it the following summer for only two weeks in the middle, and so she might be renting it by the week the rest of the time. If that happened, she'd let me know.

I soon forgot about our conversation, but the following April a letter from her arrived. If I was still interested, I could have the shack for a week at the beginning of July. The rent was twenty dollars.

Well, I told myself, push has come to shove. Peter would be in camp. I told her I'd take it. But how, I asked her, once in Provincetown, would

I get there?

She said she'd arrange for Charlie, a man who had another dune shack and also a dune buggy, to pick me up, along with my dog, and my stuff.

At that point, I'd been involved with Al for a couple of years. Just before I was to leave, he got an assignment to do some filming in England and invited me to come with him for the week. I had at that time never been to England and rather yearned to go. But it was my dune week. I felt that if I didn't go to the dunes now, I probably never would, and I felt certain that I would eventually get to England. So I turned Al down and flew to Provincetown.

I spent my first night in Provincetown at Norman's. Charlie arrived early in the afternoon of the next day, July 3rd. After kissing my parents goodbye, (they were visiting for the weekend) I piled into Charlie's jeep with my Welsh Corgi, Bouncer, two bags of groceries, and a suitcase with a few clothes and books. On the way out, Charlie told me about his shack, a three-story construction he'd erected himself. When we arrived at Thalassa, he gallantly deposited my stuff inside and led me down a small hill in back to show me the well.

Unfortunately, the well wasn't working. So we got back in the jeep and drove down the beach to Euphoria, Hazel's shack. She filled a couple of gallon containers with water, and the three of us returned to Thalassa and conferred over the well. As I remember, they determined that there was a broken part on the pulley mechanism. Hazel said she'd replace it after the weekend, but meanwhile, I had enough water for a couple of days.

I pulled out the bottle of Scotch that I'd brought and we made a merry dent in it while they regaled me with stories of their lives on the dunes. When her children were little, Hazel had spent whole summers with them in the Coast Guard house, summers that sometimes lasted for four or five months. That was in the '20s or '30s. Now in the 1960s, she spent at least six months of the year in her shack.

The day was cloudy and very quiet, and our little party seemed to make the stillness surrounding us palpable. It felt right, the desert island I had expected.

On Sunday I woke to a brilliant blue, to the sun, and to the sound of sight-seeing buggies laboring through the sandhills behind me. Then the steady shrill hum of the sight-seeing plane cut through the air. I got up and went out to look at the ocean. Spread along the beach were several fishermen casting their lines, their vehicles beside them.

Wryly, I thought, so much for my fantasy of a remote, unpeopled place.

But it was Sunday, the 4th of July. On Monday, everyone was gone and the dunes felt wild again.

Thalassa was nothing if not snug. Its dimensions were about 8 feet by 12 feet, maybe less. A single bed filled one wall and a table and bench stood under the window on the opposite wall. Between them was about two feet of space, which, if one had overnight company, would be occupied by a foldup cot stored in a corner of the shack, in which case it would require some serious gymnastics to get free of the bed. A two-burner hot plate at one end of the shack was fed through the wall by some form of liquid gas in a container attached outside. A few pots and pans had been provided. There was no indoor plumbing. The privy was a few feet from the shack—a small wooden structure that contained a wooden bench with a hole. There was no door, but a slight rise in the dune sheltered it. One could not see the beach but the view of the sea was glorious. Since there was no electricity or refrigeration, I had brought canned and a little not too perishable fresh food. To light the dark, there was a kerosene lamp on the table. I had been advised by Hazel to bring a lot of matches.

I also brought several books. And a Greek grammar. I'm not sure why I thought this week would be an ideal way to start the study of a difficult and not very useful language. In any event, I never got beyond the alphabet.

There turned out to be a great deal to do. In addition to getting water from the well, I would every couple of days take the waste from my meal preparations down to the beach where I would burn up as much as possible and bury the rest in the sand, all somewhat time consuming, and probably not environmentally sound. Still, it made me feel that I was dealing with life on an elemental level. I also swam a lot and took long walks on the beach and gazed out at the ocean more than I read. Perhaps because it was so reminiscent of childhood summers by the sea, I kept feeling as if a limitless future lay ahead and had to remind myself that I was pushing forty. But living with the mystery of the ocean and the sweep of the sky instead of my usual daily habits and concerns made me conscious of the cosmos and how extraordinary it was to be a part of it, no matter how small and finite I might be.

One day, to replenish my larder and get some fresh food, I walked with Bouncer across the dunes and into town. Poor thing. In the heat of the day, the sand not only burned his paws but since he was so low-slung even his belly felt the heat. He kept looking at me as if I were crazy, but he wouldn't leave my side.

I stopped in to see Norman, who told me that Mother before she returned home had been so upset about my week on the dunes that she kept asking him what was wrong with me and why was I doing it. He finally became so annoyed that he said to her, "Because Mom, unlike you and me, Barbara is sane, so she can stand to be alone." Mother was probably as surprised as I was to hear she wasn't sane, and while it might not have alleviated her worry, it did silence her. Norman then told me that he had once rented a shack and gave up on it after one night. He couldn't bear the isolation.

One afternoon toward the end of the week, coming back from a beach walk I found Charlotte Gilbertson sitting on the dune outside Thalassa. She was Beverly's friend, and someone I hardly knew. She looked a little wilted from the sun.

"Why didn't you wait for me inside?" I said.

"Your dog wouldn't let me in."

Fierce old Bouncer. I couldn't help laughing.

I brought out the Scotch, and over the next few hours Charlotte and I became friends. It delighted me that she was so interested in shack living. In fact, in that one visit she became so enamored with Thalassa that the following year she rented it from Hazel for the entire summer.

I too wanted to return and when, at the end of my July week, Hazel mentioned that the shack would be available in early September, I decided to come again. Peter would be home from camp, and because his school started later in the month, it seemed like the perfect way to end the summer.

He has always remembered that week fondly, though to me it hardly seemed like a roaring success. The first couple of days were great. It was Labor Day weekend and we had lots of company. My friend Adeline and her three sons, and one or two Provincetown boys with whom Peter was used to hanging out. Maybe Norman and Beverly came. I remember that Al did—he was just finishing a month of vacation in Provincetown. But on Monday, Labor Day, as the sun was setting, everyone went back to their winter homes.

Peter looked at me and said, "Now what do we do?"

He did not feel the charm of burning garbage or lugging water from the well. He wanted friends. Hazel sweetly invited us to dinner one night, which did prove interesting. Digging in the sand she had found part of a Meershaum pipe which she thought dated to the seventeenth century—a remnant of the Pilgrims. Peter found that exciting. Dinner became a bit problematic, however. Hazel was cooking swordfish kebabs on an authentic Japanese hibachi. Unfortunately, she had lost the grill and simply let the ends of the skewers rest on the rim. Fish chunks kept dropping into the coals, and seeing the hungry eyes of my child, I kept fishing them out with my bare hands.

Most of that week, however, Peter was bored. He kept dragging me into town where for him the action was. Finally, near the end of the week, I left him with Norman and Beverly and went back to the shack for a last sweet day and night alone.

I didn't see Thalassa again until about thirty years later. I had taken some friends for a walk across the dunes to the ocean. Somehow I lost the trail we usually took, and we ended up at the beach just in front of the shack. I was thrilled to have an unexpected chance to share with my friends this relic of my past, and we climbed up the dune to get a better look. Just as we reached the top, a young couple came out from inside. Embarrassed, I apologized for disturbing them, and my friends and I quickly took our leave along the unmarked path I had walked so many times in the summer of 1965.

As we trudged away, I said, "I'd forgotten how small Thalassa was."

I think that in a way Thalassa had merged in my mind with the immensity of the ocean, the sound of the waves, the expanse of sky, the miles of beach, and all the dunes.

In Search of Mother's Age

B rooklyn Heights was never more beautiful than it was that September in the weeks after Mother died. The weather was perfect, the light golden, and the tree-lined streets and brownstone houses more vivid and handsome than I'd ever seen them. For the first time, I was able to imagine myself living there if I were ever forced to leave my beloved West Village.

What surprised me most about emptying Mother's apartment and tying up the remaining few loose ends of her life, was that the chore made me happy. It was, I realized, my way of mourning her, of putting in perspective the sour agonies that had accompanied the deterioration of her last few years.

Not everything got done that month. It was almost a year before I arranged for her footstone (she'd had the foresight to erect the headstone after Dad died). The reason for the delay, for which she would have had no sympathy, was my determination to put an accurate birthdate on the stone.

The realization that I did not know how old Mother was had landed on me, memorably, ten years earlier, in 1975, on the day that her sister, my Aunt Jenny, was buried. Oddly, that had been a nice day, a day of epiphanies, one of the days I include in my private version of "This

Is Your Life." To attend the funeral, Norman and I were to drive out to Long Branch, New Jersey. I'd agreed to meet him at his house on Columbia Heights in Brooklyn. So as I walked along Clark Street from the subway station, I was not expecting to see him, and for a brief instant the man I saw coming toward me from the direction of the river was not my brother but my father—the same gray hair, the same build, the same deliberate gait of someone lost in his own thoughts. How long was the moment? A second? Half a second? Since my father had been dead for two and a half years it was long enough to make my skin prickle before I realized with a small shock that it was Norman walking toward me and that he was no longer a young man. He was 52.

On that perfect spring day, we reached Long Branch with half an hour to spare before the funeral, and Norman suggested we take a look at the ocean, the happy focus of our childhood summers. The hotels we'd known—the New Howland, the Scarboro, the Vendome—were all gone, replaced by garden apartments and kitsch motels. But the boardwalk was still there, and the pier where we'd played Skeeball or taken a ride on the Whip, and of course the beach and the rough Jersey surf where we'd spent most of every summer day. We walked out on the pier. It was quiet and lovely at eleven in the morning of an offseason day. We leaned over the railing and watched the waves and suppressed a yen to eat a hotdog. We hated to leave.

At the funeral, in the usual inaccurate eulogy by a pompous rabbi, we were offered a piece of information—that Aunt Jen was 85 years old—which I did not much notice in the moment. But at the cemetery, as we milled around after the interment, I looked at Aunt Rose's grave (she had died the year before) and noted with surprise that on the recently installed footstone, her date of birth was given as 1893.

I pulled Mother over. "Rose was five years older than you. How come you always told me there were only two years between you?"

Mother answered easily enough. "I felt so guilty for marrying first that I always tried to make her younger than she was."

It seemed plausible. Mother had a number of irrational guilts, and you could never convince her that she was wrong.

Everyone repaired to Adele's house for the post-funeral spread. With all of Mother's family buried in Long Branch, Aunt Jen's daughter, Adele, who lived nearby in Red Bank, was the one who did the receptions—first Dad, then for Aunt Rose, then for Aunt Jen, and later for Mother.

Cousin Sylvia, Jen's other daughter, had come in from Hawaii. She and Adele and Norman and I were reminiscing, and Norman said, "I didn't realize Aunt Jenny was eighty-five."

"In fact," Adele said, "she was older. But she began lying about her age because she didn't want to retire at sixty-five. She was actually eighty-nine."

Norman looked puzzled. "Well, then how old is my mother?"

Sylvia said, "My mother always said she was nine years older than your mother."

If Sylvia was right, it meant that Mother was then 80. But for many years she had said, and I'd believed her, that she was born in 1898, which would have meant that, in the spring of 1975, she was only 77.

That was the moment in which the question of Mother's age took up permanent residence in my brain. I suddenly remembered that over the years the date of her birth had inexplicably changed. When I was a child she had told me that she was born in 1901. Later, perhaps during my adolescence, it had suddenly become 1899. Still, later she said 1898 was the year of her birth. And there she stuck.

Strangely, each time it changed, I'd accepted the information without question. I'd simply readjusted in my mind the age she was when I was born. I'd believed her. Now, suddenly, I thought, I don't actually know my own mother's age!

Norman was gleeful. "God, how marvelous if Mother is eighty. For eighty, she's in great shape."

As if on cue, Mother walked over to us, and Norman, who could never resist an opportunity to tease her, began a small inquisition on the subject of her age. It didn't get very far. She didn't even deign to defend herself. She just walked off in a huff.

Norman and I looked at each other. Now we *knew* she had been lying. "Wouldn't it be funny" Norman said, "if Mother turned out to be older than Dad."

We both laughed. Mother had always seemed much younger than our father, who, we had been told, was born in 1892. And she was younger than Aunt Rose, who, as now writ in stone, was born in 1893. If Sylvia was right, Mother would have been born in 1895. Why, I wondered, did she find it so necessary to lie? Why did this straightforward, practically on the nose woman, who was almost devoid of personal vanity, find that, at the age of about 80, she still needed to lie about her age to her grown children (who would be cheered by an increase in her calendar years, since it boded well for their own futures)? It boggled my mind. Norman took a more melodramatic view. "For a good woman," he said, "she feels too much guilt. There's got to be some awful secret she's been hiding all her life."

Over the next ten years, I made desultory attempts to pry the truth out of Mother. It became a kind of game. I still see the two of us in her living room. I would be sitting on the red velvet couch. She would be in one of the aqua velvet club chairs, the fabric thinning with the years as she spent more and more of her time in it. Very soon, I realized that frontal attacks didn't work. A question like "*Why* won't you tell me how old you are?" was answered by a bland, "But I have," or a giggling, "Why do you care?" To the latter, I could not help but answer, "Because how can I ever hope to know what happened 10,000 years ago if I don't even know my own Mother's age." This she found hilarious, as I knew she would.

But I was serious. I am, in fact, fascinated by pre-history, and for some years I had been marveling at the fact that we know almost nothing about people living as short a time ago as 10,000 years.

I became more devious. She liked to talk about her childhood, and I would ask innocent-sounding questions, like how old had she been when Aunt Jen got married or Osie was born. Sometimes I tried a one/two punch, like how old had she been when Aunt Beck got married, and a little later, what year did Aunt Beck get married. She never missed a beat. Her answers were always consistent with 1898, or her memory conveniently failed her. Looking back on it now, I suspect it was a game I didn't wholeheartedly want to win. Mother's ability to deflect me was so impressive, so nearly heroic, that I think it would have saddened me if she had ever given herself away.

She began to have trouble paying bills, and so I began to help her. In some paperwork we were doing, Dad's date of birth was given as 1891 instead of 1892. I pointed it out to Mother. She didn't seem surprised.

"For Chrissake," I said, "why did he bother to make himself a year younger?"

"Oh, it had to do with an insurance policy he was applying for." A standard answer, but it made some sense. I had a dim notion that the premiums for some life insurance policies were based on five-year categories, and during the Depression, a small difference in a premium would have been important.

So Dad had been a year older than we'd thought—81 instead of 80 when he died. Yet I was still no closer to knowing how old Mother was.

After her episode of congestive heart failure in 1981, the game became less fun. She moved less and less, under the belief, I am sure, that if she didn't move at all she would live forever. Her brain seemed to deteriorate along with her muscles. Even her reminiscences began to lose coherence. I realized that no matter what she told me now, it would be suspect. I was resigned to never knowing. Then, one evening at a party in late 1983 or early 1984, a surprising piece of information jolted my curiosity again. An acquaintance, Howard Goldberg, told me that his paternal grandparents had lived in Long Branch, and his Aunt Frances, now aged 90, had been a good friend of Mother's. I did the arithmetic. Mother was supposedly 86. Four years seemed like a large age difference between close friends.

I tried the game again. I told Mother her old friend Frances Goldberg had sent regards. Did she remember her?

"Oh yes," Mother said. "We were very good friends till she accused me of trying to steal her boyfriend."

"Did you go to school together?"

Even through the thick lenses of her cataract glasses, I could see wariness flicker into Mother's eyes.

"I don't remember if we were in the same class."

"Were you the same age?"

The flicker turned into a gleam of combat. "Oh you know," she said airily, "there was probably a year or two difference, give or take. I was so hurt when she accused me. I told her in no uncertain terms that I had no need to steal her boyfriend because I had plenty of my own. We didn't speak after that." I dropped the interrogation. The image of Mother at the age of 20 or so, charming another woman's young man, was too delicious. Poor upright Fanny. I'm sure she meant no harm. But if you're sitting next to someone at a party, surely you must talk to him. And if you're having a conversation, surely you mustn't be expected to control your natural animation or your inclination to listen sympathetically (even if you couldn't have cared less). If the young man found her pretty and flirtatious just because she was being polite, that was his problem. I'm sure she felt, as she was to say to me so often when people cared less about me than I wished, "It's their loss." On the other hand, close friends were not so easily come by in a small town, and people relished mean gossip. I don't think Mother ever had a close friend again, and quite openly never trusted anyone outside the family.

Since even in her now fuzzy mental state, I was not going to trick Mother into a definitive admission, I began to think a bit more like the researcher I used to be when I worked on documentary films. Maybe I could find out what year Mother graduated from high school. I called Osie. She didn't know, but she did know the name of the school—the Chattel High School in Long Branch.

In February of 1984, I called the Long Branch school system and reached a nice woman by the name of Mrs. Holden. I told her I thought Mother probably graduated high school between 1912 and 1916. She said they had attendance records going back to the nineteenth century but much of it was in the basement, and largely inaccessible. If I would send a written request, she would see what she could do.

I did as she suggested, and a few weeks later received a copy of a report card for a Fanny Schneider who entered the high school in 1913, whose father was Jacob Schneider (wrong name), living on Garfield Avenue (wrong address) and had been born in 1900 (even younger than Mother claimed to be). I called Mrs. Holden to ask if there could have been another Fanny Schneider, unlikely as that would seem to be. In fact, there was, but she didn't think it could be Mother because this other Fanny Schneider entered the eighth grade in 1905 at the age of 13. She gave me some of the details and the anglicized name of the father (Henry, which might well stand for Chaim), and the address seemed relatively accurate.

Mother couldn't be *that* old, I thought. Maybe the family had decided to make her older than she was. She had no doubt been a bright child and they probably wanted to get her into school early. But at the age of three or four? Or was there a third Fanny Schneider?

It occurred to me that information on her sisters might cast light on the mystery, and I wrote to Mrs. Holden again, requesting any records for Beck, Jenny, and Rose. The answer, when it came months later, was that they had found nothing in the accessible paper documents, and to search the microfilm would be too time-consuming. I asked if I could do it myself and she said that would require permission from the principal.

I didn't pursue it any further. Even if I got permission I didn't know how or when I'd be able to spend the time. I was still working at Simon & Schuster, I'd just had a hysterectomy, and I was more and more preoccupied with Mother's deterioration. As she became more dependent, she grew more difficult, fighting all the time with the two young women, Ann Marie and Rose, who had been taking care of her since 1981. I couldn't bear the idea of putting her in a nursing home. Should I quit my job and take care of her myself? The thought of listening all day to the tic she had developed (she would ask, "What time is it?" about every 30 seconds or so), seemed like Chinese water torture. I knew I wouldn't be able to do it.

We lucked out. An old acquaintance in Provincetown died in the summer of 1984, and his nurse, Eva Santiago, became available to care for Mother. A firm, intelligent woman with a sense of humor, she capably fed and jollied Mother for ten months until the end.

My feelings toward Mother in those last years were often a mixture of anger, pity, disbelief, love and exasperation. And guilt about the fact that I couldn't help but hope she would die before she became a total vegetable. I felt betrayed. Mother, the rock, was disintegrating. A few of my journal entries written during the last year of her life give a sense of what it was like.

From my journal—July 21, 1984

Driving up from the city on Wednesday with Mother and Tom Piazza, a friend of my son, Peter, and of the family in general. I was so hopeful that Mother might actually enjoy herself this time in P-town. She was more in touch than I've seen her in months. And Tom was marvelous—patient with her repeated question, "Where are we now?" He kept giving detailed and different answers, teasing her about her loyalty to Peter, and helping me get her in and out of the car. When we stopped for lunch, Mother said how much she was enjoying the trip. And then after Peter picked us up in Hyannis, she got into real form, defending Peter against Tom's usual raillery (when he complained to her about the way Peter treats him, she said crisply, "You want me to shed a tear?") We all enjoyed it, Tom particularly.

Then yesterday, she began during the day to talk about how she has to get back to New York to take care of the business. I said everything was taken care of, which seemed to satisfy her. Then, just as Al and I were finishing dinner, Steve came over, looking breathless and upset, saying Mother was insisting on calling Jenny, who was Jenny? He mentioned a telephone number, which was Osie's (amazing that she remembers any telephone numbers). I went over to Norman's house and found everyone (except Norman and Norris who were out to dinner) in the bedroom with Mother, who was in her nightgown, sitting on the bed, hallucinating. Her talk was so nutty, it's hard to reconstruct. She seems to have got the idea in her head that her caretaker, Rose, is helping her run a business (she kept asking me, "do you think she'll buy it?"), and worrying that Rose is stealing (she kept asking me what Rose did with all the money. I tried entering into the fantasy but it was impossible to satisfy her. She backed me into the wall with her logic until I finally had no recourse but to straighten her out and say there was no business, that the money was what she paid Rose to take care of her. She would accept it for a minute, then go back to the "business" or "the store" where she said they were selling meat. Sometimes she would suddenly realize she was "all mixed up." Or she would accuse me of trying to mix her up. A few times she said she wished she were dead. Other times she called me an angel, repeating endlessly that her children are gems and all she cares about. Once she said, "I want my parents to take care of me" (the memory of that makes me want to weep). I've never seen her so tense, so frightened, and so pitiful. Once, indeed, she said, "Pity me." Mother! Who's always been too proud to want anybody to pity her.

I don't think I calmed her at all. Finally, she just got tired and agreed to lie down. But she was so tense she barely seemed to touch the bed. And when she started the store hallucination again, I got angry (partly deliberately, since anger seems to be the only thing that snaps her out of it). Norman rushed in when he heard my voice rise and I had to hiss at him to get out and let me handle it. She finally seemed okay and I left her.

I don't know whether she's close to dying or whether it's just her fear of dying. A lot of it I think is that she's almost blind and so she must feel as if she's in the dark, and she was afraid of the dark when she was a child. Was it her prescience of how she would end?

Norman thinks she must be feeling very guilty about something she once did, but I'm not so sure—if true, it was probably something from a previous life. As Norman said last night, "This is the reward for a virtuous life?"

Visited Mother briefly this morning. She seemed somewhat back in touch—kept asking me how I slept after our "exciting evening."

From my journal—August 5, 1984

Brought Mother home with us on Tuesday. She keeps saying she's dying to whoever is around, and has become terribly clingy. She calls several times a day, even on good days, and she's driving me crazy with Rose. She fought with her within half an hour of arriving, and I'm beginning to think that Rose does indeed treat her meanly, or at least indifferently. But Mother's abusiveness toward her is so ugly that I can't control my temper when I hear her calling Rose names. Yet when it comes right down to finding someone else, Mother always decides to make do. I really don't know how to handle it. I'm appalled at her being locked in this misery in her last days, but I don't know how much of it she is causing herself. She goes in and out of hallucinations so fast I never know what to expect next. I really have to train myself to take each day at a time, and be prepared for a crisis every time the telephone rings. Most of all, my role seems to be to jolly her out of her bad moods. It's enormously distracting. I feel as if I'm dealing with the rest of my life—work particularly—superficially.

At least Mother gets along with Ann now. She called me today and said she wanted to leave her something, would I take care of it? Only she called her Rose.

From my journal—January 9, 1985

After complaining about a new sense of apprehension and dread and a long litany of family ailments—Adeline, Norman, Danielle, Peter, Al, and myself, I wrote: Only Mother stays healthy. It's almost comic the way everyone around her, including the people caring for her, can be sick, and she never catches so much as a cold. Otherwise, she seems to deteriorate weekly. Less sight, less sense, less hearing. I used to feel as if she had, by strength of will, protected us all, and now as she goes down the drain, so goes the family. Yet I can't bear the sight of her waning away, losing touch with all the things that give life point, sinking bitterly, yes bitterly and ungraciously into the grave. I can't understand why she wants to go on. Please God, don't let me go that way.

From my journal—August 29, 1985, 7 a.m.

Mother died yesterday at about two in the afternoon.

I haven't really been able to grieve yet. Nothing like a death to elicit one's executive abilities—the closer to you it is, the more demands on them it makes. Norman was in Provincetown and flew in. He and Al and Eva and I had dinner together. Norman brought up the question of who should do the eulogy. I reminded him that after Dad's funeral he had complained to Mother about the absurdity of the rabbi's eulogy, and she had said that she would like Norman to do her eulogy, and he had said he would.

We knew she was going, but to transpose Adeline's famous comment on marriage—no amount of preparation is worth a damn...

None of the relief I thought I'd feel. Just numb.

What I'm finding hardest to cope with is the feeling that there's nothing there. I got to the apartment about half an hour after she died. I kissed her and stroked her face, but already her body—that poor cadaverous remnant of her body—seemed abandoned. And all afternoon I had no sense of her presence, as if she had left not only her body but her house.

Has Mother already found another life? I would have thought she'd stick around with us a while and not go gallivanting so soon.

Yes, I finally feel something. Abandoned. How normal.

From my journal—August 30, 1985, 8:30 a.m.

Waiting for the limousine to take us to the funeral home.

I woke at 6:00 this morning, thinking about Mother, and all the things I couldn't think to say to the rabbi last night. Oddly and unexpectedly, it made me feel good to look at her in the coffin, even though there was no real likeness. As Norman said, she finally looked like a Jewish princess in the East 80's. The hair was still beautiful, and she was serene and haughty, and it gave me a sense of peace to stand there and look at her.

It occurred to me this morning that the most extraordinary thing about her was how she remained utterly primitive in her emotions, Victorian in her values, and yet grew increasingly flexible and sophisticated in her attitude toward her children and grandchildren. And all this without a trace of schizophrenia.

The most agonizing thing to bear these last few years was that as she grew increasingly helpless, not only her ability but even her desire to protect us seemed to disappear. Today I feel as if her spirit may come back to protect us once again.

From my journal—September 2, 1985

The funeral was very satisfying. Dan Rous, the cantor Grace Jaffe found for us was young, intelligent, sensitive and dignified. He has an excellent voice and read and sang the prayers and psalms—in Hebrew and English, and tried to give some sense of Mother's family and of how the grandchildren felt about her. He got a few things wrong, but that was all right since he had the sense to say in advance that he was a stranger and please forgive him his errors. Then Norman got up and talked about Mother. He was marvelous. He managed to portray her character with love and respect and humor, and without an ounce of sentimentality. I'm sure it was just what Mother wanted.

Ever since the funeral I have felt as if she has come back. It's as if freed from that body she was trying so hard to keep, her spirit is once again able to protect us. Norman and Peter feel the same way. And I have the crazy notion that the reason I couldn't feel her Wednesday and Thursday was that she was visiting Sue. When Sue called me Thursday night, she was reconciled to not getting here in time for the funeral because Mother dying on her birthday was a message to her as if she was being visited!

It's not a palpable presence I feel—just her spirit. It's lovely and I hope it lasts.

Shirley and Adeline seemed to think that I would miss the irritating responsibilities because they had become so much a part of my life. But it's like all that has just melted away. What I miss is the knowing she was there, but separate. Now it's as if I must incorporate her into myself.

Months later I incorporated into my sewing chest a few of Mother's things, including her thimble. As I tried it on my finger, it brought back the feelings of childhood as I watched her sew, and a rush of tenderness for her, and the familiar ache of 'temps perdu'. While I will never again feel so protected, I don't think I will ever entirely lose the feeling.

Absorbing those parts of her I wanted for myself was only part of it, however. I had never thought about her so intensely, and I began to have dreams in which I was writing her biography from inside <u>her</u> head. I had begun to inhabit her mind.

Meanwhile, however, I had to order the footstone, and since the dates would be "writ in stone," I wanted them to be accurate. I began to pester the Long Branch high school again about letting me search their records but after several months of polite but useless phone calls, I gave that up and went off on another tack.

Adele and I had begun to talk a lot by phone. Among other things, we discussed the houses in Long Branch that the Schneider family had lived in while Mother was growing up. I remembered Mother talking about a couple of them, especially the house on Morris Avenue, with grounds so extensive and flowers so beautiful that they had to hire a gardener. It was too late now to ask Mother why, strapped for dough as they so often were, it never occurred to them to do their own gardening. But I thought I knew the answer. It was considered manual labor. And then there was Kingsley Court, a summer hotel consisting of three Newport style 'cottages', that the family had bought in 1922, and which I'd heard about for as long as I could remember. Both Adele and I got interested in the details and decided we'd look up the records in Freehold.

On June 16, 1986, I took the bus to Red Bank where Adele picked me up. In Freehold we ate lunch on the porch of an old hotel, reminiscing about the family. It felt much further south than New Jersey. Adele, who's about 10 years older than I am, had several stories I'd never heard before. One was about the family moving into Kingsley Court. She said it was in the fall of 1926 or 1927. Her family was there. My family was there. Grandma and Grandpa and Aunt Rose were there. Aunt Ann, my father's sister, and her husband, Dave Kessler used to come down on weekends. But as the weather got colder, so did the house which was large, drafty and uninsulated. The furnace couldn't cope. It conked out. In December the pipes burst and everyone moved out, most of them moving into the small hotel that my Uncle Joe and his wife, Sarah, were running.

Adele also told me much about Aunt Beck that I hadn't known before. I had always been aware that Aunt Beck was in many ways the most extraordinary of the sisters—a woman of great intelligence, determination, ability, and character. In the pre-feminist days of the '30s and '40s, Mother used to say, "If only she'd been a man, she'd have been able to do anything." She was like one of those nineteenth-century Southern ladies who, during the Civil War, took over the running of the plantations and held everything together while at the same time they managed to maintain their ladylike manners and grooming. I never heard Aunt Beck raise her voice. The story about the cemetery which Adele told me that day was quintessential Beck.

The only Jews in Long Branch before my grandfather Schneider and his family and friends arrived were German Jews. The German Jewish cemetery was either not welcoming or, more likely, not considered orthodox enough. So when my great grandmother, Leah Kamrass, (Grandpa Schneider's mother-in-law) died in 1898, she was the first person buried in the orthodox cemetery. Her youngest daughter, Minna, dying a few years later in childbirth, was the second, and lies next to her. My grandparents died in 1928 within months of each other. However, they were buried not side by side, but in separate rows, because the congregation believed that orthodoxy required keeping men and women apart not only in the *schul,* but even after death. This continued until Beck's husband, Louis Shapiro died. She wanted a plot for the two of them. The "elders" demurred. It would set a precedent and everyone else could do it too. "Very well," said Beck calmly. "I understand, but in that case, I'll have to bury him in the reform cemetery." Because Louis had been president of the congregation, this was too scandalous to contemplate. And so the temple administration caved in. Beck had her way and incidentally desegregated the cemetery in the process.

Adele's admiration for Beck was boundless. "Do you know," she said, "Beck was the first Republican Committeewoman in the state after female suffrage was passed."

"Republican?" I said. "In *this* family?"

"Oh yes," she said. "Both she and Louis were Republicans until the Depression. And my father was a fervent Democrat. Whenever they got together, they had political arguments, which, except for my mother, they all loved."

After lunch, we went over to the Hall of Records. It had the feel of an old library—brown and beige and lots of wood. For the real estate record, we were sent to a long narrow room, its walls lined with bound books of documents. It wasn't very comfortable. High tables, no chairs. We went through eight or ten H. Schneiders until we found that the Morris Avenue house had been purchased in Uncle Joe's name in 1906, and transferred to Grandma in 1914, presumably when Joe got married. I asked Adele why in the world it was bought in Joe's name in the first place and she guessed because he spoke English, but I still didn't get the logic of that. We couldn't find any record of its sale, but it was probably sold in 1922 when they bought Kingsley Court.

Adele wanted to do everything very fast, whereas I would have liked to linger and mull and maybe make copies. Her impatience distracted me and I almost wished I'd come alone. Until that is, we came to the record of the sale of Kingsley Court, and she provided me with one of the day's comic moments.

"Adele," I said, "they sold Kingsley Court in 1925."

"Impossible," she said. "They owned it when my family lived there in 1926 or 1927. And anyway, they didn't sell it. They lost it."

"But Adele," I said, "here's the document."

She was unimpressed. She insisted they owned it, at least through 1926. That she should be so wedded to her own memory gave me an inner giggle.

Mother, too, always talked about having 'lost' Kingsley Court. Perhaps what she meant was that they had to sell it at a loss. The price was $65,000, of which they got 20 or 25 in cash, and perhaps they had to pay off a second mortgage. One sad little note. The record indicated that before they could sell they had to get their own deed rewritten to include the riparian rights to the beach across the street. In other words, they hadn't known that they were entitled to use the beach. Perhaps if they had known, Kingsley Court would have been more of a success.

Thinking now about how large a part of the family psyche the loss of Kingsley Court became, I suspect that until that time they had felt themselves to be inexorably upwardly mobile. Despite the hard work, maybe because of it, they could see that starting with nothing they had built a business of first a store and then added on a hotel. They had gone from renting to owning their own home, the rather elegant property on Morris Avenue. And in standard American entrepreneurial fashion, they had invested the profits in a still grander establishment—Kingsley Court (even the name indicated something about their expectations). Mother's feelings about the place were probably best evidenced in the story she told a number of times. A limousine stopped there one afternoon in Spring, the passenger came in, said how nice the place looked, and asked if he could get some tea. He was the Lieutenant Governor's father. Mother said they weren't yet open for the season but she'd be happy to serve him and proceeded to do so as if she were in her own home, providing him not only with the tea but also with her company. She was absolutely thrilled to be talking to somebody she considered to have such prestige. So it must have seemed like a comedown when they were reduced to just the butcher shop, and had to rent the summer hotels they ran, and live in the winter in Joe and Sarah's rooming house. When the Depression arrived, the hotel business turned into a losing proposition. Mother was glad to leave it and move to Brooklyn. But I don't think she ever shook the feeling, intensified by our poverty during the Depression, as well as Dad's inability to keep a job because of his gambling, that she lived in straitened circumstances and probably always would. She certainly passed on to me the notion that money was something to be treated with respect but also that one should not put too much value on material things, that it was better not to need than to spend.

Before we left the Hall of Records, Adele suggested that we check the naturalization records of our grandfathers. We were sent to a fusty office run by a very helpful woman who quickly found the information. Our mutual grandfather had filed first papers in 1899 and became a citizen in 1903. Adele started to say something but stopped abruptly. I looked at her and she kicked me under the desk, muttering, "I'll tell you later."

I could hardly wait. As soon as we left I said, "What was that all about?"

"I'll tell you," she said, "but you must promise not to mention it to Osie (Aunt Beck's daughter) because I think it would make her angry." She paused with some dramatic relish. "You know," she said, "Your mother always said that she and Rose had been born here, and Beck and Jen in Russia, and Aunt Beck always maintained all the sisters had been born here. However, my mother told me, and I think you know she was the only one who would tell the truth, that none of the children were born here."

Wow! It had never occurred to me that Mother might be lying about that!

In Long Branch, we drove out to the cemetery. I put roses on Dad's and Mother's graves. It was hot and sunny, peaceful and pleasant. For the first time, I recorded the information on the gravestones of other family members.

Leah Kamrass (my great grandmother, Ida Schneider's mother) died 12/14/98 - 66 years old
 Minna Reisman (Leah's youngest child) died 2/11/03 - 29 years old

Ida Schneider (Grandma) died 5/29/28 - Age 68
Hyman Schneider (Grandpa) died 11/22/28 - Age 69
Joe Schneider (Mother's brother) died 1962, Age 77
Rose (Schneider) Paley - 1893-1974
Jenny (Schneider) Michelson - 11/8/88-5/30/75
Flora (Reisman) Hollander (Minna's youngest child)
1903-1979

There was no way of knowing if any of the birthdates were accurate, except for Flora whom we know was born just before her mother died. But if at the time of her death in 1975 Jennie had been 89 as Sylvia said, she had to have been born in 1886, not 1888. So Joe, who would have been born in 1886 if he were 77 when he died, had to be older since he was the firstborn and Jennie was the third.

So they all lied. Or maybe they just didn't know. It was tricky, in fact, because they were never sure of the exact date since it involved transposing the Jewish calendar and/or the Julian calendar the Russians were still using when they were born. Osie once told me that Mother had said she was born in late December. I suspect she told us January 2nd because, not knowing the exact date, Mother figured she might as well take advantage of stretching a few weeks into another year.

Since it was almost a year since she had died, I felt increasing pressure to give the stonecutter a birthdate so he could finish the headstone and we could put it on her grave. As I was discussing the problem one night during a family dinner at Norman's, Steve suddenly said, "When I was about eight years old I asked Grandma when she was born, and I had the feeling from the way she answered that she was telling me the truth." We all pounced. "What did she say?"

He relished the drama. "I still remember," he said slowly. "She said 1894."

114

A breakthrough! Impossible to imagine her telling anyone that she was older than she actually was. She must have been born no later than that. It was of course hard to believe that she would give a grandchild the information I had begged her for. But then I hadn't yet started to pester her for it as early as 1973 when Steve was eight. Perhaps it salved her conscience to tell a child (who would probably forget) what she had for so long been hiding from the rest of the world.

I called up the stonecutter and gave him the date.

But now there was another mystery. Had Mother been born here or not? That summer, a year after she died, I finally began to go through her papers, which included a handwritten memoir she had once done at Norman's urging. I hadn't before felt the urge to go through it because Norman had said he'd found it disappointing. I know why. It was not dense with colorful detail. Much of it consisted of opinions and pronouncements. But that was so like Mother, and indeed the whole thing was so much in her voice—straightforward, no-nonsense—that it was like having her around again. I loved it.

Also, it turned out to be full of tantalizing hints, though no answers. She said she was 12 or 13 when the Morris Avenue property was bought, which I now knew was in 1906. That would push her birthdate back to 1893 or 1894. She also said that Minna was about 18 when she came here with Grandpa. Since Minna was 29 when she died in 1903 (at least that was the age on the gravestone) it would mean that Grandpa came in 1892. But since Mother, Osie, and Adele had said that Grandma came a couple of years after Grandpa, 1892 knocked all the gravestone birth dates into a cocked hat. If Rose had really been born here in 1893, Grandma would have had to come earlier than 1894, or Mother and Rose would have had to have been born before she came, and Mother no later than 1892-3. Or perhaps Grandma had been pregnant with Rose when Grandpa left, and Mother was born here a year or so after Grandma arrived. According to Adele, Jen had said that Grandma was pregnant with Mother when Grandpa left Russia, and that was why she hadn't come with him. If that were true, and Grandpa left in 1892, Mother would have had to have been born in December 1892 or January 1893 (assuming that she was born in December or January).

I realized I was going to have to look for the dates of their arrivals. It seemed at first like mission impossible. I called the Immigration Service and got treated to the first of the interminable recordings the government and most other large organizations used at that time. Tape 3 told me how to obtain documents: I would need Form G639 or G641 for genealogy research. Available by mail or in person at the nearest Immigration Office. $15 for filing. The taped voice sounded more like Hal from the film 2001, than a real human being, but by dint of waiting out the tape, I did, at last, get a live person at the other end of the line. He said the forms didn't provide much help or information. I would need a date first. I asked if there were any Ellis Island records. He doubted it but said the National Park Service would be able to tell me. Also, the New York Public Library and the National Archives might have records. I might want to talk to the New York City Health Department or the New York Historical Society.

In August, I went to the New York Public Library, a place I love. The Genealogy Division was the size of a small local library, the shelves filled with tantalizing masses of arcane reference volumes and books of local history. The librarians knew what you were looking for almost before you told them, and were graciously happy to tell you how to find what you needed. I lucked into a most knowledgeable lady and found out that while there were no Ellis Island records (they were destroyed in a fire) the manifests of all the ships arriving in New York were on microfilm and available in the Reading Room. They were even indexed by name of the passenger, but only up to 1840 and from 1897 to 1902. Alas. For the intervening years, I would have to go through the microfilm year by year. She made a great suggestion, however. If I knew where they were living in 1900 or 1910 I could go through the censuses, which were now open for those years. One of the questions asked in the censuses was when they had arrived.

Unfortunately, the central New York Public Library didn't have the census records for New Jersey. I could find the 1900 census at the Schomberg branch in Harlem, and both 1900 and 1910 were available at the local center of the National Archives, which was then located in Bayonne, New Jersey.

I called the Bayonne National Archives and got the directions for getting there—a train, a bus, a long walk and another bus. It would take me at least an hour and a half. I decided Schomberg was easier but put it off because, as a small white woman, I felt venturing into Harlem might not be safe.

I went back to Mother's memoir.

Reading her account of her parents, I began to feel a gnawing curiosity about them, particularly my grandmother. Some years before I had once said, "You talk about Grandpa all the time, but not Grandma. What was she like?"

Mother pondered a bit, then said shortly, "She didn't work."

From the photos, I had always pictured her as a workhorse, even a peasant, and so I said, "How could she not? With all those kids?"

"Well," Mother allowed, "she did the cooking. But nothing else."

Given the size of the household—five children, a husband devoted to scholarship, brothers, nieces and in-laws who often came to visit, as well as at least one or two of the Talmudic students my Grandfather liked to have around, the cooking might well have been a full-time job. But Mother's extraordinary one-liner was more or less confirmed by Osie, who added, "she was very intimidating, very opinionated, but very much the lady."

I was so stunned by these descriptions that I discussed them with Rhoda, my oldest friend. Rhoda laughed at me. "Of course she was a lady. She saw herself as the rabbi's wife."

Of course. But by Mother's own account in her memoir, when Grandma first arrived in this country and they opened up a grocery and meat market, Grandma had not only run the household but had functioned as a caterer, providing cakes and appetizers for sale in the store. She must have worked like an ox. Her lady days probably only came later when they moved to Morris Avenue and always had a hired girl to help with the housework and perhaps the cooking. Before that, the daughters had to help, and Mother remembered with some resentment that she and Rose had to make all the beds before they left for school.

One evening, I asked my cousin, Cy (Beck's son) about our grandparents. He was about thirteen when they died, but unfortunately, he'd not been very interested in them as a child, or even able to talk to them much since, unlike Osie, he never learned Yiddish. He said he had often wondered why all the New York rabbis used to come to hear Grandpa resolve theological disputes even though Grandpa didn't want to be a rabbi. He'd finally decided that Grandpa didn't really believe in God. It's probably true that Grandpa's concept of God was far from orthodox since from Mother's account he always spoke of Spinoza as a great thinker, and the only religious notion she seemed to have imbibed was a pantheism of the sort for which Spinoza had been excommunicated. So Cy may have been closer to the truth than either Mother, who said Grandpa had claimed being a rabbi was like having 50 bosses (the congregation), or Osie, who said that he had thought it a parasitic way of life. (The latter reason seems particularly spurious since Grandpa was always scornful of "political Jews" and he had no qualms about exploiting his own children, albeit lovingly. He always expected them to work in the store and to take care of the yeshiva *bochers* he charitably invited into the house for extended stays.)

About Grandma, Cy had even less to tell. He had the impression that nobody much liked her. This was not true. Adele, for instance, claimed she adored her. It was Louie, Cy's father, who didn't like her because she had opposed his marrying Beck, and later, Grandma was furious with him when he talked Jenny out of marrying a rich old man. No doubt he transmitted his own feelings to his children. Beck suffered. In 1957, when she was dying, I went to visit her, and she talked to me about how painful her early years with Louie had been because he didn't want her to spend time with the family she so dearly loved.

In any case, it seems to me that Grandma, even as Osie described her—"very opinionated and very much the lady"—had a definite impact on her daughters since Mother was opinionated, and Beck was a lady—with a will of iron.

Osie, reminiscing about the Morris Avenue house three-quarters of a century later, could still describe it in detail, including the Torah Grandpa owned (a private Torah was probably almost as rare then as it is now) and the leather-upholstered Mission furniture in the parlor, inexpensive at the time. She also told me how the family got into the hotel business. Part of the Morris Avenue property was a 40-room summer house on the other side of the street. The first summer they owned it they rented it out to people who ran it as a hotel. Grandma, who, to make extra money, had sometimes taken in boarders, now decided it would be more profitable to run the hotel themselves. That building, called the Maple Hotel, burned down a couple of years later.

But they were hooked. In 1915 or 1916, Beck heard that the people running the large, elegant Scarboro Hotel were giving up their lease. So she and Louie took over the lease and bought the hotel a couple of years later. Grandma and Grandpa ran a hotel called the Philando until they bought Kingsley Court. During the Wilson Administration, Long Branch was the seat of the summer White House, and business was good for all of them in those years.

To my own surprise, I realized that I was involved in something I had thought would never interest me. I had always thought of genealogy as the sole preserve of those attempting to connect their families to the Mayflower, and as the child of more recent immigrants, I think I protectively scorned an activity that implied I didn't rate. But trying to find one simple fact about Mother, had led me to wonder about the lives of people I had never known or thought much about before, namely, my not so distant forebears, my grandparents.

Willy-nilly, I was doing genealogical research.

Early in September of 1986 I finally screwed up the nerve to venture up to Harlem. It turned out that Schomberg Library at Lenox Avenue and 135th Street was directly across the street from the subway station, so all the courage I had summoned dissolved into a small giggle. I was quickly ensconced in front of a viewing machine with three rolls of microfilm at my side. As I didn't know the exact address at which the family had been living in 1900, I was going to have to scroll through all of Monmouth County to find Long Branch, and go through all of Long Branch.

Along the way, I began to feel a strange falling away of the 86 years that separated me from the time when all this information had been recorded. There was something so intimate about the hand-written forms, the handwriting changing with each census taker. Familiar names began to appear. There were the Reismans, living on North Broadway in Long Branch when Minna was still alive. The census stated that she had arrived in 1891. Aha! She was supposed to have arrived with Grandpa. So he too should have come in 1891.

I came across Dr. Slocum, who had delivered Norman and me. Mother had always spoken of him with great respect, writing in her memoir of the awe and admiration she felt when she entered his house for the first time and discovered a world of Oriental rugs and antique tables and lamps.

Isaac Goldberg, the father of the friend with whom Mother had quarreled, also lived on Broadway. Frances was listed in the census as having been born in 1893. Another aha! They were approximately the same age.

Four hours into the search, weary and worried, I came to Rockwell Avenue, and there I found an entry for "Snyder." Despite the spelling, it was obviously Mother's family. It said Hyman had come in 1891, was 40 years old, and had been born in October, 1859. Grandma had come in 1894 and was 42, born in January 1858. They had been married for 20 years, had 6 children, 5 of whom were living. Their birthdates were given as:

Joe—August, 1880
Beck—September, 1882
Jennie—September, 1885
Rose—June, 1890
Fanny—December, 1891

I nearly fell off my chair in the effort to squelch both a shout of triumph and my disbelief both at what I had found and that I had found it. It was the Eureka moment, the culmination of what I still think of as the day I fell in love with documents.

Still, I could hardly trust my own eyes. I really had not believed that Mother could have been that old. Eighteen ninety-one! Yet it made sense. If Grandpa came in 1891, Grandma probably was pregnant with Mother, and as Adele surmised, it was probably the reason she had not come with him.

At last, I could guess why Mother wouldn't tell us her age. Because she undoubtedly never told Dad, she probably felt that it would be disloyal to him if she told us, even after he died. Or maybe she felt that she really had rewritten history.

That night I called Norman to tell him. He was delighted. Ever the novelist, he carried it a step further. He was convinced that Mother was hiding some other deep secret, like an earlier marriage. I didn't buy it. Lying about her age to Dad seemed like sufficient reason for guilt, and then she'd always attributed any disaster that befell her to her original sin of marrying before Rose had. Though how she could hold onto that guilt when after all she hadn't married until she was 30 (and Rose hadn't married until she was 50) still astonishes me.

I also called Mr. Ardoline at the Long Branch Monument Company to ask if I could change the year of birth on the footstone. He said changing it would be costly and not very satisfactory, and I decided to leave it the way it was. That way Mother won a little. And since Rose's stone said she was born in 1893, the 1894 date would at least keep Mother in her proper chronological position as the youngest in the family. Though it did seem a bit of a shame that it was too late to assuage Mother's marriage guilt by engraving her in stone as older than Rose.

I wrote in my diary the day after Schomberg that I had an idea for a story about the development of an obsession. I was going to call it "Documents."

And then I realized that the information in the census might be suspect. It was a document, but it was a subjective document (as are most), and so I couldn't possibly know how accurate either the interviewer or the interviewee might have been. Was it Joe or Beck or Jennie who gave the information? Unlikely that it was Grandma or Grandpa, as their English was limited. Certainly, the months of birth were doubtful. Osie later insisted that her mother's birthday was December 24 or 25, since Beck had always said she was born at

Christmas. And Jennie's gravestone gave her birthdate as November. I had to remind myself. They all lied. Except maybe Jenny. Whether born in September or November, she would indeed have been 89 when she died in May of 1975.

I realized that I needed to find out exactly when and where Mother had been born. If I could find Grandma's arrival in the passenger lists, I would then know which of the children had arrived with her, and how old they were at the time. (I think now how naive of me to believe that the ages listed would necessarily be correct.) The prospect of going through passenger lists, however, was daunting enough to make me procrastinate a bit. I went back to the telephone. I called Lily Brauer, Mother's cousin, and the only member of Minna's children who was still alive. She couldn't pinpoint Mother's age, but she had been born in 1900 and thought Mother was at least 8 or 10 years older. All the Reisman girls had loved Grandma. They always ran to her with their troubles. In fact, Lily's older sisters, as well as Flora, the youngest, had often lived at Grandma's house.

It occurs to me that there's another thing Grandma provided and passed on to her daughters—a place of haven. People came to stay or visit because it made them feel good, or at least better. The Reisman girls came. Her mentally unstable sister-in-law, Uncle Ike's wife, would periodically appear on the doorstep and stay for a couple of weeks until she felt able to cope with her own family again. Later, from the accounts of both Mother and Lily, Beck's house became a magnet for all her sisters and cousins. And I remember how, much later, in the 1930s, I loved the Sunday nights when we would pile into the old Chevy and travel for almost an hour through the streets of Brooklyn and over the bridge and all the way to 87th Street and Park Avenue, to have dinner at Beck's apartment. I'm not sure why it made me feel so good. Perhaps because Osie was for me the image of glamor, and Beck's aura was graciousness and class, and it was Manhattan, not

Brooklyn. Just being there gave me intimations of another world and the idea that it was not totally inaccessible.

I also called Bob Lucid, who was planning at the time to write Norman's biography, to tell him about my census find, and learned that he had discovered in Norman's basement, letters Mother and Dad had written to each other before they were married. Their courtship had been conducted almost entirely by mail, and she had saved the letters, tied up in packets with pink ribbon. Bob brought them to me the next time he came into New York.

Since most of Mother and Dad's courtship took place by mail, I now had the opportunity to discover the plot. I already knew some of the details, that they met one weekend in Lakewood early in 1920. How almost immediately after, Dad went to New Orleans to take a job, and how Mother, who was always trying to fix Rose up so that she would herself feel free to marry, urged Rose to answer a letter he wrote to them. When Rose refused, Mother answered the letter herself, and she and Dad began corresponding. Mother kept all his letters. Unfortunately, Dad did not save hers until the following October. However, by inference, she found his letters so terrific that she decided around June of 1920 that she was in love with him and, no doubt encouraged by his urging her to be frank, she told him so. I wish I could have seen that letter. I think he panicked. In any case, he wrote her that she was just a child and couldn't possibly be in love with him since she didn't really know him—after all they had met only once. She must have answered angrily because in his next letter he said that he didn't think she wanted to hear from him anymore, and he did not write again from New Orleans. But in September he left his job and moved back to Brooklyn, and then wrote to ask if he might visit. Obviously, she said okay because he went to Long Branch for a week and by the time he left they were unofficially engaged. He then went to Milwaukee where he'd taken another job, and except for a two-week trip east in April, during which they officially announced their engagement, he stayed there until August 1921. During this time they wrote to each other about twice a week, and even after Dad came back east for good, there were occasional notes, as he was living again with Ann and Dave while he looked for work. They were married in New York City by three rabbis in February 1922.

As I read, I found Mother and Dad so much the way I remembered them as being that I was continually suffused with the contradictory familiar emotions they so often evoked in me, of love and irritation, of disapproval and pity, of admiration and dislike, of interest and impatience. What struck me most was Mother's capacity for faith and belief. She was the romantic one. In the first letter that Dad kept, she told him how special he was. Dad's answer was sweet. He knew he was not what she thought and that she didn't know him at all, but I think at least for a while he hoped that he would become the man she believed him to be. He wrote back that he hoped he wouldn't disappoint her. Of course, he did. And Mother, true believer that she was, just transferred all her belief to Norman and me. As I read their letters, I burst into tears. It was like reading a Sherwood Anderson story—the crazy beauty of people's sad lives.

In the letters Mother sometimes referred to herself as the Rock of Gibraltar, and indeed we often called her that. It was easy to liken her to a mountain—all there to see. The metaphor for Dad, on the other hand, would have been a tidal pool—smooth and charming on the surface, and teeming with a secret life in the shallows beneath. The truth is that Mother wasn't all there to see, either, or I wouldn't have been spending so much time these past years trying to understand her. What was most startling about the letters was how young they seemed. They were both getting on toward 30, but they seemed so immature. Dad whined a lot about headaches and colds and all the letters he had to write, and Mother complained and worried when his letters didn't arrive on time. While they both worked hard and took pride in what they did, they thought of work as onerous and believed they would be happier playing.

Even though he was working, Dad seemed to be having money problems, and I suspect he was gambling. He often told her she would be marrying a poor man (her response was, "Any fool can make money"), and it was quite a blow to him when in an early 1920's recession his salary was cut (Mother's reaction—they didn't appreciate him sufficiently). He was certainly worried about his prospects for getting a job in New York, but he never made a serious attempt to get Mother to join him in Milwaukee, and she made it clear she didn't want to leave her family. I also suspect that she was afraid of venturing into a Gentile world. And while Dad would have been much more willing to do so, all of his letters to South Africa were forwarded through Ann and Dave because they didn't want his mother to know that he was no longer living with them.

On the whole, I found myself more irritated with Dad than with Mother. He kept calling her a child when she worried about him or chided him for not writing enough. But to me he came off as a condescending, manipulative brat who in one letter could flatter her, whine about his cold, and let her know of all the women he's surrounded by—but not to worry, he's a changed man. Of course one cannot quite blame him for calling her a child, since if she had not actually lied, she almost undoubtedly must have implied that she was much younger than he. Since ten years later she was still telling us that she had been born in 1901, I wonder if that's what she originally told him.

Years later, I read the letters again and felt more sympathetic to Dad. He would have liked her to know him as he really was, but as he wrote her, "this dear little girl...so obstinately refuses to listen to anything I wish to tell her about my 'other' self—the 'unmasked' self of me! Yes, dear Fan, with your constant reproaches that you won't have me 'run myself down' I don't really know what I dare and what I dare not write you?" To please her, he said he would "shut up". How torn he must have felt between the attraction of her adoration and his fear of losing all the complexities and spices of life, not to mention losing his wayward nature. No wonder in the years that followed he had to live a secret life. In fact, we all did. Norman and I never talked to Mother about the things we did that we knew she would not approve of, and I always believed that she did not really know me.

Dad often accused her of loving his letters or the idea of love, rather than himself. Mother never got a clue. She never questioned her love for him and so she playfully accused him of being jealous of his own letters. It amazes me that he didn't wriggle out of the engagement, but somewhere along the line, he seemed to fall in love with the idea of getting married. For once, I think, he was trying to be a good boy. He knew it would please his family. The letters make clear he was Grandma Mailer's favorite, and so Mother's adoration might well have seemed like something he could live with, undeserving as he knew himself to be.

His ambivalence, if not panic, was evident in his reaction to her disclosure of her feeling for him when they had been writing to each other for only a few months. He did not keep her letter, but he wrote a short note saying he must think about it before replying. He liked her "frankness" (he had been urging her to be open and frank, which was no doubt what emboldened Mother, with all her Victorian primness, to declare herself). He encloses a couple of snapshots of himself in tennis clothes, "which will perhaps show you your unwisdom of bestowing on me the kind 'thought' that you do. I don't deserve it!" (What a tease he was. He looked marvelous in tennis clothes.) The letter he promised was dated five days later. He says he can't help her "liking" him, as well as her frankness, but "I know—know *too well* that such 'regard' of yours for me is impossible—so utterly impossible that I simply can not—and *will not* take you seriously!...such 'feelings' as you wish to convey you hold for me *can not* be possible.... There isn't a speck of intention on my part to in any way hurt your feelings or, in a sense, to 'slight' your admirable frankness...I...admire you for your very frankness itself, and it's because of that that I want you to be on 'guard'—not to say anything that *I know* you cannot feel. Remember, after all, you only met me once. At a time too when the surroundings were pleasant. Is it not possible, therefore, that any such 'attraction' emanating from under such circumstances, might be dissipated under different conditions?. . .I think...you're inclined to be a girl of impulse...." He also encloses a couple of clippings warning against marriage. One of them: "If you *encourage* yourself to fall in love with someone, you will be building an ideal, which may not be like the character of the man you think you love." (His underlining.) At the bottom, he wrote, "Something that almost takes the words out of my own mouth!"

So despite all his pomposity and condescension, he had a pretty clear view. However, he also wrote that he would like to visit her when he once again came north.

On the second reading of the letters I also found that despite knowing the story so well, I was more engaged by the details of the plot. Half of me was reading as the family researcher I had become in the intervening years, ready to pounce on little clues I had not noticed before, and part of me was reading an epistolary novel. Indeed, I found myself frustrated by the elisions that occurred when Mom and Dad actually got together, and I could only guess at what had transpired.

It was almost the end of 1986 before I began to go through the passenger lists. Over the next few months, spending two or three afternoons a week in the North Reading Room of the New York Public Library, I managed to go through 10 rolls of microfilm of the manifests of all the ships arriving in the Port of New York from January

1, 1894, to September 17, 1894, and I was beginning to despair of ever finding Grandma's arrival. It was grueling work, and very frustrating. Dozens of ships arrived every month, and each one from Europe had hundreds of steerage passengers—long pages of name after name, all hand-written. Often the handwriting was almost impossible to decipher. Some of the pages had been so under- or over-exposed that they were too dark or too faint to read. And some had been torn or worn away even before they had been photographed, leaving big holes in the image. I guessed that window light had been used as sometimes names were obscured by grids of dark shadows that resembled window frames. Because the names were so often difficult to read, I began to scan the nationality column, checking only those who were Russian, but worrying all the time that they might have lied about that too. After an hour or so of scrolling through a roll of microfilm, I would find myself falling asleep.

And then there were the machines. Some of them were balky. Always some were out of order. In some, the image was blurred, and in some, the light was too poor for the more inadequately photographed pages to punch through. The machines were very much in use and it became a worry each time whether I would be able to find one that was not only working but working well enough to make the film legible.

Examples of my notes give a sense of the problems:

12/31/1986—20 ships listed for 7/6/1894 to 8/3/1894

7/27/94—Persia out of Hamburg (A lot of it is so dark, it's illegible)

7/27/94—Normannia out of Hamburg (Shadows make much of this illegible)

8/3/94—First Bismarck out of Hamburg - #335-344 missing

1/7/1987—20 ships listed from 8/4/1894 to 8/17/1894

8/10/94—Lahn out of Bremen (most of it is unreadable—thick

writing, blotted and smudged)
8/16/94—Havel out of Bremen (most of it too faint or background too dark to read)
Very good machine—4th table, last one on left, facing South.

Inevitably, I was missing a lot and I began to worry that the listing for Grandma's family was on one of the pages I couldn't read or that I had inadvertently missed it during one of those times when my eyes glazed over. A time or two a family of Schneiders would excite me for a moment, but the names and sexes of the children would turn out to be wrong.

I allowed the library research to lapse for a while. My husband, Al, and I took a trip to Spain and then began to prepare for our first full summer in Provincetown. I did finish reading the courting letters, which confirmed Dad's birthdate as 1891 since he mentioned his 30th birthday in 1921. But the only reference to Mother's age was in a letter Dad wrote in which he said that he was disappointed in a photo she had sent him because "You seem to have become thinner in the face, Fanny dear, and appear older than I believe you to be." I didn't get back to the library until we returned from Provincetown in the fall.

Meanwhile, I found myself mulling over Mother more and more — who she had been and my own relationship with her. I came across a short memoir by Doris Lessing in which she wrote about the frustration of trying to understand her mother only after her death and it was something I felt I could have written myself.

In fact, much of what I read would trigger echoes and memories and questions. While reading Elizabeth Frank's good biography of Louise Bogan, I suddenly realized that one huge lacuna in my understanding of Mother was that I hadn't a clue as to whether or not she enjoyed sex. Norman, years ago, thought she'd never had an orgasm. But I wonder. Perhaps orgasms were the big secret of her life. Dad once confided in

Norman that of all the women he'd known Mother was the best. Was he just being loyal? One of the ironies of their relationship was that despite all his womanizing he never managed to make Mother jealous. I remember her telling me 'that' was one thing she never worried about. Even when he pawed women in front of her, she believed implicitly in his fidelity. It was only her pride that was affronted. It was family shame she felt, not jealousy.

I asked Osie once if Mother had ever discussed sex with her, and she said no. I wonder if she ever discussed it with anyone. In fact, she talked so little about her feelings for Dad, and there was so much friction between them, that most of my life I had not thought of them as ever loving each other. So I was dumbstruck by something she said to me a month or two before Dad died. He was in the hospital, and she spent every day with him. I spent a great deal of time there too, to keep her company. We took a break one day in a coffee shop down the street. We both knew he was dying—it may have been the day the doctor told us there was no hope. And suddenly, as I sipped my coffee, Mother said into the silence, "I keep remembering when I loved him." I think what surprised me beyond the information that she had indeed once loved him, was that she was, for the first time in our lives, being intimate with me.

Perhaps it was my own fault. I may have preferred her propriety—it gave her the strength and authority of the rock we always felt she was. Only now I am no longer sure she was really so monolithic.

On the other hand, she played the role so well and so long, it may have become her existential being.

It amazes me that Mother never used the similarities between her correspondence love affair with Dad and mine with Jack Maher when she was trying to convince me that marrying a Catholic wouldn't work. Did she feel no empathy? Or did she simply think it was unseemly to discuss your emotions with your children? Or was she wise enough to know that when it comes to love, nobody else's experience seems to have relevance to your own? I do remember her saying, "You're in love with love." Exactly what Dad had said to her. Like mother, like daughter, it had no effect on either one of us. And in any case, my youth was not really the issue. Everyone then was marrying young, and if Jack had been Jewish, she would have been happy to accept him. Or if I had been older she might have hesitated to oppose the match out of fear that I would become an old maid.

I dreamt about her a lot in the year after her death. In one dream Mother and I were on a bus on the way to a museum and somehow we went too far. We started to walk back. She was compos mentis but very old and infirm, and I ended up carrying her. She was as small as a baby and I felt very tender and close to her. I woke up achingly sad but somehow comforted as if I had succeeded in remaking her last years into something prettier, in which her helplessness was only physical instead of irritatingly senile, and I was strong and motherly instead of childishly resentful of the switch in our roles.

I also began to see family patterns repeating. I was struck by the parallel between Norman's large family and the nine children Grandma's brother Harris had, and that he, like Norman, had evidently dominated them. Mother often said Uncle Harris squelched his children, thanked God she wasn't one of them, and couldn't understand why her mother thought he was so special. All of which reminds me that Peter, much as he admired and respected Norman, couldn't help commiserating with anyone in the difficult position of being his child. And much as Norman was adored, I don't think any one of us was impervious to how overwhelming he could be.

Why did Grandma adore her brother? Was it simply because he was the oldest male (though younger than she)? Was she grateful to him for being the first to leave Russia and perhaps urging the rest of them to come? Or did he perhaps as a young man have a vital and fertile

132

mind like Norman's?

The only time I ever met him, I was a very young child. Mother took me to a house even further out in Brooklyn than where we lived. We sat with his daughter, Sarah, in a room with the shades drawn. It was dark and gloomy. "Uncle," as Mother called him, came in to say hello. He was sour and severe and he stayed only a few minutes. And Sarah did indeed seem timid and depressed. Is my memory accurate? Or did I simply sense Mother's unhappiness at being there and her own take on the atmosphere?

Perhaps Grandma respected Harris because of all the men in her family he was the only one who seemed able to cope with the world and had a modicum of success. He had a going business—I think it was mattress ticking. Whereas her husband, her son, and her other brother Ike, were all sweet unworldly men. It leads me to believe that her attitude toward men was split. There was the eastern Jewish tradition in which men were to be nurtured while they studied and lived the life of the mind and women were there to provide physical and financial support. On the other side of the dichotomy was the desire of a good bourgeoise to have a strong capable man supporting her. Mother certainly subscribed to both. She always saw the men in her own family as tender flowers in need of much care. At the same time, she enormously admired men like Uncle Dave whom she saw as great material successes. How marvelous it must have been for her to have a son like Norman who could fulfill both ideals.

Phone calls with my cousins began to be dominated by my family questions and their reminiscences. One common theme was how little any of the immigrants had revealed about life in Russia before they emigrated. On the Mailer side, Steve Chipkin said his grandmother would always deflect any conversation that veered toward the subject. And on Mother's side, a conversation with my cousin Sylvia was typical. She said, "What does it matter if it's not right? I rather like it the way my mother gave it to me." The 'Who cares?' syndrome. I realized that most of my relatives thought my pursuit of the truth was a bit nutty.

Back in New York, on October 1, I went once again to the New York Public Library to research the 1894 passenger arrival lists.

I started on the eleventh roll of microfilm for that year, covering arrivals from September 18 to October 6. I slogged through 16 ships with names like Dania and Wittekind and Furst Bismarck from places like Bremen and Hamburg and Rotterdam. Very soon I began to feel haunted by the specter of fruitless years in front of a microfilm machine, ending only with an acceptance of defeat.

And suddenly, there it was! Arriving on October 6th, on the S.S.Veendam from Rotterdam, a whole list of Schneiders. There could be no mistake because with them was Leah Kamrass, my great-grandmother.

Kamrass—42 (No occupation, Destination N.Y., 3 pieces of luggage
    Chaje (Ida) Schneider—30
    Jossel (Joe)—11
    Blume (Beck)—9
    Schene (Jenny)—7
    Rochel (Rose)—4
    Feige (Fanny)—1

Hard to believe I'd found it—these ordinary entries embedded in all those handwritten names—the indisputable evidence that they had arrived on a certain ship on a particular day in October 93 years ago. But there it was. And Mother was on it, her listed age closely confirming what Steven had told us she had told him—that she was born in 1894. The subdued library sounds around me seemed inadequate to the moment. Triumphal horns would have been more appropriate.

As I examined the information, I realized that while, yes, they had undoubtedly arrived, all the ages given for them seemed out of whack. Highly unlikely that Leah Kamrass was only 12 years older than her daughter, Ida. Besides, on Leah's stone in the cemetery, it said she died in 1898 at age 66, so she was probably *sixty*-two when she arrived. And according to the 1900 census, in 1894 Grandma was at least 35, Joe was 14, Beck 12, Jenny 9, Rose 4, and Mother almost 3. And Sylvia had confirmed the census ages for Beck and Jenny.

I also soon saw that there was another problem. If Mother had been only one year of age in 1894 and Grandpa had come in 1891, she could not possibly be his child.

I called Norman that night to tell him what I had found. Convinced as he was that there was a skeleton in the family, he said, "That's it. Mother was illegitimate." I didn't think that likely given the family's hidebound Victorian attitude toward sex which we spent much of our lives rebelling against. But it did make me more curious about my grandparents. Suddenly there was the possibility of complexities in their relationship I had never before considered. Grandpa obviously loved Mother and depended a great deal on her. If she were illegitimate, did that make him a saint? Or was he guilty for having left first? Perhaps it was a purposeful separation. But that was not likely either since supposedly Grandma's sister Minna came with him.

Months later Norman changed his mind and decided that Mother probably was Grandpa's child. But I was never again to think of my grandparents as writ in the stone of family myth. I realized how little I knew of what they did and how they felt. Could they both have had affairs and suffered basic guilts? After all, they were only in their early 30s when they were separated for two to three years. On the other hand, if Mother was illegitimate, then Grandma's ability in the face of such a scandal to maintain the force of character and community standing that she reputedly had, would add a tinge of awe to her image.

I didn't believe it, but I was not unhappy speculating, and there was a kind of bleak satisfaction in realizing that the old saw was true—the more we learn the less we know.

About that time I had another dream. I was trying to get permission to go to a well at the bottom of which I knew were valuable historical artifacts. At last, I reached the well, but when I looked down I realized it was too deep and I could never get to the bottom of it alive. The dream was obviously symbolic of my frustration with the contradictions in the documents I'd found. But I was not about to give up. I wrote in my journal, "I'm beginning to understand why adopted children have such a thing about finding their biological parents. I've come to feel that way about Grandma and Grandpa."

A few days after I found Grandma's arrival record, I made the trip to the National Archives in Bayonne to check the 1910 census.

It was a two-hour trip—the Path train to Jersey City. Then a 40-minute bus ride (marveling at how much Bayonne looked like the Brooklyn of my childhood). From the bus stop where I got off, it was a 15-minute walk to the military base, at the entrance of which I had to wait for still another bus to take me to the Archive building. I felt as if I had traveled to the Midwest, despite the sight of the New York skyline looming across the bay. It seemed so close but as ghostly and unreal as a scrimmed backdrop.

In a poorly ventilated corner of the library, I developed a nausea as bad as seasickness, a syndrome caused by staring intently at the moving lines of print as one scrolls the machine. But I did find the Schneiders before I had to stop. Once again, the dates and ages confirmed nothing.

Herman (did the information giver think the name

136

**was more American than Hyman?) aged 50, married 30
years**
  Ida—ditto
  Joe—27
  Jennie—20
  Rose—18
  Fannie—16
  Their arrival dates were given as 1892 and 1895

Beck, married in 1906, was no longer living there.

Well, we *know* 1895 is wrong. And everyone's grown younger than they were in 1900. Joe's age agrees with the arrival record, as does Mother's. But Rose and Jennie are younger than in 1894, while Grandma is older—50—which is closer to the 1858 date of birth given for her in the 1900 census.

One cannot but suspect that whoever was giving the information either didn't know or had no great desire to tell the truth. At the very least, he or she was inattentive to arithmetic as the arrival dates given for Grandpa and Grandma would certainly have made Mother, if really 16, illegitimate. My guess is it was off the cuff, and approximate was considered good enough.

I wanted to throttle them all. Instead, that spring, I went back to the New York Public Library and the awful microfilm machines, determined to find Grandpa's arrival date. I didn't know if it would prove anything, but I was in too deep to stop. What had started out as a search for just one bit of truth, i.e., Mother's age had turned into a desire to explore the lives and characters of people who until then had existed only at the edges of my consciousness. Various scenarios presented themselves. Facts, I realized, do not necessarily establish the truth. They sometimes only enlarge the possibilities for interpretation.

The ship arrival records of 1891 and 1892 were even worse than those of 1894. Again and again, my notes complain of illegibility caused by holes or blots, indecipherable handwriting, poor photography. The machines, too, seemed to deteriorate, or else more people were using them and it was increasingly difficult to find a good one. When I would find a machine that worked well and a listing written in a clear hand, I would sometimes forget about what I was looking for and simply enjoy the pleasure of reading the names. All those lists of names of people I had not known! Perhaps because they were handwritten, all the familiar names, those Shapiros and Goldsteins and Edelmans and Cohens began to give their owners a presence that the people sitting around me did not have. Like a time machine, those pages of names would suck me back a hundred years, and make me feel so intimate with the aura of that time, that I could hardly believe I knew so little about it.

Through most of 1891 and a few weeks in 1892, I still had not found Grandpa's arrival. Or at least I didn't think I had. I came across a few Schneiders, but always the names or ages were wrong. I found a Chaim Schneider, 31 years old, who arrived on April 2, 1891, on The Nevada from Liverpool. But his occupation was listed as Laborer. I thought it unlikely that Grandpa would have described himself that way, but it was possible that he said he was a worker so the authorities wouldn't believe he was unreliable. And there was no one with him—no Morris, no Lena, no Minna Kamrass. Mulling it later, I realized that it might be the family lore that was wrong. Perhaps they didn't come with him. Maybe they all came alone. I wrote in my journal, "Another fact evaporating. Depressing." However, I continued to look for all of them, continually haunted by the dread that I had missed the listing or that their records had been obliterated.

We went to Provincetown for the summer and so for a while, I was blessedly cut off from the microfilm machines. However, a visitor to the family, Sue Moschen, turned out to be a serious genealogist, and I began to get from her a sense of how many avenues of research there were. What I did not realize was that I was entering a world which I would sometimes feel was as extensive and complex as the human circulatory system, where one could wander endlessly through arteries and veins and dead-end capillaries of information. Some dim intuition, triggered perhaps by a proselytizing gleam in Sue's eye, did elicit from me a few jokes about not planning to make this a life work. But at the time I thought that by checking out other records first, I might be able to bypass, or at least limit the scope of my ship arrival research.

First I tried to get Grandpa's naturalization record in the hope that it might contain information on when he arrived. The Freehold Hall of Records told me to call the Immigration & Naturalization Service in Newark. And so began my education in the depersonalization of modern life. For five days I listened to one tape after another, each of which would list options—7 options, 5 options, 12 options, 3 options, and each time I would choose one, I would get another list of options. Newark told me to call New York. New York said to leave my name and address if I wanted forms. In desperation, I called the National Archives in Bayonne, where a man actually answered. He told me that they don't have New Jersey records, only federal records, but I found it so exciting to talk to a real person that I kept asking questions just to keep him on the phone.

I called the Newark INS again and discovered that if I waited through the twelve minutes it took to get through all the options, there was, at last, an offer of human assistance. I pressed "3" as instructed, was told to wait 25 seconds. At the end of 25 seconds, I got...a dial tone. Cut off. I tried again. This time, after the 12 minutes and 25 seconds had elapsed, I got another tape saying all lines were busy, and suggesting I call some other time. Five days later I did at last get to a live human being, who told me that they have no records prior to 1906 and suggested I call Bayonne.

I did call Bayonne again and was told that they have only the declarations of intent and Freehold must have the final naturalization papers. So I called Freehold and the person I spoke to insisted they had nothing but the intent petition and was unresponsive to my insistence that during my visit two years earlier, I had seen Grandpa's 1903 naturalization paper. I could only assume that having pulled the record then, they had misplaced or never refiled it.

I called Sue Moschen and she was full of suggestions—the Mormons, state and county censuses, gazetteers, even archives in Russia. She said she'd try to find some organizations that might be helpful to me.

Around this time I heard a funny poignant story from a man at a dinner party. He was a doctor, and, as often happened at that time, when anyone asked me what I was doing, I began to talk about my genealogical quandaries. He found this particularly interesting because recently one of his patients, an old Jewish woman, realizing she was dying, had gathered all her children around her to make a deathbed confession. She said, "You always wondered why I didn't come to this country at the same time as your father. Now I have to tell you the truth. It was because I was pregnant by another man." The kids were unimpressed. "Yeah, ma," "Come on, Ma," they said. The poor woman had been hiding her shame all those years and now they simply refused to believe her! They preferred to believe it was senile fantasy.

I realized that emotionally I had been discounting the possibility that Mother might have been illegitimate. Like the children of the woman in the story, I found it too difficult to believe what I did not wish to be true. I wanted to keep my grandfather. He was too interesting and admirable a man to give up on easily. I had always been pleased by the knowledge that he had considered Spinoza a great thinker because he believed that God was not a being, but existed everywhere, in everything.

Everywhere, in everything. Almost the exact words Mother would use when she and I had arguments about religion. She really didn't have a religious bone in her body, but she had the habits of long years of ritual, and she didn't approve of atheism, since it denied Judaism. I would say, "Well what is God?" And she would answer, "I believe what my father always said, that God is all around us and in everything." I would shout, "That's pantheism, you're a pantheist, and Spinoza was excommunicated for that." Her huffy answer was, "You can call me anything you want—I'm still a Jew."

Of course. And so am I, since in fact, one doesn't have to believe in God at all to be a Jew. Growing up in the 1930s in a Jewish neighborhood in Brooklyn, increasingly aware of the menace of Hitler, as well as of the blatant discrimination in the world beyond Crown Heights, I was in some ways as ghettoized as my grandparents had been. I even remember thinking at the time that I was like a pea in a pod. The world felt Jewish even though I knew it wasn't. I assumed that in the world at large, I would always be an outsider. But I also felt morally and intellectually superior to most of the rest of the world, particularly to those on the inside. Some of this naive and almost smug sense of self-worth came, possibly, from the incredible ability of the Jews through all the centuries of oppression and diaspora to maintain the notion of being God's chosen people. But mostly it came from Mother's family. I once asked her why, in Long Branch, her family was so particularly looked up to by the rest of the Eastern Jewish community. She thought about it for a few moments, then said, without any doubt at all, "Character."

So they believed in themselves and their own importance. Much like the Wasps.

In fact, the family seldom thought anyone was quite as good as we were. Not only did we know that we were expected to be better and smarter than everyone else, we pretty much thought we were. One of my childhood friends once astonished me by disputing my choice of the game we would play by saying, "you always act like you're the Queen." In fact, that <u>was</u> the way I felt. The surprise was to discover that the ranks might rebel.

I began to identify with Grandpa. He was in so many ways the epitome of the outsider, who never expected to be anything else—a brilliant man who, despite arriving here in his early 30's never learned English well enough to use it functionally; an ordained rabbi who would conduct a service only if there was no one else to do it because he so disliked institutional authority; a scholar of the Talmud whose knowledge and understanding was enough to make him an arbiter of theological disputes among rabbis, and yet, if Cy was right in his interpretation of their discussions, absolutely open about his own apostasy. For the first time, I began to understand what it means to be a "Talmudic scholar", and how Grandpa could have spent his life at it. How easy to get lost among the trees as one juggles interpretations, and what sense of power and pleasure if a sudden shaft of light makes a connection that illuminates "a truth". All those tiny glosses probably had for him the same aura as documents have for me. And I wonder if my own reluctance to join any establishment other than the family comes from him.

He was not without guile, however. When a poor woman came into the store to buy some meat he would always try to sneak a few extra ounces into the order without Mother seeing it. This not only fed his compassion, but since Mother usually did see what he had done, it had the added advantage of making her want to keep him out of the store. So he was encouraged to stay home, where he could study and think.

He was fortunate. He had been born into a tradition in which if a man lived the life of the mind, it did not matter if he was ineffectual in the world. It was an honor to be attached to him and women did the work. However, in capitalist America, some resentment must have developed. Grandma wanted her daughters to marry not scholars, but rich men. And Mother couldn't help admiring successful businessmen like Uncle Dave, though she always considered her own men delicate flowers.

In February of 1989, I went back to the ship arrival lists and scanned all of 1891 and 1892 that I had not already done. Nothing. Just my usual complaints about machines that did not work, machines that gave me a stiff neck, indecipherable handwriting, bad light, and poor photography that obscured the information. At times, there were so many other people working the machines, that none were available. One day, however, I discovered Seat 179. Its machine was marked out of order. I tried it anyway and found that the only problems were a sticky rewind and a focus that needed a lot of jiggling. But the clarity was better than most and for the next few weeks, I was able to use it every time I went to the library until, unfortunately, the Out of Order sign came off.

My failure to find Grandpa did not really surprise me. When one did find what one was looking for it seemed little short of a miracle. One day I heard the young man at the next machine say, "I found them." And the mixed tones of astonishment, awe, and delight, with which he uttered those few soft words, so exactly matched the vibrations of my own experience, that I said, "Isn't it wonderful." He had found his great grandparents in the 1900 census, and so we held a short celebratory conversation.

About this time I received a letter from Sue Moschen with a flyer for a publication called *Genealogical Resources In The Metropolitan Area*. Little did I know when I immediately ordered it that I was entering a new magnitude of involvement. How naive of me not to realize that my name would now be on a mailing list that would spread to every genealogical and Jewish publication and organization. Before the book arrived I received a subscription invitation from *Avotaynu, the*

International Review of Jewish Genealogy, and a membership invitation from the New York Jewish Genealogical Society, which also published a quarterly publication.

I went to the Jewish Division of the New York Public Library to check a few back issues of *Avotaynu.* The first one I read had an item about why the majority of South African Jews are Litvaks and referred to a book called *The Jews in South Africa,* from which I learned that the major immigration of the Lithuanian Jews to South Africa started in the 1880s as a result of Czarist oppression and appalling congestion. From 1881 to 1910, 40,000 eastern European Jews emigrated there and the "overwhelming majority" were Litvaks. Most of them came from the province of Kovno, and one of the main towns from which they came was Ponevez (Panevacys), the place Mother had told me Dad's family came from.

In the Spring 1989 issue of *Dorot,* the quarterly of the New York Jewish Genealogical Society, I also found an article on Jewish migration after 1880 which stated that "Children's ages were often falsified to obtain a lower fare." A good reason for Mother to have been listed as one year old when she was quite possibly older.

I was hooked. I subscribed to *Avotaynu* and joined the Genealogical Society.

More and more I wanted to know who my grandparents were. Who was Grandpa? In one view, the archetype of the timid Jew, but also the saintly, kindly man, the revered intellectual, brave enough to come to a foreign land and work at menial entrepreneurship, too afraid of violence to stay in New York (a gang of young thugs once overturned his peddler's cart, which was what induced him to leave the city), orthodox in his rituals, but on the edge of apostasy in thought. Who indeed was he? And Grandma. Was she the moving force? Did she send him ahead with a yeast formula she had developed in the hope that he would sell it or turn it into a business, or because she wanted to join her beloved brother, or because after 10 years of marriage she knew there was no future for them where they were? Did she hope that her yeast formula would make them rich in that land of opportunity? And why did she do nothing with it herself? Was the language barrier ultimately too much of a problem for them both?

And what about Dad's parents? For the first time, I was beginning to think that I should find out more about Dad's family and that I might be able to. I called *Avotaynu* and obtained the address for their South African representative—I. L. Meyerowitz. I wrote to him inquiring about census, naturalization, and ship arrival records. His answers were generous in space and effort, but the gist was that South African census records gave little in individual specifics, and shipping lists were sparse, and limited primarily to those traveling first class (how annoying to be stymied by British snobbery). However, there were naturalization records in Pretoria.

A phone call from Steve Chipkin in June 1989, made me decide to write to his mother, Pearl, to enlist her help in checking South African records. So I sent her copies of all my correspondence with Meyerowitz, as well as a long letter explaining what I was doing, and asked a number of questions about the family that I thought Aunt Ray might be able to answer. Ray was the only one of Dad's siblings who was still alive and compos mentis.

Pearl, alas, was not interested in doing archival research—it seemed too academic to her. She would, however, pass on my questions to Aunt Ray. But that, too, proved fruitless. Much later she reported that Aunt Ray's response was the all-too-familiar, "Who cares?"

I decided then that Dad's family was probably a black hole and went back to my Schneider grandparents. I began to investigate my grandmother's Kamrass family and found out that Harris' youngest child, George, was still alive. My first phone call made me realize that he was confused or senile. But his wife, Fanny, blessedly, was not, and she had learned a lot about the family from George's mother. She also had Harris' naturalization documents, and she sent me a copy. It was a bit of paydirt and presented me with a new puzzle. According to the naturalization papers, Harris was born on December 18, 1860. Since he was younger than Grandma, it made me think that the 1900 census was more accurate about the facts than 1910; therefore, another reason to believe Mother was born in 1891.

The naturalization paper also stated that he had been born in Denenberg, Russia. Denenberg? Where was Denenberg? And what kind of name was that for a Russian town? Over the next few weeks or months, I checked the Family Finder, gazetteers, encyclopedias. There were no Denenbergs. Not until six years later did I find the likely explanation. Another name for Dvinsk was Deneburg. Perhaps then Dvinsk (or Daugavpils, as it is now called) was the Kamrass hometown. Was Grandma Schneider born in Dvinsk? Who, then, had lived in Utena? Was it the Sack family of my great grandmother Leah? Once again—another fact, another question.

In her letter, Fanny Kamrass also wrote that Harris arrived in March 1888, in time for the Great Blizzard, and that he came alone. (Mother had always said that his brother Ike came with him.) At last. A small definitive period of time in which to search the passenger lists. Fanny thought Harris had arrived within a couple of days of the blizzard, before or after. I was sure I'd find him and went off to the library. The blizzard hit on March 11, 1888. I checked the ship arrivals from 2/17/88 through 3/28/88. And once again I hit a wall. No Kamrass.

Meetings of the Jewish Genealogical Society always made me feel that I was discovering new approaches, but these new approaches came with problems that I realized could be insurmountable. For instance, a session on tracking naturalization papers led me to think I might find some interesting information on Mother and Dad if I could find their naturalization papers. I didn't know where or in which court they had been naturalized, but that led me to wonder how Mother got a passport when we were going to Europe in 1948. We had gone together to the Passport Office, and after we made out our applications, Mother sat me down to wait for her while she went to talk to someone dealing with problem applicants. She had no birth certificate. She claimed the original had been lost in a fire at the Belmar Town Hall, and any copy had been lost when the Maple Hotel burned down. Did she use her naturalization papers to get a passport?

When I worked on TV documentaries I always loved the serendipitous nature of research, the way tangential sidebars often led to unexpected insights, or how one lead, though disappointing, might tip another, which would suggest still another, until at last—with some amazement—I found what I wanted. So despite the fact that in terms of my original primary purpose, just about all the tangents I went off on ended in blind alleys, I never got bored. Sometimes bemused, sometimes afraid I might be missing a vital clue staring me in the eyes, sometimes losing track of what I had already done. But never bored. Also, as soon as I realized that I wanted more than Mother's date of birth, that I wanted to understand people and a past I had never given much thought to before, almost everything became grist for the mill.

That spring of 1990 I went off on a lot of tangents.

To give some credence to my suspicion that the reason Mother had been listed as only one-year-old on the ship manifest was to save money on the fare, I tried to find out what the fare schedules of the Holland-American Line had been in 1894. To begin with, I went to the New York Public Library. Two librarians in the Economic Division were stumped by whether or where one might look for such information, but tried hard to be helpful. First, they sent me to the catalog. The Holland-American Line entry said, "See: Nederlandsch-Amerikaansche Stoomvaart Maatschappy." Of course, most of the titles were in Dutch and I realized that I couldn't even guess which, if any, might be of use. One librarian called the Science Division since it too handled the subject of Transportation. They had menus from the ships, but no fares. She suggested I check with the Genealogy Division, and as a last resort call the Dutch consul.

The Genealogy Division had nothing. In the library's Reading Room I obtained a book in English about the history of the Holland-America Line. It had nothing on fares, but it did tell a little about a tariff war that had been going on in 1894. I went to the Business Affairs Division and looked at the 1894 Journal of Commerce. Nothing on the tariff war, so I looked at the shipping ads. The Veendam had charged $50 and up for first-class passage, and $38 for Cabin Class. There was no price listed for steerage.

I called the Dutch Consulate, which gave me the address of the Holland-Amerika Lyn in Rotterdam, to which I wrote. A month later I received an answer with a sample page from the S.S. Amsterdam bound from Rotterdam to New York in 1900, steerage class. There *was* fare variation according to age—full fare, half fare, and free fare, but no information on the age at which each fare kicked in. And I didn't know if the fare schedule in 1894 was the same as it was in 1900.

In 1990 I went on to other possibly helpful tangents. I wrote to the Board of Elections requesting my parents' 1928 voter registration record. They sent me the 1929 record, which stated that Dad was naturalized in Freehold, New Jersey in 1926. He gave his age as 38, which corroborated his birthdate as 1891. Mother gave her age as 31, so maybe she had always told Dad that she was born in 1898, or at least she was telling him that then, though she was still telling her children that she'd been born in 1901. In the record, she also said that she was U.S. born and she didn't even admit that she'd had to be naturalized after she married Dad.

Discussing this latest tidbit of information with Adeline, we realized that Norman had been born while both Dad and Mother were British citizens, and Adeline pointed out that if he wished, Norman could reclaim British citizenship. I called him the next day to tell him. He cracked up. He said if the reviews on his next book were bad he just might do it. "On the other hand," he said, "the reviews are usually even worse in England." He laughed again. "However, I might consider it if they give me a knighthood. I would really enjoy the literary world in New York having to address me as Sir Norman."

My mulling went on. In pondering why Mother was listed as only one year old when she arrived in 1894, though she was probably closer to three, it occurred to me that she might well have been suffering from malnutrition and thus was small enough to seem that young. As a grown woman she had slightly bow legs and was the shortest of all her siblings, so she might have had a poor diet and stunting in her first few years.

When it came to establishing facts, I felt more and more that nobody else gave a damn, and maybe they were right. I was struck by a review in the New York Times of Frank Kermode's *The Uses of Error*, which quoted from the book—"The history of interpretation, the skills by which we keep alive in our minds the light and the dark of past literature and past humanity, is to an incalculable extent a history of error." Even with documents, so little in them is identifiable as fact that willy-nilly we end up having to interpret the possible fictions they contain, and if life was more fiction than fact, perhaps my lust for documents was misplaced. But I could not stop hoping that enough more facts would emerge to convince me of the most likely story.

Perhaps I should explain the rather complicated and cumbersome, but personally agreeable process with which I was working. I was keeping three sets of records. In 4x6 memo books I noted anything of interest that came out of the books, articles or genealogical journals I read, and the JGS meetings I attended, as well as any research I did. I also kept a telephone log, and so had a record of my conversations with Adele and Osie. My personal diary contained thoughts and ideas triggered by what I was doing. Using my typewriter (I did not yet have a computer) I had started to transfer all of this to 4x6 cards. Everything was dated and so, in the writing, I could keep this tale of what might very well turn out to be an exercise in futility, in chronological order.

Talking to Norman about work, he said he could no longer imagine not working hard, that work was what he most wanted to do, and I said I too felt happiest functioning. We agreed it was Mother coming to roost in both of us.

When the local branch of the National Archives moved to Varick Street, just a fifteen-minute walk from home, I began to visit it more often than the library. Checking out the 1920 census for Mother's family, I found everyone had grown still younger. My grandparents were now only 58, rather than 60+. Rose was 24, which would have made her birthdate 1896, and Mother, bless her heart, was only 21. Since this census was taken after the winter when Mother met Dad, I suspect that she was the one who talked to the census taker. Rose was likely away, studying or teaching. Very possibly Mother had told Dad that she was only 21.

I also checked out the 1905 and 1915 New Jersey censuses. They were deliciously cockeyed. The birth dates given in 1905 were pretty close to those given in 1900. By 1915, Mother and Rose had lost three years. And from 1915 to the 1920 U.S. Census, they had only aged one year each. In 1915 Mother and Rose were listed as born in the U.S. History rewritten. Since I knew they were on the boat, there seemed little reason to believe any of the information in the 1915 or 1920 census records.

There was still the nagging question of whether Mother was one year old or almost 3 when she arrived here. Adele told me that Grandpa didn't know his wife was pregnant when he left, and that he felt very guilty that she had to give birth alone. According to Adele, he always spoiled Mother a bit because of his guilt. But wait a minute. Why should Grandpa have felt guilty if Grandma hadn't told him she was pregnant? Because he didn't bring the family over sooner? Because Grandma was the one who really kept the family going? Irrational guilt? Or maybe he didn't feel guilty. One cannot rule out the possibility that Grandma might have had an affair after he left and therefore fudged the date of Mother's birth. Or maybe she was raped by a Cossack, and that was why Grandpa felt guilty about having left her. (Norman would have loved that. Or half loved it.) And if Mother knew, or suspected, that could have been the terrible secret Norman felt she had. But according to Mother, Grandma did bring all their vital records and supposedly they went up in smoke when the Maple Hotel burned down. Maybe Mother's "terrible" secret was simply that she knew she hadn't been born here and she lied to Dad about her age. It seems the most likely explanation. Or maybe her guilt was caused by what she said when anything bad happened—she was being punished for having married before Rose. Or maybe she didn't feel all the guilt Norman thought she had.

Sometimes I think she felt more deprived than guilty. In her last years, she began to express resentment about the lost opportunities of her youth. For the first time, she was thinking more of herself than us—her children. Over the years she had sometimes said that before she married, a businessman from New York was so impressed with her abilities at the hotel that he offered her a job in his store. She wanted to do it, but her father said where would she live? She wanted so much to go, that even though she detested Uncle Harris, she said, "I'll stay with Uncle." Grandpa never said she couldn't go. He said, "Oh Feigele, you'll be lonely, it's no good working for someone else, here you're loved and needed." He made her feel they couldn't do without her at home. When she told me the story in earlier years, she would exhibit a slightly smug pride in having had such a close-knit loving family, as well as in having been a good and supportive daughter. But in her last years, she would say, "He should have let me go." I found myself bothered by this and tried to give her back her old perspective. I would say, "But Mom, if you had, you never would have met Dad, and Norman and I wouldn't be here." My egocentrism was no match for hers, lately acquired though it might be. She was filled with a yearning for the might-have-beens of her life.

If you were to ask me now, when do I think my mother was born, I'd say, most likely, the end of 1891. That I do not definitively know the date, does not mean the search was futile. The search led to a greater good—meditations on the lives and mysteries of grandparents I never knew, and a connection with the past that enlarges the present. While Mother might have hated what I was trying to discover, perhaps she would have appreciated how much I learned and how much I loved her. Even though I always felt that we did not really understand each other, as if our thoughts and feelings had different textures, still how much of her I absorbed—the love of family, the love of function, and the belief that one's children are more important than oneself.

Dad's Family

I t was probably inevitable that my research into Mother's family would eventually make me ask myself, "What about Dad's?"

Because it seemed too British for a family from Eastern Europe, I had always wondered how we had the name "Mailer." I had even speculated that since my Mailer grandfather was a house painter, and the word for painter in Hebrew is "maile" or "maler," that upon arrival in South Africa, when asked his name, he had misunderstood and told them his occupation.

To alleviate some of the frustration I felt because I had not been able to determine the date on which Grandpa Schneider had arrived in this country, I decided to look for Dad's arrival. I knew he had come in 1919 and ship arrivals in that year were indexed.

Not so fast. I found an Isaak Mahler, an Isaac D. Miller, and an Isak Maller, but the years of arrival and all the ages were wrong. The librarian said that if he traveled first or second class, he might not have been indexed.

A few days later, I talked to Bob Lucid, a professor at the University of Pennsylvania, who was then doing research for a biography of Norman. He told me that Dad came on the S.S. Baltic which arrived in New York on November 10, 1919. (88 years later, Norman died on that date). The reason I hadn't found Dad in the index, Bob explained, was that on a printed program for the ship's party, his name was listed as J.B. Mailer. A letter Bob found from a South African official had spelled Dad's name as Jaac. Out of sheer orneriness, I checked the index the next day for Jaac Mailer. Still no listing. But since I now had the information, I wrote to the National Archives for the ship's passenger list.

In research at the Jewish Division of the New York Public Library, I found a book called *The Jews in South Africa*, in which I learned that the major immigration of Lithuanian Jews to South Africa started during Czarist oppression in the 1880s, and was amplified by the overpopulation that had occurred in the course of the century. Meanwhile, the discovery of gold and diamonds in South Africa transformed its agricultural society into one in need of storekeepers and craftsmen. Since Jews in Russia, generally barred from the professions, were primarily merchants and artisans, South Africa became a new and attractive destination for emigrants. Those who made the journey wrote back about how good things were, and more people followed. From 1881 to 1910, 40,000 Eastern European Jews went to South Africa. Ponevez, the town in Kovna province from which, according to Mother, Dad's family hailed, was a main source of these immigrants.

In *Avotaynu*, the Jewish genealogical publication I had subscribed to, I found the address of the South African head of the Jewish Genealogical Society in Johannesburg, I. L. Meyrowitz, and sent him a letter requesting information on census, naturalization, and ship arrival records. His answer was generous in space and effort, but the gist was that South African census records gave little specific information, and shipping lists were limited primarily to first class. There were, however, naturalization records in Pretoria.

I decided to write to Pearl Chipkin, the wife of my first cousin,

Mervin, because their son had told me that she was taking classes in Jewish history. Since she lived then in Johannesburg, about an hour's drive from Pretoria, I thought she might be willing to take the trip. I sent her copies of all my correspondence with Meyerowitz and a long letter of explanation, and asked a number of questions about the family that I thought our Aunt Ray might be able to answer (Ray being the only one of Dad's siblings who was still alive and compos mentis, albeit very deaf).

Pearl, alas, did not share my enthusiasm for archival research. She would, however, pass on my questions to Aunt Ray. Unfortunately, that too proved fruitless. Much later she reported that Aunt Ray's response was the all too familiar "Who cares?"

I was beginning to think that I'd reached a dead end. But one day, late in February of 1990, Adele Becker, my maternal cousin, called to tell me that a young man who had come into their hardware store in New Jersey, had told her that he was related to Norman's South African family. His name was Averell Eisner. I called him right away and learned that his mother, whose maiden name was Shapiro, had told him that Norman was named for her grandfather. He didn't know whether his great grandfather was related to Grandma Mailer or Grandpa Mailer, but he would try to find out. A few weeks later we had a marvelously confused conversation (there are times when genealogical discussions sound like nothing so much as senile nattering). The source of our family connection, he said, was a Schappersnick family living in Libau, Latvia, in 1895. The name meant hatmaker, and indeed they were a family of hatters. His great grandfather, Nochom Melech, was the man after whom he claimed Norman was named. As we talked we mistakenly assumed that the name 'Melech' was the source of Mailer. Averell further informed me that Nochom Melech Schappersnick emigrated to the United States in 1900, and changed his name to Shapiro. Two other male siblings came to Brooklyn, while the fourth,

Tzvike, went to South Africa. He thought Tzvike was another brother. What neither of us knew at the time was that Tzvike is a girl's name.

It made no sense. Grandpa Mailer's given name was Benjamin. And if he was Tzvike, how did he get from Schappersnick to Mailer. Also, who had lived in Ponevez, where Mother had said Dad's family originated? Besides, if Dad and Aunt Ann had uncles here, how come Norman and I never knew of them? How come our parents never talked about them? Or did they? Had we been out to lunch? Or was it all too improbable to be true?

Hours after the phone call I suddenly remembered that Norman's Hebrew name was not just Nochom, but Nochom something. Dimly, it came back to me from the few months I had spent at Hebrew school when I was ten, that Melech was a word heard often in Hebrew prayers, as in Melech Ho'olom, King of the Universe. Of course! That was why Norman's English name was Norman Kingsley. I called Norman to check. Yes, his given Hebrew name was Nochom Melech. But he thought it inconceivable that we would not have known if Dad had uncles and aunts and cousins here. "Somebody has been reading about me and is fantasizing a connection. Tell them," he said, "that we know all our family came from Lithuania."

Of course, I *knew* that we didn't *know* much at all.

I called Averell again and explained that Melech was a given name. He found it hard to accept because he wanted to believe it was connected to Mailer. I let that go and told him how unlikely it was that we would have been unaware of first cousins of our father living in the same city.

"Well," he said politely, "I understand there were a number of family to-do's." In other words, there had been a falling out.

I called Adele, who never forgot anyone she ever met or heard about, and got the first bit of corroboration of the information Averell had given me. She did remember meeting a cousin of Dad's, whom she

156

thought was a niece of Grandma Mailer. In fact, she had wondered over the years what had become of her.

When I told Norman that Adele remembered meeting a cousin of Dad, and Averell's belief that we had lost contact because of a family quarrel, he laughed and said, "That explains it. Dad must have borrowed money from them."

All doubt about this new family connection was soon erased by my discovery of the ultimate proof: a document. Mother had left many photo albums and boxes of family snapshots. Six cartons of them had been sitting in our basement for years. At some point, I asked Peter to bring them up and they sat in my bedroom for another few years. Finally, realizing that they would need some organization, I started to go through them. A small box surfaced. It contained some photos, and at the bottom, some papers. Among the papers was Dad's London application for a U.S. visa, dated October 1919, as he was being mustered out of the South African Army. He said he was an accountant and had been born in Capetown in 1891. (I would later discover that the family didn't get to South Africa until 1900.) He said he was going to the U.S. for business purposes, so he must already have decided to look for a job in the States. Besides his sister Ann, he said he had <u>maternal</u> cousins who were U.S.-born. So the Schappersnicks/Shapiros were Grandma Mailer's family.

This document just came out of a box, but I felt as if I'd dug an artifact out of the earth. Not only was I indulging my yen to be an archeologist, but I was also once again trying to imagine what life had been like for this other set of grandparents. I began to feel more connected to the past, and I sensed how extraordinary it was for the Jews to have survived over so many millennia.

But what to do with all the photos? Many of them were in albums I remembered from my childhood, large old-fashioned horizontal leather-bound volumes of black paper, to which the photos were glued.

Some of them were fading, and I realized I needed professional advice on how to preserve and store them. A visit to an archival supply business gave me only an inkling of how difficult and time-consuming this would prove to be. First, I would need to remove all the photos from all the albums. Then, the black paper that remained glued to the backs of the snapshots would have to be carefully scraped away by moist cotton Q-tips and a special scraping tool. The first photo I worked on took me about ten minutes to clean. And there were four or five hundred of them!

When I first sat down with the oldest album and spent an afternoon looking at photos of my South African family, photos taken in the 1920s and 1930s, I got depressed. All these aunts and uncles, so young then, were now gone. And I was now as old as my grandparents had been then.

I realized it would take months to clean the photos. Not only that. I was also the last living being who had the patience, the knowledge, and the desire to identify the who, the when, and the where, for each photo. (I was to become obsessive about the accuracy of my identifications, irritating Norman considerably when he couldn't determine for me whether a photo of him as a toddler had been taken in 1924 or 1925.) To my delight, though, I often found after cleaning that there were legends on the backs of the photos, some written by Mother, providing clues to the people, dates, and even places. I became adept at matching scene and hairstyle and dress and dredging up my own memories of people and places. On the back of a small photo of Grandma Mailer as a young woman, I hit a bit of pay dirt—the name of a photographic establishment in Ponevez. No date. But it confirmed some relationship to the town—Grandma, Grandpa, or both. Shuffling the photos around, over and over, hunting for clues, I began to feel very close to the people in them, some of whom I'd never met, so many of them now dead. It was almost like reading a novel that had never been written. I could only guess at the events and who the people were. For instance, Dad's sister Bertha, who died in 1929, and who looked in the pictures as if she might be depressed or mentally slow, and who my father never talked about. Peering at the people, marking the details of each snapshot's particular moment, I began to feel as if their moments, 60 or 70 years earlier, had crossed the boundaries of time. They felt palpably present in my moment.

Once again I talked to Averell and he put me in touch with his great aunt, Florence, who, he thought, might be helpful. When I asked her where the family came from, she knew of no other place than Libau. She stunned me, however, when she said that in 1974 she had written Norman a letter and sent him a photo of Nochom Melech for whom he had been named. And Norman had replied and thanked her.

As soon as I hung up I called Norman. He had no memory of it.

"How could you forget a thing like that?"

"Barbara, I write about 750 letters a year, which means that since 1974 I've written about 12,000 letters. How can you expect me to remember?" Florence had said that she'd send me a copy of the letter and it came a few days later. It was indisputably Norman's signature. He not only thanked her for the photo but also wrote, "I remember my father from time to time would talk about Louis Shapiro (her father) and it's my recollection that they used to visit one another many years ago." Was he merely being polite? Or was it possible that while only recently he had been adamantly sure that Dad had never mentioned any cousins, twenty years earlier he still remembered events from our childhood that I had been too young to be aware of?

In any case, where was the picture of Nochom Melech? Norman thought he must have given it to Mother. I went through all the pictures again, thinking I might have missed it.

No luck. Had Norman thrown Nochom Melech out? Not until a year later did it occur to me that since the picture came with a letter,

159

it might be in Norman's papers. All his correspondence had gone into the Archive, so I asked Bob Lucid if he had ever seen it. To my astonishment, he had just recently come across it and he sent it to me for the picture album I was assembling.

As for establishing facts, I felt more and more like the proverbial "voice crying in the wilderness." Nobody else seemed to care, and maybe they were right. But if life was more fiction than fact, perhaps my lust for documents was misplaced, and my search for "the truth" a big waste of time.

I could not accept that. What I could accept now was that fiction and fact, interpretation and trust, weren't opposites. They were inextricably intertwined.

Therefore I kept rummaging around in the libraries that Spring of 1991, looking for Latvian and Whitechapel records at the Mormon Library, and passenger lists and census records at the Public Library, hoping to find some snippet of information about Nochom and his family, and his brother Adolph on Suffolk Street in 1900. Nada. Niente.

In the midst of my research into Grandma Mailer's relatives, I finally asked myself the obvious question—didn't Grandpa Mailer have any brothers or sisters? After all, in those days, hardly anyone was an only child. But given the expanse of years and geography separating this grandfather and myself, it seemed unlikely, no, impossible, that I would ever discover any relatives he might have had.

Then the impossible happened.

In March of 1995, Norman did an evening with Charlie Rose at the YMHA. At the reception that followed their talk, I saw Norman in conversation with a man I didn't know. As I wandered near them, Norman grabbed my elbow and said, "I'd like to introduce you to a cousin of ours—this is Stanley Young." I realized that Norman had just met him, and I asked Stanley how he was related.

He replied, "On your father's father's side."

I pounced. "I've been looking for you," I said.

It wasn't exactly paydirt. It was more like opening up another can of worms. Stanley's paternal grandmother was a sister of Grandpa Mailer. So there was at least one sibling. But Stanley knew nothing about Ponevez or Libau. Indeed, he thought the whole family had come from Warsaw. And he had no idea what the family name might have been other than Mailer. But I did find out that he still had one living aunt, a first cousin of Dad's, and she was coming from Florida to New York in a couple of weeks.

Stanley showed little interest in my genealogical obsessions, but he put me in touch with his sister Gladys and his cousin Elinor. Elinor was the daughter of Dad's first cousin Florence, the one who was coming to New York. Florence was the youngest of seven children, and her mother was Grandpa Mailer's sister. She had come to the United States with her parents in 1923. Some of her siblings had emigrated here earlier, but they were all gone now. Elinor lived on Long Island. I called her and we agreed that when her mother arrived we would get together.

Meanwhile, I called Gladys, who lived in Montreal. I was startled that she, of whose existence I had been unaware before, that she remembered Dad.

She said, "I was very impressed by him because he was the only one of the adults in the family who didn't have a *mittel* European accent." She also remembered that the red fire engine Norman had as a toddler was passed on to Stanley. The accents perhaps explained why Mom and Dad, accent snobs, weren't eager to get closer to that part of the family, but it boggled my mind to find out that Dad had visited them often enough for her to remember his South African accent, and that they had been aware of us all these years, while I had never known of their existence.

161

Gladys also told me that when Dad was in Poland with the Joint Distribution Committee in 1947, he tried to find her aunts and uncles (Dad's cousins) who had remained in Warsaw and that he had reported that they were all lost in the Holocaust It seemed extraordinary that I had never heard about this. Or had I? I asked Bob Lucid to check the archive for any letters Dad may have written to Mother from Poland.

Bob reported that he had found all the letters we had written while Dad was in Poland, letters between Dad and Norman, Bea, Mother and myself, and none of them made mention of his searching for relatives. Mostly they dealt with how we would all be getting together in Paris. Bob said, "They're full of bounce." I laughed and said I'd like to see them anyway, if only to appreciate how totally self-absorbed we were. I couldn't help but feel the pleasurable ache I always get whenever I remember the excitement of those days, and how inexorably past they are.

Elinor's mother, Florence, arrived, and I went to Long Island to meet them. Florence was in her 80's and her memory was fading, but she did remember that when she was 8 years old she went with her mother to Ponevez to visit another sister of Grandpa Mailer, a woman whose first name was Chava. She had a vague memory of having been on a farm, so perhaps they lived outside the town. Or maybe there were just some chickens in the yard. Florence had no idea what this sister's married name might have been, but it indicated, at the very least, that there was a Mailer connection to Ponevez, as Mother had said.

Searching ship arrival records at the National Archive, I found the 1923 arrival of Florence with her parents, Golda and Simcha. I hoped it would tell me where Golda was born. *Mirabile dicta*, it did have a column for place of birth. For Simcha, it was a town called Horoldo in Poland. For Golda—ditto marks! So whoever was giving the information, probably Simcha, didn't say or didn't know where she was born, since it probably wasn't in Poland. I could only laugh at myself banging into a blank wall again.

In the summer of 1999, the Jewish Genealogical Society held its annual conference in Manhattan, so I came in from Provincetown to attend—a week in the hot city, though thankfully, spent primarily in an air-conditioned midtown hotel.

I was excited to find that Mr. Meyerowitz of the South African Jewish Genealogical Society was in attendance. But the name Mailer meant nothing to him. However, there was a lot of talk about how much genealogical information was becoming available online. I still did not own a computer or know how to operate one. On the last day of the Conference, I went to the Society's computer room, thinking I would quickly learn how. A very sweet man, Mr. Levin, sat beside me. He worked everything so fast that in half an hour I had a sheaf of printouts on Kamrasses, Mailers and Schapochniks, but I was still totally in the dark as to how to use the technology.

A few months later, I decided to purchase my first computer, but I found the process depressing. It shouldn't have been since my friend Adeline had instructed me to get an Apple laptop. But because I was still unfamiliar with computer jargon, the store salesman was impatient and dismissive. Previously, I had sometimes worried that we might eventually lose English to Spanish. Now I realized it was worse—we were going to lose our language to geek talk.

Twenty years later, I'm on my third Apple laptop, but my family research has languished. I still receive and read the periodical publications and go to some genealogical meetings. Occasionally, I check out a lead to a name. Mervyn's son, Stephen Chipkin, who has taken an interest in his forebears, went to Lithuania one summer, and I was hopeful that some on-site research would result in some revelations. Unfortunately, he found nothing about the Mailers. It feels as if an impasse has been reached.

On the other hand, as so many times before, perhaps, perhaps...

Perhaps again, something impossible will happen.

Jack

Oe day, Peter and I, for some now-forgotten reason, started reciting to each other the T.S.Eliot poem, "The Love Song of J. Alfred Prufrock."

Let us go then you and I
  When the evening is spread out against the sky
  Like a patient etherised upon a table

I suddenly remembered that at the age of fifteen I had been introduced to the poem by Jack Maher. It was his favorite poem.

Of course. The stunning imagery mirrored the world-weariness with which, as teenagers, we were wont to view our lives. Was it because we grew up in the Depression? Jack even said at the time that his ambition was to live the life of the common man. This seemed understandable then, even commendable. It smacked of throwing in one's lot with the downtrodden masses. And since Jack was showing his sensitivity to literature, and introducing me to a wonderful poem, it didn't at that time occur to me that he identified with Prufrock because he felt he was not so special.

I grow old, I grow old
  I shall wear the bottoms of my trousers rolled

I loved those lines, though I wondered what they meant since I didn't
yet know that one shrinks as one ages.

At fifteen so much is baffling that it didn't occur to me to ask. Nor
did I ever think that Jack might feel more ordinary than I did. So it
was with some dismay that 63 years later I discovered that he had not
become an interesting man.

But back to the beginning. After all, it was a sweet first love, based
on two shy teenagers discovering we had some interests and emotions
in common.

I regret that I neglected to ask him while he was still alive if he
remembered the day that we met. Norman had induced our mother
to allow me to go visit him in Cambridge for a football weekend, and
he had asked Jack to be my date. Norman and Jack had met in one of
the lecture halls where the seating was alphabetical, and as Mailer and
Maher, they were seated next to each other. Probably under Norman's
influence, Jack followed him in comping for and being invited to join
the literary magazine, *The Harvard Advocate*.

There were a few moments that weekend that I've never forgotten. I
was wearing new high-heeled shoes, and after the game, as we walked
back along the Charles, the uneven footing of the grassy bank made
me stumble. Jack suggested I take off my shoes, and I did, discovering
when we got to the bridge that there were so many burrs in my
stockings that I couldn't put the shoes on again. So Jack and Norman
made a chair out of their arms and, with all of us laughing, carried me
across. Sitting in Norman's Dunster House suite, Jack spent an hour
extricating the burrs without tearing the stockings, grateful, I suspect,
to occupy himself with this bit of business. I still remember how he
looked—sweet-faced and intent.

We hardly talked to each other until after dinner when we all went to the usual after-game dance. He didn't dance. And although I loved to dance, myself, I didn't expect intellectual boys to dance, so it was okay to find a quiet spot in a stairwell. That was when we discovered that we both loved train rides, landscapes and literature, and had both experienced the moments of ineffable yearning and hope that they evoked. For the first time, I felt I had rapport with a boy. We were delighted with each other.

Norman sensed it and the next morning, he asked Jack if he would like to squire me around so he and Bea could have some time alone. Jack took me to visit Bruce Barton Jr., another member of *The Advocate*, who lived in relative splendor in Lowell House and impressed me as the epitome of the Harvard Man. The two boys talked, about jazz among other things, and I listened.

Because the war was on, we were all living very much in the moment. Who knew if we'd be alive in a year? We hankered for meaning more than for a career. Jack expected to go into the Army soon. So he had stopped going to classes and didn't finish the term. When he went home at Christmas, he knew he would not be coming back.

After the weekend, I returned to Brooklyn in love with Harvard. I remember the sense of unreality I felt on Monday as I made my way around classes at Erasmus Hall High School in Brooklyn. For three years, ever since Norman's freshman year, I had dreamed of going up to Cambridge for a football weekend. Now it had happened and it had been better than any of my daydreams. Cambridge, I knew, was where I belonged.

Jack and I began to correspond. He sent me the Cornford translation of Plato's *Republic*, which cued me to the notion that a particular translation had importance. I read it carefully and wrote him that I found Plato somewhat fascistic. He found that odd but interesting.

When he left school at Christmas, he came to Manhattan with

Norman and the three of us sat in his hotel room and talked. At the time, Norman was high on Otto Rank's theory of the claustral complex and convinced me that his intensity and my calm were due to our birth experiences. We both saw Jack off at Grand Central. To say goodbye, Jack leaned his forehead against mine and looked yearningly into my eyes. We had never kissed.

I'm not quite sure how we decided we were in love with one another. I think Jack wrote to Norman that he had fallen in love with me, and Norman, once again acting as *deus ex machina*, passed this news along to me. I hadn't yet thought myself in love, but my eyes must have lit up with the thrill of being loved, and Norman jumped to the conclusion that I too was in love. He asked if he should tell Jack. Accustomed to accepting Norman's take on everything, I said yes.

I wish I still had the letters in which Jack and I professed our love. I cannot now even imagine how we did it. In any event, Jack went into the Army, and I got accepted by Radcliffe. Because of the war and the desire of male students to get as much college as possible before they were drafted, Harvard instituted an all-year three-term system. Since it was academically aligned and geared into Harvard, Radcliffe followed suit. As a consequence, I was to start at Radcliffe come July.

Before going overseas, Jack was given a furlough and he induced his parents to meet him in New York. It was the end of June. Norman, having graduated, and not having yet been drafted, was still at home. Jack and his parents were staying at the Waldorf Astoria. They invited us to meet them for dinner in the Starlight Room, which at the time was very posh. Jack's parents were large people, they looked very Irish, and naturally, they drank. We ordered cocktails. The only cocktail I knew the name of was an Orange Blossom, so that was what I ordered. My first drink. By the middle of the second round, I felt a bit woozy but soldiered on. Mr. and Mrs. Maher had managed to get two tickets for the next night to the new Broadway sensation, *Oklahoma*, and told me how sorry they were that they had not been able to include us. I wasn't unhappy as I was so cluelessly snobbish that I thought going to a musical was the height of tacky. Besides, it would give Jack and me a chance to be alone.

Indeed, we spent the next evening in his room. On the bed. But when it came right down to it, we were both too scared to do more than neck.

We did a lot of that in those three or four days. One afternoon we went to the Metropolitan Museum, wandered around for a while, then went outside to Central Park where we rolled around in the grass for the rest of the day. One more soldier and his girl.

Knowing my parents would disapprove I didn't tell them how involved with Jack I was. I suspect his parents were not too happy about me, but since he was about to go off to war, they wanted to indulge him.

At home, packing to leave for Radcliffe was a big deal. Aunt Ann came over to show me how to use tissue paper to keep the clothes from creasing. (They creased anyway.) I had only one square clumsy suitcase, which I had chosen because it didn't look like other suitcases. It proved quite difficult to carry and my father said he would take me to Grand Central on the day I left.

That was a problem.

My departure day was also the last day of Jack's furlough. Unwilling to miss any possible time with each other, we'd decided he would ride up with me, get me to my dorm, have dinner, and take the train back. We agreed we'd meet at the train gate.

I didn't reveal this plan to my parents as I feared it would make them realize how involved I was. So I was seriously dismayed when my father said he would see me off. I said it wasn't necessary, that I would really prefer to go alone.

"Nonsense," he said. "You have this heavy suitcase. I'm taking you."

When we got to Grand Central, I asked at the information kiosk for the gate number. I could see the gate from there and could tell by the number of people waiting that it hadn't yet opened.

"Stay here," I told my father, "I have to go to the ladies' room." I hung out in the bathroom as long as I felt I could, and when I returned to my father, saw with relief that the gate was now open and Jack would have gone through.

Usually one needed a ticket to go past the gate, so I figured the gate was where I would say goodbye to Dad. But once again I ran into trouble. It was July 1st, and lots of people were sending their children off to camp, so the guards were letting parents through. I guess I looked young enough to be one of the campers.

"It's okay, Dad," I said, "I can take it from here."

"Don't be silly. I'll help you get a seat and put your luggage on the rack."

Panicked at the thought of his seeing Jack, I went into the first car we came to. There were a few people ahead of me in the aisle. Then suddenly, there was no one. No one but Jack, coming straight toward us. I must have looked horror-struck because he abruptly swung around and started to walk in the other direction. I looked back at my father. He was just maneuvering that blessedly clumsy suitcase from the vestibule into the aisle and had not seen him. The three of us marched up the aisle—Jack in his soldier's uniform, myself trying to look as large as possible, and my father. Finally, Jack managed to get a few people between us, and I grabbed the first empty seat.

"This is good," I said. "Thanks so much, Dad. You don't have to wait any longer."

My father looked at me a bit quizzically, a bit disappointed. "You're sure you're all right?"

"Of course." Taking a cue from something I figured Norman would have said, "and I hate long goodbyes."

Reluctantly, Dad kissed me and left. I waited a few seconds, then went to the exit to make sure he was gone. He was still standing on the platform outside the car, looking puzzled (when I later told the story to Norman, he said between laughs, "Yes, when Dad got home, he said that he didn't know what was wrong with you, that you had been behaving very strangely.").

I went back to my seat, and after the train pulled out, Jack joined me, the two of us laughing and laughing—for a long time after, I had only to think of Jack, myself, and Dad marching up the aisle—to dissolve into giggles.

It was almost two years before I saw Jack again. We wrote to each other three or four times a week, hundreds of letters. I didn't have to worry that he might get killed because he was posted to Puerto Rico to teach English to the local conscripts. I went out on dates, but if a boy became too interested, I let him know that I was in love with a soldier overseas. Because of the war, the process had begun in which Radcliffe was integrated more and more into Harvard. Instead of the professors repeating their lectures to classes of just Radcliffe students on our campus, we Radcliffe girls trooped over to Harvard Yard to join the somewhat diminished number of boys.

My only disappointment at Radcliffe was that the war made college life seem somewhat tangential, and it never quite lived up to the intellectual glamour with which Norman had described it.

In the spring of 1945, Jack got a month's furlough and came to Cambridge. It was already the beginning of the end of the war. VE day arrived while he was there.

He got a room in a rooming house off Garden Street and we spent a lot of time there. Of course, given the parietal rules, I had to be back at the dorm by midnight, so we didn't spend a night together, but I did, at last, lose my virginity. We were sure we were in love. I had no doubt that I was in love for all time. In fact, I was a bit of a prig about it. Jack once said to me that we might some years hence find that our feelings had grown stale. "If that happens," I said, "I'm sure we'll be able to work on it and work it out." He hugged me. Which I did not deserve. How little I understood how much could change with the passage of time.

It's interesting that I remember that exchange. Did he? I doubt it. Sixty years later I was appalled to find how few if any, memories we had in common. He talked of experiences we had in bed of which I had no memory. The only one that I never forgot was not so much sexual as emotional. It was an overwhelming sense of flowing one into the other. For years it was the touchstone for me of what one should feel when one is in love.

In any case, I was a true believer. Jack's furlough ended. He was sent to North Carolina. When school ended for the summer I fudged my return to Brooklyn and took the train to spend a couple of days with him. The trip triggered an episode that still makes me wince. A couple of letters from Mother arrived at my college house after I had left, and my roommate, Phyllis sent them to me enclosed in an envelope addressed to me as Mrs. Jack Maher at the address in North Carolina I had given her. Of course, it didn't reach me in time, and sometime during the summer, the whole thing was returned to Mother, including the envelope. When confronted, I confessed that I had been sleeping with Jack. Mother was furious but relieved that I wasn't actually married. In one comic note that captures the sexual attitudes of the time, she told Bea that I could still do better. Meaning, of course, that while I might be damaged goods, I could still marry a Jewish man.

I had to promise that I would not go to bed with him again. It was ridiculous.

The war ended in August and Jack was mustered out of the Army in the next few months. For the spring term, he came back to Harvard, and finally, I had the college experience I had wanted—a civilian campus, a boyfriend, the informal socializing and intellectualizing. We even took a course or two together.

In those months there's one day I remember in great detail. It was a beautiful spring day. In the afternoon we went to a concert at Boston's Symphony Hall. Afterward, we walked back to Cambridge along the Charles. The water sparkled in the late afternoon sun, the air felt perfect. Jack began to skim stones across the water. He tried to teach me, but I was an utter failure, so bad that we fell back onto the grass, laughing. We had agreed that since we had goofed off all day we would study when we got back. But then, crossing Cambridge Common, we ran into some of my housemates. They were on their way to the U.T., the movie house in Harvard Square. We said goodbye to them, walked on a few yards, then looked at each other, and without a word, turned and ran after them. The movie was *Murder My Sweet* with Dick Powell, based on the Raymond Chandler crime mystery, *Farewell My Lovely*, and because of my mood, one of the most enjoyable movies I've ever seen.

Sixty years later, when, in a letter, I wrote to Jack about that day, he replied, regretfully, that he had no memory of it.

During those few months in Cambridge, Jack made a dumb decision. He decided to transfer to the University of Minnesota. His older sister's best friend was married to the head of their Journalism Department, and they convinced him that since he wanted to be a journalist he should get his degree there. We planned to marry when he graduated.

So we parted in June of 1946. He went back to St. Paul. I graduated the following January and went back to Brooklyn.

We kept writing letters. Many many letters. In one he told me he was seeing a girl, but it was not a romance. He even wrote that he kissed her once and she said, "You do that like you shouldn't be doing it." I didn't worry. My mother seemed like much more of a problem.

One awful day Norman and I were sitting alone in the apartment on Pierrepont Street, talking about what strategies I might pursue. Mother, who had come home unexpectedly, heard us as she was about to open the door. She entered in a rage, yelling at both of us, no doubt feeling totally betrayed. And suddenly she was on the floor, crying with pain, looking like she was having a heart attack.

I said, "Okay, I won't marry him."

We got her into bed. The doctor came and diagnosed a heart attack. (All these years later, I wonder if there might have been some collusion since she never had another episode and indeed was as strong and healthy as the proverbial ox.) I wrote to Jack and said that it could never be.

Norman thanked me. He thought I was being noble and didn't know if he could have done it. I didn't feel noble. Mainly, I was angry. Besides, I hadn't really given up. Somehow, I thought, Jack and I would yet get together, whether it was in two years or ten. I decided I would wait until Jack graduated and if he didn't then come in search of me, I would look for him.

For a while, I heard nothing. Then, two or three months later a letter came. He was writing to tell me that he had formed an attachment to the young woman he'd been dating and that he was going to marry her.

I was devastated. How could he so quickly have fallen in love with someone else? And what of my own feelings? The love I had so totally believed in had simply dissolved and disappeared. What I realized was that I couldn't love Jack if he didn't love me. In fact, it was possible that I had only been in love the whole time with the idealized image of myself that he reflected. I wrote him a furious letter telling him exactly that—though later I was greatly ashamed for having done so.

Hurt as I was, and disappointed in both of us, I also felt relieved. At least I would no longer have that particular battle with my parents.

In truth, though I could barely admit it to myself, I was sneakily excited. The future was once again an unpredictable adventure. Underneath whatever else I was feeling, I had little doubt that I would fall in love again.

Now, sixty-five years later, I wonder how I could ever have been such a true believer. Perhaps Mother had been right. A true believer if ever there was one, she once insightfully said to me about Jack, "It's not what you think it is. You're just in love with love." Not surprisingly, hearing this from her infuriated me, all the more so when I realized she was not wrong. Many years later I came to understand that she had been right to prevent the marriage, though for the wrong reason—because if Jack had been Jewish she wouldn't have objected.

In the end, though Mother may have been a true believer, she was also a realist who viewed marriage as a contract, as much between families as between two people. Also, she was probably pretty dubious about love after all Dad's gambling and lying.

Once I got over the initial shock, I went on happily enough with my life, and for years assumed that Jack's life too was satisfactory. In the 1980s, when Peter Manso was doing his biography of Norman, I suggested that he might want to interview Jack, if he could find him. He did and gave me the awful news that both of Jack's children had died. That seemed to me like more pain than anyone could bear, and I felt I had to tell him so in a letter. I never got a reply.

When we did make contact nearly 60 years after we had last seen each other, it was by pure happenstance. Shortly after Al died in 2005, my classmate, Barbara Norwood, came to dinner bearing a current copy of *Harvard Magazine*. My own copy was sitting with all the other periodicals I hadn't read for the past difficult year, and no doubt would soon have been discarded, unread. Barbara had noticed an item in the Class Notes. A John Maher, class of 1945, was living in a retirement facility in Arizona, editing the in-house magazine and looking for news from anyone he'd known at college. I knew Jack's real name was John, and it seemed unlikely that there was more than one John Maher in the Harvard Class of '45. I also knew he'd been a journalist. But Arizona?

I hesitated at contacting him. When Peter Manso had tracked Jack down in the 1980s, he'd learned that Jack's wife felt he would have been much better off if he had married me instead of her. She couldn't bear to hear my name. If she were still alive, they would not be happy to hear from me. And while I wasn't looking for a new lover, it still seemed tacky to look up an old love so soon after Al was gone. But I did want to know how he was. So I told Norman about the item in Class Notes. Maybe he could call?

Norman did call and was rather surprised that Jack didn't exhibit much enthusiasm, but was rather formal and restrained. Jack's wife had died some years before and they did talk about me. Norman gave him my number.

And then he didn't call me. It occurred to me that maybe he was afraid to. I let some more time pass. Finally, I called him. He sounded wary. But soon after that, he sent me a letter, and we started to correspond. The letters were largely about our current circumstances and what we were reading.

Eventually, he began to talk about his marriage and its many traumas. It was worse than what I had previously learned. In the early years, his wife kept getting pregnant and the babies, three or four of them, all died at birth due to a diabetic problem she developed during pregnancy. Finally, a daughter was kept alive. A son, his wife's by a previous marriage, whom Jack had adopted, was killed in his teens in an automobile accident. The daughter, when she reached her mid-twenties, committed suicide.

My God, what a blighted life. I felt enormously sorry for him. And somewhat puzzled. He talked about it all without affect—no anger, no sorrow. Did he think it would be unmanly to express such feelings? Was he too proud to show any sorrow for himself? Or had he just been hit too many times to feel anything?

What could that marriage have been like? From the little he told me it sounded as if his wife had called all the shots. After they finally had a daughter who survived childbirth, his wife no longer wanted to have sex, claiming she associated it with dead babies. At least that's what Jack told me. Since they were only in their thirties, it hardly made sense. I asked him if he hadn't in that case been attracted to other women. He said yes, but that he felt he couldn't cheat on his wife because of what she'd been through. I suspect it had more to do with his own shyness and fear of rejection. Or maybe they did occasionally have sex, just not as often as before.

Jack's wife determined not only their sex life but also how and where they traveled. She was afraid of flying, which meant they only traveled by car and were never able to leave the country. After their daughter's death, she decided she no longer wanted to live in Long Island. So Jack gave up his newspaper job and they moved back to the Midwest. Fortunately, after relocating, he discovered he enjoyed teaching. But his wife's health suffered in the cold climate, so they moved again, this time to Arizona. I suspect that with each move they made, Jack became more provincial.

Was it passivity? Was it guilt? He said he hadn't ever been greatly in love with her. I asked why then he had married her. He said, "I hoped I could make her happy, but it turned out I couldn't." In those days, unmarried sex often produced guilt, and so very soon after they started their affair she expected him to marry her. When Jack said that he didn't know if he was ready, she ranted and raged until he acceded.

Did she, by the intensity of her needs and emotions provide him with a substitute for his own lack of them? Or did she just make him feel needed?

I never pressed Jack on any of this. I think I felt that if I didn't maintain a certain patina of politeness, I might get more embroiled than I wanted to be. Perhaps I feared that he had constructed a shell, that probably it was fragile, and that it would crack if tapped.

After Jack's wife died sometime in the 1990s, he moved into an independent living facility in a retirement community 30 miles south of Tucson. He made a number of friends there but of course, they kept dying off. His sister also died, and he felt little connection to anyone else in his family. He kept busy editing the in-house magazine, and he made much of the family of a young woman who had cleaned the house he had owned. I met her and her parents—a gutsy, earthy family with more elan than most of his acquaintances at the Posada. But basically, he was alone. And lonely.

Letters, emails, and phone calls continued. At the time I was coping with various medical problems, culminating in a hip replacement. I wrote to Jack that I would be out of touch for several weeks while in the hospital and rehab, but gave him no details. So, a few days after the operation, feeling depressingly isolated as I lay in the inside bed in my hospital room, I was delighted to get a phone call from him.

"But how did you know where to find me?"

He pointed out that as an old newspaperman he was adept at digging up information, and of course, in this instance, all he had to do was call Norman. Nonetheless, I was touched. A few weeks later, he asked for a photo. I dug up a couple of recent pictures—a black and white photo in which I looked serious and interesting, and a color snapshot in which I was smiling. I debated which one to send. I even asked Norman for his opinion. He recommended the pretty one, so I sent it.

Jack, who now went by John, claimed to be blown away. He sent me a picture of himself. As I had expected, he was fat and almost bald.

He began to lobby me to visit him in Arizona. There was a weekend in October when the town held a big parade, and he gave an annual lunch party for all his friends at La Posada. I should come for that. At first, I said it was out of the question. I was too busy settling Al's estate and organizing a retrospective show of his photography and collage. But I realized that Jack wanted to show me off, and I was amused at the notion of being a trophy former lover. After the sorrow and strain of the previous months, I had a sudden urge to be frivolous. What the hell. I decided to go.

He met me at the Tucson airport. It was pretty clear to me after our phone calls, letters, and emails, that I wasn't going to fall in love with him. But to meet again after sixty years seemed in itself a breathtaking proposition. Perhaps that's why I wasn't prepared for the intense dismay and disappointment I felt when, in the minute between our spotting each other and our hugging, I realized that he was approaching me with the mincing little steps of a geisha.

He was to tell me later that he walked like that because his balance was bad. He had no inkling of what a turn-off it was. It also symbolized the readiness with which he seemed always to allow his life to be constricted.

The three days I spent with him in Green Valley were not exactly a barrel of laughs. I did find it interesting because it all felt rather strange. I was both amused and sad. Amused because he was so blatantly showing me off, but I also grew a bit weary and lonely as I tried to be polite and gracious to a quickly passing bunch of strangers. I wanted to comfort Jack because of his terrible life, but in truth, I found myself somewhat bored. Epitomizing my visit was the big parade he'd so hyped. We sat on low beach chairs, holding umbrellas to protect ourselves from the sun, while an endless parade of kids from every school in the surrounding countryside marched past. They all carried flags, and the elderly denizens of the town (Green Valley being a retirement community) kept bobbing up and down to salute. It went on for four hours. Jack sensed my astonished boredom and apologized for having kept me there to the very end. I said that someday if he liked parades, he'd have to come see the annual Gay Pride parade in Provincetown.

I strained to keep things light and polite. I think I feared where probing might lead. Careful as I was, it didn't matter. On the day I left, over cups of coffee in the airport, Jack said, "I'm in love with you again. Perhaps I always was."

I felt stricken. I'm sure I must have looked it. I said we really couldn't be more than friends. To sweeten it a bit I said, "Maybe even loving friends." A mistake. He latched onto that and cheered up.

On the plane home, I spent a long time contemplating my dismay. I remembered the title of a Delmore Schwartz story—"In Dreams Begin Responsibilities." And I thought, in frivolity begins responsibility.

Once home, the phone calls began. He called me early every morning, almost always as I sat down to breakfast. Given the two-hour time difference, it meant he was calling soon after he woke up. He would always start by singing a song, anything from "When Irish Eyes Are Smiling" to "My Darling Clementine" to Tom Lehrer, of whose songs he seemed to have an endless supply. He had a nice voice and feeling as if I had been transported into a 1930's Hollywood musical, corny as it was, I had to laugh.

The calls were usually brief. He might tell me about how hard it was to get anyone at La Posada to turn in the piece they'd promised for his magazine, or how much he hated all the memorials he had to go to. He certainly wasn't eager to hear what I was doing. Saying goodbye, he would say "I love you", but so flatly, so by rote, that it didn't sound as if he was feeling anything. I even wondered if his good friend Todd had told him, "Don't lose this one. Tell her you love her. Every woman falls for that." Or was it that he had for so long suppressed anguish that it was difficult to express any feeling in words?

I have to admit that I enjoyed getting some male attention. But mostly I found it both sad and a bit ridiculous. Still, if my role in his life was to give it a new fillip, so be it. I knew he was dining out on this renewal after 60 years.

During 2006, we visited back and forth every few months. I went out to Arizona again in February. He came to New York in April. I went with him to the Grand Canyon in June, and he came to Provincetown in August (alas, there was no Gay Parade the week he was there). I limited the visits to a week because at the end of that time I couldn't wait to be alone again. He would marvel at how comfortable we were with each other. Which I suppose meant he was not usually at ease with other people, or at least not with most women. But I was not in need of comfort, and I would have preferred to inspire him. True, it was easy to be with him, but he infused me with a mixture of tenderness, disappointment, pleased vanity and irritation.

I didn't quite realize it at the time, because he didn't complain, but his health, which had not been good for years, was further deteriorating. More and more he was able to do less and less. When we went to the Grand Canyon, he couldn't walk the length of a short level trail or go down a flight of steps to an observation point. When we went to Bisbee toward the end of 2006, he couldn't cope with the hills and just stayed in the hotel. We went to Taos in the spring of 2007, where having walked one block from the hotel he became so winded he had to sit down for some minutes and then barely made it back. It was clear he could no longer make the trip east, and I had come to detest the plane trip to and from Tucson.

In the beginning, I tried to be helpful. Since the car culture in which he lived was obviously not good for him, I urged him to get some physical therapy and exercise training. He made a stab at it but he just couldn't take it seriously.

A few weeks before I went to visit him for the second time, in

February of 2006, Todd Furniss, his best friend, and his collaborator on the monthly magazine died suddenly. I knew this was bad, but I don't think I fully understood what an enormous loss it was for Jack. The *Resort Report* had been giving him an undeniable sense of some clout, as well as an occupation, but he didn't feel that he could do it alone. He did finally find someone to handle the graphics. But Todd was the last of the good friends he had made at La Posada. Now they had all died. He was left only with the widows, with whom he remained friendly and caring, at least as much as his accustomed reserve would allow. He also began to live in a fantasy world of what might have been. After Eden was born he liked to think of her as a surrogate granddaughter.

I think he loved my aura, but I doubt that he had a clue as to who I had become. Perhaps for both of us, it seemed too dangerous to plumb the depths of another. When he came east to visit, he obviously enjoyed my family and friends and concerts in New York and the quirkiness and beauty of Provincetown. He often said to me, "You have a wonderful life," but I can hardly blame him for not wanting to hear about how much I enjoyed it. I suspect he would have preferred me to be lonely and needy—as he was.

The last trip I made to visit Jack was in the spring of 2007. From Green Valley, we drove to Taos, New Mexico. Barbara Furniss's sister, Pat Tressler, lived there, and meeting her saved the trip from being an almost unalleviated pain. My suitcase got left at the motel in Truth or Consequences where we had spent a night en route. The town had actually once been called Hot Springs, but in 1950 rechristened itself when the radio program "Truth or Consequences" promised to air its tenth-anniversary broadcast from the first town that renamed itself for the program. That most southern area of the Southwest seemed to me so unattractively arid that I couldn't help but think in my snotty Eastern heart, "But living lives of quiet desperation of course they would have wanted color, even tacky color." When we discovered that my suitcase had been left behind, I was perhaps angrier than I should have been because I thought Jack should have noticed when he loaded the car that my suitcase wasn't there. Since we didn't realize it until we were checking into the Taos hotel, it was too late in the day to find out from the motel whether it had been found. But when Pat came to our room to welcome us, she was such a delight that I immediately cheered up. She told me where I could go the next day to buy some inexpensive clothes. She even offered me a nightgown, although since she was a foot taller than me, I laughingly refused.

Jack had spoken to me of her, and not always with approval. Unlike her sister, she had lived an unconventional life. Perhaps it was her sister's disapproval that he had picked up on. Pat had been an actress, had even been promised a part by Fellini in one of his movies, but had only ended up having an affair with him. At some point, she got fed up with playing in stock companies, and on a spur of the moment whim, had purchased a property she heard about while having lunch in a small New Mexican town that she was passing through. The building was a mess, but with some hard work, she'd turned it into a bed and breakfast, getting business strictly through word of mouth. I gathered that she'd run it rather like a personal salon, until, beginning to feel her age, she'd sold it and moved the twenty miles or so to Taos.

We had a few meals together and she and I walked around the Indian reservation while Jack sat in the car. On our last evening, she came to our hotel for a drink and I discovered that she had known my friend Merle Debuskey some fifty years or so earlier, when they had both been starting out in the Off-Broadway theater.

I also spent a lot of time by myself, since I realized on our one abortive attempt to visit an art gallery near the hotel, that Jack simply could not walk around. Alone, I wandered into jewelry and craft shops, rather desultorily looking for gifts. I tried unsuccessfully to find the hotel where I had eaten fried strawberries forty years before while visiting the town with Al. I marveled at how totally transformed Taos seemed from my memory of it.

Still not realizing how much Jack was failing, I felt annoyed at the lack of companionship. We had planned to take a different route back to Green Valley, but after my suitcase was found at the motel in Truth or Consequences, we retraced our route and spent another night there. On the last day of our return trip, I fumed again. Passing through a sizeable town, I noticed that the gas looked low and suggested we stop to fill the tank. Jack said no, we'd wait till the next town. It turned out that there was no town, and no filling station for many, many miles. When it looked like we might not make it, Jack finally set the cruise control to fifty to conserve what we had. On a Southwest highway, this was a speed slow enough to be a traffic hazard. I smoldered as cars whizzed past us. The vast emptiness of that part of the country was both awesome and a bit terrifying, given our predicament.

We did eventually make it to the next town, but the first service station we stopped at was locked up. I ran into a restaurant next door and asked where we might find gas. They directed us to another station not far away. With a sigh of relief, we pulled up to a pump. Jack, as was his wont, went to the office to offer his credit card, then came back to the car looking totally distraught. "The office is closed," he said.

I said, "You can put your credit card into the pump." I pointed to another pump where a man was doing just that.

Vast relief and a new experience for Jack. I didn't know whether to laugh or cry.

Despite my increasing irritation, I had no intention of not seeing him again. At the very least, he had become my charge. But home in New York, there was both more fun and more dire matters. The specter of the next air schlep to Tucson made me think, "I'm 80 years old. I shouldn't have to do this." I expected I would anyway, but the time just never seemed right. Norris was in and out of hospitals, and

Norman was failing, until in November of 2007, he died. Then there were the preparations for the memorial several months later.

Meanwhile, Jack and I continued to talk almost every day. He spoke of coming to New York or Provincetown, but I said it wouldn't work if he couldn't walk. His doctor said his muscles were atrophying and put him on physical therapy again, but it was clear to me that he couldn't or wouldn't work at it. Gradually, his complaints mounted. He had mysterious bleeding in his knees; he was using a walker; he was diagnosed with the beginnings of Parkinson's. Eventually, he could no longer function independently and was moved to assisted living, where at least he had the company of Barbara Furniss. But she soon had a diagnosis of bone cancer, and he knew she did not have long to live.

Just before Norman died, Jack came down with pneumonia and was sent to the hospital. He was there for a month until he was discharged to the nursing home at La Posada. But a couple of weeks later he relapsed and was sent back to the hospital. While there he complained to me that he had run out of reading matter, then said that when he had nothing else to do, he simply lived over in his mind the wonderful times he'd had with me. I was unable to respond. I could only ache at the chasm between our feelings for one another.

When he returned to the nursing home he didn't sound good, but he still occasionally sang a song for me, and he was still hoping to get back to assisted living. Within a couple of weeks, however, it was clear that he never would.

By the end of January 2008, he was wheelchair-bound and had almost stopped asking me to come. He was using oxygen all the time.

By May, his other widow friend, Rosetta, was also moved into the nursing home. But unable to afford it, she had to leave La Posada. Jack would soon have no good friends left.

I still intended to visit, maybe in September. I even discussed with

Pat Tressler the possibility of meeting her there when she visited her sister. In July, however, Barbara Furniss died, and so Pat would not be going again to Green Valley. The thought of negotiating a trip by myself—the plane, then bus or taxi, and a motel room in a place where other than Jack, there would be no one else to spend time with, so depressed me that I kept putting it off.

And Jack kept deteriorating. The strange bleeding began again. Then an intolerable itch, and worst of all he began to throw up almost everything he ate. His heart and his kidneys began to fail. Through it all, he managed to maintain an admirable equanimity. He would still occasionally sing something.

By now, I was doing most of the calling, and would often not be able to reach him. At times, he was somewhat incoherent, sometimes delusional. For a while, he even became convinced that we were planning another trip to Bisbee.

Then, on April 12, 2009, a week before he died, he calmly told me that everything was shutting down and we would not be going to Bisbee after all. Sounding perfectly clear and compos mentis, his voice strong, he heartbreakingly said he was only sorry he would never see me again.

A few months later, talking to my oldest friend, Rhoda, about how sad his life had been, I said I hoped I'd given him a little happiness.

She had not approved of him. Rhoda can be judgmental. When she met him during the week he'd spent with me in New York, she had said he was too old for me. "Why," she asked me now, "is it so important to you to make people happy?"

I laughed. All I could say was, "I guess it's my art form."

But the question hangs with me. Is it because sometimes I can? Is it a way of giving back for how fortunate I feel my life has been? Or is it just the extraordinary joy that someone gives you by allowing you to make them happy?

The Summer of 1950

The evening I watched the TV News and saw continual images of an enormous vehicle barreling along a street by the sea, I said to myself, that looks like the Promenade des Anglais. Indeed, it was. And the truck was plowing into the crowds of people who thronged the avenue, leaving in its wake a trail of carnage. Another terrorist attack. This time in a seaside resort—Nice, France.

Earlier that day, I had received the news from my son, Peter, that his father, my ex-husband, Larry, had broken his hip. Since Larry was 95 years old, his prognosis was very bad.

The confluence of these two events plunged me back into the summer of 1950, the summer that Larry and I got married. We married in Nice, and the night before our marriage we stayed at the Hotel Negresco. Situated on the Promenade des Anglais, it was the most elite hotel in Nice, and Larry said we had to stay there because it looked like a wedding cake.

Gazing out the window on the morning of our wedding, we saw a crowd of people standing along the Promenade, waiting for the Tour de France to go by. Sixty-six years later, as I watched footage of the terrorist attack in the same spot, the image of that sunny August day came back to me.

For days after the attack, there was news about it. At the same time, Peter was going back and forth to Boston to see Larry, knowing he wouldn't last long, but not knowing when death would happen until the morning he was gone. All those weeks, and much of the time since I have found myself remembering scenes and moments of that long-ago summer in 1950.

Why were we getting married in Nice?

Well, 66 years ago my mother was still operating under the Victorian moral code in which a girl remained a virgin until marriage. Returning to New York after four years away at college, I realized that as long as I remained in the same city as my parents, I would be expected to live at home until or unless I got married. If I moved out, it would mean to them that I planned on having unmarried sex (they weren't wrong), and so it was unacceptable.

My first two years after college I did live at home, first in Brooklyn, then in Europe when my parents and my brother and his wife, Bea, were there. I loved Europe—the livable pace, the beauty, the art, the more sophisticated sexual attitudes. Despite the battering that Europe had taken during the war, Paris still held for any American who wanted to be a writer, the aura of the Lost Generation that Hemingway and Fitzgerald had evoked so vividly in the 1920s. Still, I also felt that I was an outsider and I had no real desire to be an expatriate. So when my family returned to Brooklyn, I joined them. At the same time, I had also realized at the rather advanced age of 22, that I was going to have to run away from home.

In the spring of 1949, I went to visit my good friend, Adeline, who was living in Chicago, then wrote Mother that I had found a job and would stay there for a while. The job was my first and only as a waitress—I needed the income and I thought it would be good for the jacket copy of the novel I was writing.

Chicago reminded me of Brooklyn, or rather what Brooklyn might have been if it hadn't had Manhattan across the river. But the similarity between my native city and Chicago ended there. Though I liked to think of myself as intelligent, I was easily baffled by people who were not familiar, and mid-westerners seemed to me as foreign as the French. After a few months, I decided to move on to the West coast. Norman had just relocated to Hollywood for a bit, and he invited me to stay in the house he was renting. I toyed briefly with the idea of staying on. I even applied for a job, which I didn't get. But finally, feeling that I had no more rapport with most of the Americans I met than I'd had with the French, I thought I might as well go back to Europe and sip espresso in cafes while I wrote my novel.

With that as a goal, I returned to New York, living once again at home, while I made plans to sail to Europe in the spring. During the intervening six months, I got a job, saved some money, and saw old friends. At a party, I met Larry. It wasn't love at first sight. When he called me the next day, I had difficulty putting a face to the name. However, I liked his voice. As I remember, our first two dates were mostly about eating good food at restaurants like the Russian Tearoom. On the third date, he took me to a square dance and I felt like we were beginning to connect. He too was writing a novel, while taking a course at the New School with Hiram Haydn. I found him physically and sexually attractive. Soon we were having an affair.

Brought up in a more than comfortable home, Larry always found it natural to have a good time. We ate well, often used his parents' subscription seats—fourth row on the aisle at the Metropolitan Opera House—and tooled around in his father's Cadillac. It was all more luxurious than what I was used to. I was having a good time.

One day we both noticed an article in the New York Times, announcing the first Pablo Casals Bach festival in Prades, France, and gleefully realized that if we signed up together, it would cost no more than going separately, and we would, in addition, get the ten

LP records they were planning to record. For the two of us, the tab for three weeks of concerts in June was $100. I was leaving in March. Larry would come in May when his writing course was finished.

I left as planned. He came in May, having arranged to buy a little Renault, and pick it up in Paris. It was just one of the ways in which Americans at the time took advantage of the European need for dollars. For the French, access to buying a car was very limited, since not that many were yet being produced. But an American could buy the French car for about a thousand dollars, and then, when leaving the country, easily sell it to a Frenchman willing to pay at least as much.

As we drove down to Prades, Larry regaled me with an account of all the things that the naturalist, Henri Fabre, had written about insects, and he impressed me not only with how intensely interesting bugs are but with his own passionate enthusiasm for the subject.

The landscape was enchanting. The highways were narrow two-lane roads, winding through towns and valleys and mountains. One evening, in the Massif Centrale, we bought some charcuterie and bread in a small town, and at sunset pulled just off the road and took our food and wine to the edge of a promontory beside a waterfall that fell into a stream a hundred feet below. It was breathtaking, and for a city dweller like myself, the epitome of what I had always imagined romantic mountain scenery to be.

In two days we reached the Pyrenees. Most of the people attending the Festival were staying in Vernet-les-Bains, a spa town at the foot of Mt. Canigou. But some friends in Paris had told me about a small inn a kilometer or two further on. It was literally at the end of the road. Beyond it were perhaps eight or ten small stone houses, lining the trail that started up the mountain. The village was called Casteil. The inn was run by a Spanish exile and his lovely, overworked wife. For about two dollars a day each, we had two rooms and three very good meals. Of course, there was no bath and no hot water. When we asked our host how we could bathe, he suggested the stream nearby. The stream proved to be too shallow and ice cold (there was still snow at the top of the mountain), so we went occasionally to the spa in Vernet, which had a huge shower room that could be rented, together with an anteroom furnished with a dubious looking bed.

It was an extraordinary three weeks. In Paris, a month earlier, I'd met a member of the orchestra, the violist, Milton Thomas. He'd gotten my number from Galy Malaquais in Los Angeles and he insisted so winningly that I keep him company while he waited in the station for his connecting train, that I had gone to meet him. By the time his train pulled out, I felt as if we were new old friends. As a result, when Larry and I were in Prades, we were able to go not only to all the concerts but with our Milton connection, to any rehearsals that we wished to attend as well. Along the way, we got to know some of the other musicians—Alexander Schneider, for one, and Margaret Bourke-White, the photographer, with whom Schneider was having an affair.

My only problem was the altitude. The weather was splendid, clear, and never too hot. But I had a hard time staying awake. Whenever I tried to work or read, my eyes would start to close, and I napped almost every afternoon. The only thing that kept me awake was movement, so Larry and I often got into the car and just drove—very slowly, on very rocky roads. What astonishes me now, is that it never occurred to me to go back to the area that Barbara Probst and I had landed in when we left Spain two years earlier. It was not many miles away, and it could have helped me with the details and the mood for the novel I was working on.

When the festival ended, we made our way by car along the southern edge of France, and a few days before the end of June, we drove into St. Tropez. Having decided that we needed a place where we could settle in and get some work done, this looked ideal. Very quickly, we found an apartment. It was on the top floor of a 5-story building that overlooked the quai. It had a bedroom, a kitchen, a bathroom with toilet and sink, and cold running water. In the living room was a beat-up upright piano. The piano was what sold us—or at least me. After the festival, I wanted to practice again. We rented the apartment for the equivalent of $150 a month. Although it was likely more than we would have spent in a hotel, Larry thought it a bargain compared to resort rents near New York. To solve the lack of a bath, we joined the local tennis club, called the Lawn Tennis Club, though it had only clay courts. The showers, like the sinks in our apartment, were cold water. Fortunately, the weather was warm. And Larry would teach me to play tennis.

Since we couldn't move in until July, which was still a couple of days off, we continued to drive east along the Corniche d'Or, past Nice, to Villefranche sur Mer, where we found a pretty pension high on the Corniche. Our room had a window surrounded by bougainvillea, and with a view of the Mediterranean below. In the morning, writing a letter home, I said to Larry, "What should I use as a mailing address?" I didn't have to explain to him that a street address rather than a hotel would look suspicious.

"Well," he said, "we could get married."

I took a couple of deep breaths. We'd been having a very good time, and the sex was great. We were in love. I said, "Okay."

At the time I did not consciously think about the practical reasons for saying yes. But I knew that when we returned to New York, if I were married, I wouldn't have to go home to Brooklyn. And in 1950, at the age of 23, I felt I was already pushing the old maid envelope.

Adding fuel to my decision was my delight at the prospect of getting married far from home, with no family and no ritual folderol. I was dead set against ritual in those days. In fact, I was downright snotty about it.

We immediately sent telegrams to our parents announcing our intention. We went into Nice, and Larry walked into a store and talked to a sympathetic woman behind the counter. She told us we must get married in Nice, as it would be much easier there than in St. Tropez. First, however, we would have to establish residence. For a small sum, she would be happy to say that we were living with her. I'm not sure whether she was right about the comparative bureaucratic regulations of the two towns, or whether she was simply trying to make a buck. In any event, she convinced us. We then discovered that there were other hoops that required fairly frequent trips to Nice, and the days quickly stretched into a month. We even had to publish the banns. Larry tried to cut out the ten-day delay involved, but when he pointed out to an official that we didn't know anyone in Nice, so who could object, the man said we were not respecting the laws of France and threw us out of his office.

I'd been living in a few cotton skirts and tops. I needed a dress for the wedding. If there were any elegant stores in Nice at the time, we certainly weren't aware of them. But we did eventually find a store that had in its window a simple sleeveless dress with a small cape. It seemed appropriate. I didn't want white, but the colors the dress came in were rather garish, so I bought the white. We also needed a ring. For some reason, I didn't want just a plain band. We found a jeweler who said he'd make me whatever I wanted. I tried to describe to him what I had in mind, but I guess my French was not quite up to the task, because the ring he crafted looked like a machine gear, and was much too thick. It was a long time before I got used to it.

As it turned out, it was just as well that we were forced to post the banns. Larry wrote to friends of his whom I hadn't yet met, Pat and Buddy Richmond, who were living on Lake Como in Italy. A telegram came back—WEDDING FORBIDDEN WITHOUT US.

My heart sank until I realized it was not from any parent. Good to their word, Pat and Buddy met us in Nice the night before the wedding. Afterward, they returned with us to St. Tropez, and stayed for several days. The only thing I remember about their visit was a celebratory dinner we had that was unlike any other I've ever experienced. A small notice had appeared, probably at the cafe next door, for a new restaurant in a tiny ancient village just a couple of kilometers from St. Tropez, and set in the middle of rather dusty fields. We were intrigued and decided to try it. The restaurant was in an old stone house, where we were ushered into a small room with a table and two benches covered with pillows. It felt like a Hollywood version of ancient Rome. We didn't order. The food just came. By the time we had consumed the delicious main dish of couscous and a couple of bottles of wine, we were more than happy. We also thought we were finished. But then came the cheese, a platter of at least half a dozen different kinds, arranged artfully with leaves and twigs. After that came a large bowl of fruit, decorated with flowers. We began to worry about the cost. Pooling whatever francs we had, we waited anxiously for the bill. As I remember, we had the equivalent of about twenty dollars. Miraculously, it was enough, and we didn't mind at all that it was the most expensive meal we had all summer.

Before they left, Pat and Buddy urged us to visit them at Lake Como, and it was decided that when our lease ended on August 31st, we would all travel through Italy together.

We had been married on August 1st. On August 10th, Larry's 30th birthday, his parents arrived in St. Tropez. His mother, Adele, had wanted an excuse to take a trip to Europe and so there they were. Oddly, for his birthday present, instead of giving him a gift, they gave me a diamond ring. I was astonished. Larry was upset. His father, Jack, then informed us that they wanted us to have a Jewish wedding ceremony. Now I was upset. A diamond ring was bad enough. But a wedding ceremony! To my surprise, Larry said, "Oh let them have it."

So Jack, who was effectively executive, imported a rabbi from Nice. The rabbi arrived in a three-piece suit, which was several layers more than anyone else in our seaport resort was wearing. He was not very happy, and rather disapproving as he looked around our apartment. The first thing he said—in French since he spoke only French and Hebrew—was that we needed witnesses. Larry offered his parents as our witnesses. No, that would not do, said the rabbi. We would have to find real witnesses, and they must be Jewish. Larry said we didn't know anybody in St. Tropez who was Jewish. Grudgingly, the rabbi relented, saying we could get non-Jews. So Larry and I went down the five flights of stairs to our landlord in the perfume shop.

"Thank God we're in France," I said. An American landlord would have been shocked to find out we hadn't been married when we rented the apartment.

Our landlord and his niece said they would be happy to come.

Upstairs we went. Now the rabbi informed Larry that we would need a glass.

Larry said, "That's optional."

"No, it isn't," said the rabbi.

I said to Larry, "We can't break a glass from the apartment, because our landlord is coming and you know the French."

So downstairs we went again, this time to the cafe next door. Larry told the friendly owner that he'd like to buy a glass.

"I'll lend you a glass," she said.

"That's not possible. I can't return it."

"Why can't you return it?"

"Because I have to break it."

She rolled her eyes and handed him a cheap heavy glass.

Larry shook his head. "That's too hard to break. I need a wine glass." She shook her head, but took his francs and handed him the glass, saying, "It seems like a shame to break a good glass like that."

We climbed back up the five flights. At last, we were ready. The rabbi began to speak, in French, and mostly for the benefit of our witnesses. This, he explained, was not the way things were usually done. He described the chuppah he thought we should have had. Jack, who understood French, did not seem to mind, and Adele understood none of it. Larry and I suppressed giggles.

As I remember, Jack and Adele stayed only a couple of days. Adele got rather into the spirit of the place. Realizing that her city dresses were not the fashion in St. Tropez, she wore just a navy blue slip with spaghetti straps, and actually looked quite chic. She also made the local hairdresser happy, because she thought that what they charged her for a set was so little that she passed out hundred franc bills to everyone in the shop.

As young lovers, we were content to spend most of our time alone with one another. Except for bumping into Alexander Schneider and Margaret Bourke-White in our cafe one afternoon, we saw no other Americans in town. I do remember that, as we raved to them about how wonderful St. Tropez was, Schneider said, "Ach, but you should have seen it before zee war." The only other person we came to know a little bit was a gypsy guitarist, who like ourselves, was a transient local.

His name was Pata, and we heard him before we saw him.

Walking down a street one night, the sound of wonderful jazz played by guitars seemed to come out of the ground, but from where we couldn't tell. A night or two later, we were walking along an adjacent street and heard the same wonderful sound issuing from what was obviously a cellar nightclub. We began going there every night to listen to Pata and his fellow guitarist perform—until one night they were gone. Soon after, however, they appeared again, this time in the restaurant we went to almost every night (where for a little over a dollar we ate a dinner of *moules marinieres*, steak, and ice cream). We struck up a conversation with Pata, who was the more gifted of the duo, eventually inviting him to our apartment, where he wowed me by sitting down at the piano and playing. When I expressed some surprise that he knew how to play the piano as well as the guitar, he said that actually, it was familiar because he had played on a piano twice before.

One day, as we sat in our car, he approached us, saying that he had a wife and a baby he very much wanted to see, could we possibly drive him to the gypsy encampment where she was living. Larry, always open to a new and unusual experience, said we could. And so, a few days later, we set off. It wasn't far. The camp was in an open field. I don't remember any tents, just blankets on the ground. The gypsies were very friendly, insisted on feeding us, one woman complaining about the price of tomatoes, which at the time was about three cents a pound. One young man, introduced as a cousin, walked us along a path by a stone wall and showed us how he removed snails from the cracks—another source of food. Perhaps because we were speaking in French, a language none of us were native to, our discussions with the gypsies never went deeper than food and weather. Or perhaps we were just too strange to trust. Some days later Pata told us that the 'wife' and the 'cousin' had hooked up together, leaving him in the cold.

Larry decided that Pata deserved recognition and a wider audience. Toward the end of August, he suggested we make a record and take it back to the States. And so a day or two before we were to leave St. Tropez, we drove to Nice with Pata, to find a recording studio. It turned out that it was a holiday and everything was closed. Sadly, that was it. Pata disappeared from our lives. Years later, Larry wondered if Pata might have become the famous Manitas de Plata. Unlikely, but possible.

Looking back on it now, I realize how casually we were behaving. Our days were filled with going to the beach and cafes and restaurants, staring through our window at the yachts and Rolls Royces on the quai, making love, playing tennis, and indulging all the distractions that Larry was a master at finding. Beneath the fun was a small layer of depression because we were barely working on our novels.

I was not then aware of how distractible Larry was. Indeed, it was years before I understood why he had such a hard time finishing stuff and what was at the root of it. It was years before I saw the role his mother played. Adele was a difficult mother-in-law. She was always trying to dress me, feed me (once actually attempting to shove into my mouth some food that I had refused), and otherwise treat me like a doll. She had little in the way of intellectual or cultural interests. I don't think we ever had an interesting conversation. Yet, she was not without gifts. She was a marvelous cook and had great style and taste, which she funneled into nonstop shopping, to decorate, to redecorate, to clothe herself and others. In fact, she so loved to shop that when she was away from New York, she joked about having to get back to her "job" in the stores. I think she felt an enormous impulse to run things, while at the same time she felt she had no power. She was also a mess of fears, and could not bear confrontation, so much so that when watching television she always changed the channel when things began to get interesting. Her husband and sons mostly ignored her. Her other daughter-in-law was better at handling her than I was. Larry thought she was crazy. I detested her at times, but I also felt sorry for her and would listen to her patter.

Eventually, it dawned on me what having a mother like Adele would be like. When Peter was two years old I took him one day to visit Adele. She'd bought him a couple of great toys. He started to play with one and was really getting into it when she interrupted, insisting he look at the other toy. He let out a great howl and that backed her off. I remember thinking: now I understand Larry's problem, that growing up with Adele he had probably seldom been allowed to pursue anything to a conclusion.

In September of 1950, as planned, Larry and I joined Pat and Buddy for a tour of Italy. Most memorably, we went to Paestum where, as we had read in the tour guide, Greek temples built 2500 years before, still stood. It was a few hours drive south of Naples and we arrived after dark, hoping to stay at the hotel next door to the temple site. There were only three rooms, and it turned out they were all taken. But, we were told, if we didn't mind all sharing a room, there was an attic room with three beds, and they would put in another. We watched in some awe as they hoisted a narrow cot up the side of the building and through the window. Then we went to their dining room for dinner. At the end of the meal, we asked where the temples were. Right outside, they said.

Across a courtyard was the locked fence that enclosed the site. We peered through the fence for a bit, then simply climbed over it. I have never forgotten what it was like to wander alone, at night, through those temples. The roofs were mostly gone, but the columns, lit by the moon, looked as if they were still encased in marble. Walking through the temples, it felt like ancient footsteps still lingered on the floor. And with no one there but ourselves, it was as if we were the first people in 2000 years to have discovered the site.

Back in Paris, Larry and I finally emerged from LaLa Land. I think we had not read a newspaper all summer. But attending a movie, we found out during the newsreel, that the U.S was at war with North Korea. Once again, we were deep into our generation's deepest fear, the fear that began after Hiroshima, that the world, our world, would end in a nuclear war.

All these years later, we have so far escaped a nuclear Armageddon. But even if our armed peace continues, will the 20-year-olds of today be able to say in another two-thirds of a century, that they have held global warming at bay, that the proliferating terror and violence in the world today will have ended, and that they will not feel they are subject to robots and computers running the world?

I know the past seems lighter than it was. But I am haunted by my two images of the Promenade des Anglais—the benign sunny day in 1950 and the dark terror of that awful night in 2016. What will that avenue be like in 2082? Will it still exist? Or will it have slipped into the sea?

Harry in First Person

I n the video, Harry stood a little to the side of the painting and announced he was going to talk about it. At 85, he seemed to be in good shape, his face just a bit more grizzled than when I had known him. He was dressed in what he'd always worn—jeans, a work shirt and cowboy boots.

Why, after half a century, had I been seized by the urge to Google him on this particular day—on perhaps the only day, as it turned out, that the video was up on his website? Was there still some psychic thread tying me to him? Or had the impulse been prompted by a sneaky desire to let him know how well my life had turned out without him?

When I'd Googled him I wasn't even sure if he was still alive. But I was not at all prepared for what I found. Not only was he alive—he had a website! A website with a number of links relating to his art and one to a bio. Also the link to the video—the video I was now watching.

There, in the museum in Cody, Wyoming, was the painting Harry had been working on when we first met in 1960. It was a huge canvas, depicting a nineteenth-century stampede of cattle in which one of the cowboys was falling from his horse and about to be trampled. As I listened to him talk, I grew increasingly appalled. He pointed to the horizon line and said that because it slanted down toward the edge of the painting, it indicated that the cowboys were all going to hell. Had he become religious? To me, the painting depicted the danger and the anguish of life. I didn't think it was making a moral judgment. Harry stopped speaking for a moment. Then he pointed again to the horizon line and said again that they were all going to hell. And then he said it again.

I realized that he didn't know what to say about his own painting. Was he suffering from Alzheimer's or some other form of senile dementia?

The video cut off. I clicked on a link to his bio.

Apart from lurid details of his early life, far different and even worse than what he had told me fifty years earlier, the bio was couched in cult speak. He sounded nothing like the Harry I had known, who had always seemed lucid and literate. This account began with cosmic gobbledygook, then veered confusingly from past to present with some odd bits of American history thrown in. A son, introduced at the beginning, indicated that he was the medium through which the story was being told. So who was its author? A mentally compromised Harry or the son?

Upset and disbelieving, I kept reading. Harry now claimed to have been born into a mafia family connected to Al Capone and Bugsy Siegel; he also said that his grandmother ran a whorehouse and his mother was one of the whores.

Fifty years earlier, the story he'd told me was that he'd left his home in Chicago at the age of fourteen and run away to Wyoming because he was enthralled by cowboys and because his battle-ax grandmother was threatening to send him to a reform school. That had been bad enough. Now he was saying that he had left because his grandmother was threatening to kill him if he didn't kill one of the whores he'd been screwing. It went on and on like that.

Unable to bear it, I stopped reading halfway through. I had gotten far enough to find out that he had only discovered all this a few years before through a therapist who had helped him to recover his repressed memories.

So that was it. Repressed memories. But repressed memories, I knew, could be fantasies. And these particular memories had a curious overlay of megalomania.

I turned off the computer, sick at heart.

Harry had been so crucial in my life. Now it felt as if, were we to see one another, we probably wouldn't even be able to carry on a conversation. I had forgiven him years ago; now, irrationally, I was angry again. If he had changed beyond recognition... had I been forgotten by someone I could never forget?

A few days later something rather spooky happened. Weeks earlier, a broken pipe in the basement of my house had caused a small flood, and Peter and I had rescued a carton of papers which contained a file of some old correspondence, and a journal I'd kept from 1957 to 1961. I hadn't taken the time to look at any of it, but when I finally wandered into the room where I'd put the carton, I noticed the file and opened it. Sitting right at the top was a letter addressed to me as Barbara Alson, a name I hadn't used for more than forty years. I turned it over. It was from Harry in Pietrasanta, Italy. The postmark was March of 1961. So it had been written shortly after I returned to New York from the month we had spent in Italy together. It was in part an apology for an earlier letter which I had found offensive, and which he claimed had been written out of loneliness. And in part, it was a protestation of love written in purple prose—"part of my blood" and "flowing through my heart and veins"—that sort of thing. It was also quite clear that he wasn't pressing me to leave my husband, Larry. That decision had to be mine alone.

I'd forgotten that we had ever corresponded. With the jarring and altered sense of him that the video had triggered still so fresh, I was now touched to find that he really had believed he loved me. There was something awkward and honest about the letter. Despite the intense metaphors, he wasn't pressing me to leave Larry. He just urged me to be strong and brave.

Which was what I had wanted of myself at the time.

Reading the letter, on top of having seen him in the video, I suddenly found myself wanting to tell the story, the story of Harry. I knew that the journal, sitting under the file of mail, would cover a lot of it, but I decided I would write it as I remembered it and then read the journal later.

I wrote a few pages, then stopped. I was finding it too painful to tell the story in the first person. Why I'm not sure. I had long ago forgiven him—was even grateful to him. He had enabled me to end a marriage I no longer wished to be in. I was even glad he had ditched me since I'd come to realize our relationship was inevitably doomed and that a longer time together would have made the ending that much worse. Still, I had perhaps never allowed myself to realize how deeply I'd been hurt. In any case, I scrapped what I'd written and started again—this time in the third person.

I don't know why changing from "I" to "she" had such a salutary effect, but by the time I neared the end, I realized that I had distanced myself sufficiently from the agonies of that time that I was occasionally slipping back into "I".

Now, I thought, I can do it in "I." So I read the journal and realized how much I had forgotten, how much more complexity and nuance there had been, and how many people moved through my days. I began to call the journal The Document, a name somehow equal to the way it chronicled the time and the place, the *sturm* and *drang* of half a century ago. Indeed, as I read it I found myself getting impatient with the repetitious notes, the daisy petals of the love affair—he loves me, he loves me not, I feel great, I feel terrible, I feel strong, I feel weak. What interested me more were anecdotes and descriptions of the others around me, and how it all conjured up the feeling of the time, how eager we were to live intensely, to live passionately. Like so many of the people around me, I thought we were adults. In fact, we were still trying to find ourselves, to find the lives we thought we should live. Immersing myself in my long gone past, I felt as if I were reading a novel by someone else about someone else.

Nineteen Sixty. Perhaps the most momentous year of my life. During the two or three years leading up to it, I had grown increasingly discontented. My marriage had begun to deteriorate, at least partly because after Peter was born, Larry and I were disappointed in each other, he because I wasn't super mom, and I because he refused to take more responsibility for child care or domestic chores. I had housewife syndrome. I was bored and restless and felt I had married too early, that I had not given myself a chance to experience other men and other ways of life. Larry and I got along sexually, but at the age of 30, free-floating libido had kicked in, and I fell into bed a few times with other men. For a couple of years, I was hooked on a clandestine liaison with an older man to whom I felt sexually drawn but didn't much like. I knew we didn't mean much to each other. Still, the affair gave a fillip of unpredictability to my life, and I was vaguely hurt though not actually sorry when he got married without telling me in advance,

I had come to believe that Larry no longer loved me. He even agreed at one point that he wasn't feeling very much. I told him that if we didn't love each other, we ought to split up. But he didn't agree, and I didn't push it. I was afraid of how it would affect Peter, and I couldn't quite get my mind around the logistics.

Almost every marriage around us also seemed to be in a state of turmoil. Everyone was dissatisfied or desperate, and we were all going from one drunken party to another. There always seemed to be a party to go to, and in between, we discussed the scenes that had been made by others or recovered from the ones we had created ourselves. We thought the 1950s were a bust. I thought maybe life was a bust.

Enter the new decade. Larry and I had been living on a small income that he had, and he had been writing theater of the absurd plays. The plays were as good as any which we had seen produced, but he'd had no luck getting his on stage. A job opportunity came up and he took it. In February he had to go out of town for about a week, and alone on a Saturday night, I decided to invite a few friends over. It burgeoned into a party.

I invited my lifelong friend Milly to dinner beforehand and told her to come early so that I would have time to clear dishes and put Peter to bed before everyone else arrived.

Millie called to say that a man she knew had shown up in town. Could she bring him? Of course. Then she called again. Her friend was late, but on his way. Another couple of calls like this until Millie said they were actually leaving. By this time they were so late that when they arrived, I opened the door with a scowl on my face.

At the bottom of the stairs, the man behind Millie looked at me with a light in his eyes that turned my frown into a smile.

Dinner was a hoot. The man with Milly was Harry Jackson and his presence seemed to make us all come alive. Peter, who was not yet five years old, was having such a good time that he didn't want to go to bed. I understood. "All right," I said, "we'll all go up with you." Harry looked startled and not too pleased, but I hustled him up along with the rest of us. If he was going to charm a child, he should take responsibility for the consequences.

Later, at the party, according to my great friend, Rhoda, I flirted with every man I talked to. So it was not exactly a surprise when Harry called me the next day.

I felt somewhat embarrassed, and when he said that he'd like to show me his studio, I thought, "Department-of-Show-You-My-Etchings," how corny can you get? I hemmed and hawed a bit and finally suggested that he take me out for a drink.

I must have called Millie to check out whether she was still involved with him. She said they were now just friends, but told me to be careful, he could be very persuasive.

Before he arrived that evening, I had a phone call from his wife. She sounded like she was crying as she told me that he had asked her to let me know that he would be a little late. I didn't yet know that Harry was always late but never thought that he had to let you know that he would be, so I believed that he had asked her to call, and decided that he must be a bastard. When he arrived I sat at the opposite end of the room and said it was a pretty shitty thing to have done. He seemed genuinely upset, said she'd been making a scene with him and must have sneaked a look at his engagement book, and made the call after he left.

It all sounded like a mess. But he smiled and said he really liked talking with me, and even as I told myself that I best stay out of it, I moved to the sofa where he was sitting. It wasn't long before he kissed me. I pulled away even though I'd liked the kiss. We continued to talk, and each time I let his eyes catch mine, we would clinch again, and each time it was a little harder to stop. To extricate myself, I proposed we go out for our drink, and in the bar, he changed his mode to verbal love, how wonderful I was, how exciting, how unique. Before long we were back at my place, and I made coffee while he became more and more persistent until I realized that I wanted him—just not there and then. Finally, I said I would come to see him in his studio the next day.

From my journal—February 24, 1960

Harry. Where do I start? Let me start with him. He is so many things which are strange to me. The Wyoming twang which always reminds me that he has been a cowboy in the Wild West. A painter. Even stranger, a sculptor. And even stranger, a one-time abstractionist turned realist. And yet we speak to each other often in the same language. While I don't understand his work or have any definite opinion of its worth, still I see him very clearly in it, the craftsman struggling for his vision as an artist. I look at him and I think, you are strange to me, you are made up of all these bits and pieces, exciting because they are unfamiliar, you promise my curiosity at the same time that you appear to me and I appear to you for moments so beautiful and intense that I could die in them in the belief that there were nothing more for me to feel. And yet why you? You are not great, not yet, perhaps never. I know you at times too close to myself, at others not close enough. I sense in you cranks and crimps which I will find unpleasant. I look at your face and it pleases me. A square set face. Your nose is gross, but I like your beard, your reddish brown hair, and most of all your eyes, which looked at me so quickly with both delight and amusement. Your eyes I see all the time, blue, Chinese lidded, male eyes that can ravish me or scorn me or love, and I feel ravished, or scorned or loved. Yet why you? Your eyes delude with the promise of love even though I know that like everyone else you can promise nothing.

In two weeks I have fallen in love and perhaps out of love again. I don't really know how I feel now except that the initial ecstasy has been lost, and I suspect will not come back again because we have come to know each other a little.

When I went to his studio I had no particular presentiments of what to expect. Certainly I did not expect to find that he was in love with me. When he claimed he was, it seemed to stun us

209

both. I don't remember all or even some of what he said, but he enveloped me in love and tenderness and sex.

When I left him because I was picking up Peter at school, I wandered through an enchanted afternoon. It was lovely. It was spring. We met Jill in the park. I felt as if I had the most beatific and idiotic smile on my face. I was loved. And it seemed so natural. This thing which I had believed could never happen again, certainly not so sweetly, so illogically, so unexpectedly, so undeservedly, had happened to me. I was happy. I was strong. I wanted to shout it to the world. Of course I held my tongue.

I wish I could describe the way he made love to me that first day, and then again the next day, and the day after that. But he so enthralled me that the love-words, the wild fantasies, the caresses, elude my memory even as they happen. But this I know. He is the first man I have ever known who has really loved my woman's body. He has no ounce of squeamish in him. He makes me feel at times as if he could eat every part of me with relish, even my shit. He makes love to me and I know how the tips of his fingers feel to him as they touch me, and we both thrill.

Eat my shit, indeed. It's hard to believe now that I once had such a gift for hyperbole. Or that I could so readily believe he could so quickly fall in love with me. Of course, he framed it in terms of how special I was, telling me in myriad imaginative ways how he felt. Perhaps the gift and the curse of having had a fiercely loving mother was that I never found it hard to believe that I was loved.

Entranced though I was, I didn't immediately put the word love to my own feelings. I was only sure that I had never experienced anything like it before, and thought, "This should have happened to me ten years ago, but thank God it's happening to me now."

I still thought of myself as a writer. I was working on a story, and I was writing in my journal. But I was more interested in living, in experience, in connecting. I wanted to live courageously, even dangerously. At the same time, I didn't want too much damage to hit me and mine. Caution was, perhaps, my more natural bent, and though I might complain about it, I did not really want to destroy the family cocoon. I think my family was something that both attracted Harry and which he detested because he had been so deprived. He once said to me that he envied Norman because Norman had me for a sister. I was startled. Wasn't it better to have me as a lover? I never realized at the time how much of what was happening between us had to do with family, his envy of it, and my desire to break away from both the demands and the protection that my family gave me. Harry was the first lover I'd ever had whose presence made me feel intensely alive, the way Norman had made me feel when we were young. Of course with my fundamental practicality, I had always thought that Norman as a husband would have been impossible to live with, and so I felt very lucky to have him as a brother. So why did I plunge into an affair with someone like Harry? Or did I plunge?

Reading the journal, I realize that my feelings were more nuanced and changeable than I remember. We very quickly realized that we disagreed about a lot of things—my feminism for one. Having read Simone de Beauvoir's *The Second Sex* when I was in my mid-twenties, I had decided that being a woman meant fighting both the world and one's own nature. He didn't understand. That I was more interested in books than art certainly gave him pause. I often felt that we came from opposite ends of the universe. But we had moments of connection that felt extraordinary. I wrote in the Journal, "We really inspire one another so often to an intensity of feeling and expression. . .and yet it is strange that we should because on so many fundamentals (like the nature of woman) Harry and I disagree so violently that we cannot even talk in the same terms."

When Larry returned, I began to feel somewhat terrified. No doubt sensing my remoteness, he was always angry with me. I came down with bronchitis, and then with a back spasm, which laid me completely out. He had to go away again, to San Francisco for two weeks, and we agreed I would join him for the second week. As soon as he left, my back recovered.

The love affair was up and down. On March first, I wrote, "When I went to see Harry in the afternoon, it was only a week since I had last seen him, but I felt remote and raspish and wondered if perhaps we had already lost each other. And he said, 'I wonder if I've ever really touched you.'" But the next day, meeting him at the White Horse, "We were close again. . . . Feeling inspired and eloquent, I told him how he had touched me. After dinner, we went back to the studio (how I love that place, with all the dirt and mess and confusion and discomfort, but so filled with his work that it is impossible to see it all, and filled too with the glamor of anything which is so alien to the daily context of my life)."

Typical was our disagreement about meeting one night when I was planning to go to a cocktail party with Norman and Adele, and he had a dinner date with friends at nine o'clock but wanted to see me before. I said I thought we weren't going to see each other until Sunday. He said, "Well, I thought maybe I'd beg." I melted and said I'd skip the party and come to see him. As soon as I hung up I began to stew about it—he was asking me to give up my plans and was then going to desert me after a couple of hours. I called back and we had a tense conversation until he agreed that he would try to break his date too. When I got to the studio he claimed he had not been able to reach his friends, and would at least have to go and have a drink with them. It didn't occur to me that probably he hadn't even tried to contact them. What an incredible tendency I had to believe everything I was told. But that night was. . .

From my journal—March 2, 1960

. . .one of the most beautiful, most perfect times I've ever spent...
. It was like a long journey, from day into night, along a lovely
and unfamiliar path, in which each new turn and twist opened
up upon a more exquisite vista (the sex was very steamy and
satisfying) and when he left I didn't mind at all. I lay there
dreaming for a while. Then I put on his bathrobe and went to the
bookshelf. By a kind of inspiration I picked up the Duino Elegies.
I seldom read poetry. But sometime ago I read a short excerpt
from Malte Laurid Brigge and it so impressed me that I had the
feeling in that moment the other evening that Rilke was going
to have something to say to me. Harry had read most of it, and
underlined a good deal, and so it was fun reading it because in
addition to the delight it gave me, it also taught me a little about
him. When he came back I was feeling luxurious and contented,
and I pointed out a few lines to him. He picked up the book and
opened it to the Ninth Elegy. He said he wanted to read it to me
but was a little afraid to. Then he went ahead anyway. It was
extraordinary. I'd never before heard poetry read like that. He
read it very slowly, so slowly that it would have been excruciating
if I had not been caught by it. He was completely inside that poem,
and it came out word by word, every word thrilling with meaning.
He repeated a couple of lines a number of times. I still remember
them—"And we too, just once. Only once. Once, and no more." As
much meaning as it had for me though, it had even more for him
because at the end of it tears ran down his cheeks and suddenly
he was sobbing in my arms.
One part of me sees the scene and is amused at the corniness of

it all—two lovers reading poetry and weeping. But I didn't cry. At the moment I felt too wonderful even to feel his weeping, though I knew at bottom it was the loneliness which hit him. Mine hit me later.

We screwed again. It was very late and we were very tired. We talked about going home. But we started again. And then suddenly, he called me by his wife's name. The irony of it was, I didn't hear him. But he caught it and said, "I just called you Joan." That didn't bother me, since he'd been with her for eight years it seemed like a natural enough slip. But it bothered him and he insisted on talking about it. "I think I know why," he said. I asked him why. "You see," he said, "I love Joan." Something inside me curled up and died. Besides the hurt that I was not the only one, I felt dense and insensitive, because it had not even occurred to me, and I knew that he'd had to tell me because he sensed that I didn't know. He went on. "Some things happened tonight between you and me which never happened with Joan." Very calmly, because while it was the logical conclusion of what he was saying, still I didn't believe it, I said, "And so you called me Joan because you wished that I were she." "That's right," he said. I knew then what it must be like to get a belly wound. I looked at the gaping hole with horror, even before I felt the pain. It was almost incomprehensible to me that he could wish me to be anyone else, it meant that I was really not quite real to him. I felt as if the only way to absorb the pain was to fight the hot tears behind my eyes, and so I didn't weep much. But suddenly I had to get out, to be alone with it, I even began to laugh a little hysterically. I cracked, "Well, at least with you I never know what to expect next," but I couldn't look at him.

Now I wonder that I didn't ask him why, if he loved her, he wanted to divorce her.

In any event, I was incapable of feeling down for long. Two days later, "I woke up feeling wonderful...alive and good...as if I had been given back to myself."

What strikes me now is that despite the intense distress I often felt at the time, I kept bouncing back to my innate joy in life. It may not be possible to know the texture of another person's feelings, but I never tried to understand how Harry experienced life. I think now, that he was creating his life moment by moment, but there was never any carryover. Even if a moment was revelatory, it had nothing to do with the next moment. He could say to me, as he did on the phone one afternoon, "I live from you," as if nothing like this had ever happened to him before. But when I saw Harry as he was with other people, I knew he was aware and ready not only for me but for any new experience that might turn up. Once, at a restaurant in Chinatown, he almost started a fight because he thought somebody at another table was laughing at his beard, but the exchange turned pleasant, and then he was almost too ready to make friends. All through the incident I wanted only to be with him and resented the intrusion.

I was fascinated by the stories of his life as he told them to me. His life had been so different from anyone else I'd known. At the age of fourteen, he had run away from home in Chicago, hitchhiking to Wyoming because he was in love with cowboys and horses. A family there took him in, and he actually became a cowboy. His mother eventually found him but decided he was doing well and left him there. When the U.S. entered the war, he enlisted in the Marines. After landing in Tarawa, he was badly wounded and almost lost his foot. An explosion affected his head and he'd suffered from epileptic seizures ever since. He confessed to me that he'd never been able to shoot a gun at anyone, but fortunately, when his artistic ability became evident, he was allowed to function solely as a staff artist. Toward the end of the war, he was sent back to the States to produce paintings of his drawings. The actor in him also surfaced. He had a great speaking voice and a cowboy twang and so at the age of 20, he narrated a film about Iwo Jima and was chosen to be the MC on the Norman Corwin show for the opening of the UN San Francisco conference. After his discharge from the Army, he saw a reproduction of a Jackson Pollack painting, and chucking a possible career as a radio actor along with a commercial illustrating career, he decided he would go to New York with its burgeoning art scene and become a painter. Once in the city, he quickly found the Cedar Bar and the coterie of artists who hung out there, including Jackson Pollack, with whom he became friends. He soon married the painter, Grace Hartigan, but the marriage didn't last long. The semi-abstract paintings he was doing began to be shown and sold, and he was getting some recognition.

Then just a few years into it, he suddenly decided that he had gone as far as he could with abstraction, that he wanted to paint realistically, and abandoning whatever reputation he had achieved he went off to Europe to study the old masters. It was only recently that he had returned.

I was enormously impressed with his ability to surmount a ghastly childhood. And I was awed by his courage in radically changing the course of his artistic focus, though I didn't understand why he had done it. I liked Harry's early paintings with unrealistic human figures that gave the paintings a mood. The paintings and sculptures he was doing now, particularly the sculptures of cowboys and horses, seemed like a throwback to the 19th century. They looked as good as Remingtons. But what was the point? I thought he needed to develop an individual vision. But since I also felt that my understanding and appreciation of visual art was limited, I did not say much.

Harry thought of himself primarily as a painter. He had started

216

doing sculpture as a way of preparing for the two mural-size paintings he had been commissioned to do for a museum in Cody, Wyoming. Because the sculptures were so good, he was now preparing for a show at Knoedler's in Manhattan, a prestigious 57th Street gallery for realistic art. Even so, he at least once called the work he was doing "junk," and thought he needed to find a more personal vision.

From my journal—March 3, 1960

> *I am beginning to know so much about him now, of what his life has been (and it delights me because it has been in so many ways unusual) and of what he is like. I want so much to record in detail the coldness and the passion, the genuine and the phony, the kinks and the inspirations, and the vivid poetry of his fantasies and visions and stories. But there is no time now and tomorrow I leave.*

I had known Harry barely a month, but I was hooked. I was in love. However, I also felt that because I had promised Larry that I would join him in San Francisco, I had to go. The rest of my life seemed totally unpredictable. The day before I left I wrote, "I have had the thought that the plane will go down. And in a way, I do not care if it does. Norman asked me yesterday if I had premonitions of death. Actually, I have no premonition at all. It is just that I feel as if I have finally reached the top of a mountain and so it would not be such a bad time to die."

Though the plane did not go down, the flight was memorable. New York had been hit with a blizzard a couple of days before, and the airports had just re-opened. I left the house at 1 p.m. for a 3 p.m. flight. We didn't board until 6 p.m., then sat on the tarmac for another three hours. It was my first jet flight, and I was astonished by the speed at which the plane took off. After just an hour in the air, the pilot announced that we were having engine trouble and would have to land in Ft. Worth. As we approached what looked from the air like a postage stamp airport, I was certain the runway was too short, that we would never stop in time. When the reverse jets, another new experience, slowed us down, I breathed a sigh of relief.

It turned out that our plane could not be fixed. Instead, we were piled into a four-engine prop plane. It lumbered up into the air in familiar fashion, and the pilot announced the flying time to San Francisco. It was ten minutes longer than the flying time we'd heard in New York. The passenger sitting next to me said, "We're further than when we started." By the time I arrived at the hotel in San Francisco, the sun was coming up and I had been traveling for almost twenty-four hours. Through it all, I read *Siddhartha* by Herman Hesse and felt very calm. If the plane went down, well, I had lived. Living…well, living was going to get messy.

Indeed, back in New York, it soon did.

From my journal—March 15, 1960

> *Life is in the shithouse again. . .Have been filled all day with the pain I always have when Harry and I do not connect. Today was the worst. He's recovering from pneumonia and feeling weak and quite remote, and as I realized afterward all he wanted of me was a mothering, which it never even occurred to me to give since all we had was an hour and a half and I was looking to recapture the sense of inspiration we had. And so I feel as if I doubly failed. I didn't give him what he wanted and I know too that if I had made him respond to me he wouldn't have felt so weak.*

Perhaps I was right when I thought it might be better not to try to pick it up again. But I didn't want out, not yet.

From my journal—March 28, 1960

>*And in all of this, all of the time, Harry. I love him, and I feel*
>*so inadequate to it. As he said the other day, he needs so much.*
>*I wonder, even if I were free, if I could give him nearly what he*
>*needs. As it is, I often feel engorged with the helpless desire to give*
>*to him, and not knowing what or how. And I know this is pointless.*
>*I know. . .how little we give when we try too hard. We made love*
>*the other day and it was beautiful and tender and satisfying and*
>*that night life seemed enormously good and gay and carefree and*
>*open. The next day he was gloomy, torn by different pulls and*
>*pressures, and trying to reach a sense of himself. It was then he*
>*talked about how much he needed. I went away excited, as he*
>*always excites me with his shifts and his honesty, but with my*
>*own sense of strength ebbing. Then in the afternoon Peter got sick*
>*and I knew how fenced in I am by my life as I have made it...*

Because of some mysterious symptoms, Peter ended up in the hospital
for tests, so of course, that became the most important thing in my life
for two days until it was determined that there was nothing wrong
with him.

Two days later, it was all about Harry again.

From my journal—March 30, 1960

>*When I called him before and asked him how he felt, he said,*
>*"marvelous. Just marvelous." I love the way he says that word. I*
>*love his voice. So often when he tells me how he feels about me, it*
>*is like a cool rush of heaven at my throat. . . He warned me in*

*the beginning that I would find him inarticulate! And yet he is
that most wondrous of all things to me, an articulate lover. How
great to say, and so to hear one's love, as well as feel it. I am the
one who is inarticulate. I know that there are words to express
my love, but in the waves of ecstasy I am mindless...*

*Over lunch the other day he told me a story about rubbing some
anti-semitic graffiti off a wall. Then he talked about the fact that
for years he lied about being Jewish, and about his grandmother
who hated being Jewish and managed to marry a man who wasn't
(Jackson) who left her after Harry's mother was born. . . .His
grandmother opened a restaurant in Chicago, which his mother
was still running.*

*The grandmother threw Harry's father out of the house when
Harry was seven years old, after which he and his father had very
little to do with each other. Harry grew up using his grandmother's
name—Jackson—as his last name.*

That was what he told me then. How much of it is true? Was any of it
true? At that time, I never questioned any of it.

Perhaps naively, I always tend to believe what I am told. And since
what he told me about his early life was so bad, it never occurred to
me that he was making anything up, or that it might have been even
worse.

How could I not believe when I was mesmerized? Not only by him.
Also by my own feelings.

From my journal—April 1, 1960

*How many things I feel for him. It's as if I feel all the things I've
ever felt for any man I've cared about. . .Desire, excitement,
lovingness, givingness, witness. And it all comes out in an*

enormous tenderness. He remarked on this yesterday. He said he could feel my tenderness coming through my pores. That's exactly it. When I touch him I feel as if every cell is alive with my emotions.

But on the same day, I also wrote:

. . .suddenly last night lying in bed and thinking about Harry, I shattered. . .I knew that he would inevitably leave me and I felt the loneliness of that as I have never felt loneliness before. . .I wanted to wail like an abandoned child.

But of course, I was not as alone as he was. I simply did not understand how deprived he felt of family, nor did I realize how jealous he was of mine. In fact, he decided my problem was that I had never left home, and he thought that I should. I began to think he was right.

However, what he wanted from me, or any woman, was something else.

From my journal—April 8, 1960

Tuesday afternoon I went to the studio. We had a great fuck... .But afterward, talking, we got into the man-woman thing, and I began to feel torn apart by the pull in me toward being the kind of ideal woman he wants and the knowledge that he would eat me up and that finally I would be left with myself, and that self nothing without him. I found it impossible to make him understand that it is not enough to give up one's own possibilities for the sake of nurturing another's.

I also began to feel buffeted back and forth. Now that I was so in love with him, he was pulling away. Which made me say that we must end it. Which made him love me again and want to continue.

From my journal—April 14, 1960

I am going to see Harry this afternoon, and I am sitting here and thinking that I must break with him because he does not love me any more.

Later. Harry called and cancelled. Another omen?

It actually reinforces what I was feeling. I've been sitting here, angry, sad, noble, petty, making scenes of renunciation. Yet the other afternoon was wonderful, and I felt fabulous afterward. Sexually, we are blooming with each other. He said, "It is wonderful how you have opened to me." And that is exactly how I feel. At one point, though, he began to talk, terribly eloquently, about how he felt about me at the beginning. . . When he was finished I felt and said that since he no longer felt that way perhaps we should quit. He worked very hard after that at making me know just how much I attract him. And I left feeling not at all like I wanted to part.

From my journal—April 15, 1960

He hasn't called yet. I sit here and try to work and instead I think, you fuck, you shit, you bastard. And then the anger suddenly drains and I think it's not his fault if he doesn't care any more. And I feel helpless and the tears come. And then I think, but he really is a shit, capable of dropping me without a moment's feeling, he's said so himself, he said one day that no matter how much people may have done for him, when he no longer needs them, he can't be bothered. And again, I want to scream at him, "you

222

goddam bastard, you're killing me."...I am out of control.

But he must have called because the next day I wrote:

Yesterday we parted, and it was tender and sweet and lovely, filled with the air of a sudden spring afternoon. Somehow it was not quite real. I felt too good to feel the grief of it...when I saw him I just felt good. I laughed, and said, "I came to part with you and I'm so happy to see you I don't know how I can do it." It was such a sunny, warm, sparkling afternoon, with a soft sky and the air sweet and caressing. I felt tender and ready for sadness, but not at all sad. We sat on a bench, our eyes holding often and his sex coming up (Oh God, how will I do without that?) and I began to talk a little of how it had been for me, and how I did not know if I could bear the pain of not seeing him at all, but that I could not bear to watch what there is between us deteriorate. . .And then he said that he hated the surreptitiousness of it, he wanted to do things with me, not be haunted by my running off in an hour... .For the first time in the afternoon the tears came to my eyes, and I said, "Then I was right. We have to separate." We looked at each other and he said, "I love you more at this moment than I ever have before."...We should have said goodbye right away, but we spent another hour at it. On the way back to the car he asked me to come and live with him in the loft. I said what about Peter. He said bring Peter too. But I couldn't take him seriously. I really couldn't take any of it as serious.

That was the day that Harry took Joe into his home, which should have tipped me off about how badly he needed company, but I only saw it as an example of his ability to turn every chance encounter into an opportunity.

As we sat in his car saying our romantic goodbye, a bum came up begging for a handout. Harry took the change out of his pocket, looked at it, and finally emptied it into the tramp's hand. It was quite a lot, the guy began to bless him and Harry said suddenly, "Look, you want a job?" "Sure, boss." "Well, wait on that corner for five minutes and I'll be with you." The man went off and Harry said, "What do you want to bet he'll be gone?" But the guy was still there when I got out of the car and Harry drove over to meet him.

The last I saw as I went by in my cab, Harry had Joe in his car and was negotiating with him.

Why couldn't I take Harry's invitation, or rather plea, to come live with him, as a serious request? No matter how much I loved Harry, Peter was more important. It was clear to me that Harry had no idea of what it would mean to have a young child living in his loft. And this child had a father who was still my husband, and my feelings for Larry were all over the place—anger, fear, pity, and even tenderness at times.

And then there were the other people in my life. Apart from family, my friends, particularly a new friend, Jillen Lowe, who lived around the corner, and had a son Peter's age. Because of the kids, and because we liked each other, we'd been spending a lot of time together. Jillen was fun, she was impassioned, and her marriage was also in turmoil. We were both feeling that we had married too hastily, and whatever talents or potential we possessed had been tamped down. And probably, she too was experiencing the sexual bloom of a 30-year-old woman.

There was always stuff going on. Parties, of course. And openings. One night we went to what I think was the first production of *Krapp's Last Tape* and *The Zoo Story*, playing at a small Village theater. Both plays so deeply touched some personal chord that they colored my mood for days. Another night Jacques was photographing a political event at the Seagram Building, and Larry, Jillen and I sat in the cocktail lounge, getting high, laughing a lot, and feeling somehow connected to national events. Also, walking the streets of the Village on a lovely day was enough to make me feel good. Indeed, no matter how histrionically desperate I felt at times, no matter how miserable I thought I was, I kept springing back into the joy of just being alive.

From my journal—May 2, 1960

A glorious day and I feel wonderful and full of life in spite of the fact that it seems as if nothing good is ever going to happen again.

Despite our "split," Harry and I were still in frequent contact, although I often felt that we were no longer connecting. I wrote, "He makes me feel so alive, even when it's awful with him." But two days later, I recorded a couple of lovely hours we spent together.

Harry loved me again when I helped him write the biographical material and address the invitations for his Knoedler show. He said no one had ever helped him like I had, which of course made me feel good but also seemed like too much gratitude for something I found so easy to do.

Of course, after the show opened, he was for a while too busy to see me much. He was trying very hard to be businesslike about sales, about publicity, about interviews with *Time* and *Life*. I understood, but it underscored how quickly he could move on.

At the beginning of June, he told me that he was leaving for a couple of weeks in the West, and soon after that, he would return to Italy to work, probably for a year. It took my breath away. He also suggested that we should try to spend a month together in Italy to see if we would get along. I think he did not expect me to consider it. And as we discussed it in the following days, it seemed to make him love me less and less. On June 9th, I wrote: *Tuesday night Harry and I went out together into the universe, enveloped in an immortal stream of light....Today*

I feel as if we've landed on two different planets.

The push and the pull. Whenever I decided that he didn't really want me, I became the woman he did want and we would connect again. I think I always knew that I carried more baggage than Harry was ready to accept—a child and my middle-classness.

But he could not prevent himself from challenging me to prove how much I cared. And so, one fateful day, when I was about to leave his studio for home, he asked me to stay the night. He had just thrown Joe out because of some transgression that Harry was very upset about. He probably didn't expect me to agree, but I called Larry and told him I wouldn't be home until morning and I would explain why then.

I realize now how little Harry expected me to accept his challenge to stay over. Neither did I guess how nervous it must have made him. It was a terrible night. We went out for dinner, and when we came back Harry immediately fell asleep, waking up briefly a couple of times only when Joe started hammering on the door, asking to be taken in again, and Harry yelled at him to go away.

From my journal—June 21, 196

> *Harry and I talked for a few minutes. I told him that it had occurred to me that life with him might be just like trying to sleep in the same bed with him had been, lonely, exquisitely uncomfortable, and spent on the hard, lumpy mattress of which I held only a scrap. He tried to make love to me, but he couldn't, and he fell asleep again. I lay there another hour or so, then got up....At last I was dressed and ready to leave. He got up and came to the door with me. He felt very badly about what had happened. Perhaps once again I had made a mistake. Perhaps I should have woken him right away, and said, "Look I'm here, and I'm leaving in a few hours. Stay with me." But I was always holding my*

226

breath for fear of doing the wrong thing.

I was so tired, drained, hopeless, and ready to say goodbye. I couldn't say anything. He was the one who spoke. He said, "Be strong, be good, be kind. Love yourself. Love me always. Remember that I love you."

It bugs me now that I didn't have the sense to say then, "Cut the bullshit. You're the one who chickened out."

I had assumed that once I told Larry that I was in love with another man, we would split. It was not so simple. Instead, Larry suddenly found me interesting again and decided he really loved me and was ready to fight for me.

From my journal—June 22, 1960

Larry was still pissed off at what he'd suffered all night, but whatever he'd expected his reactions to be, they were thrown askew by what he hadn't expected—first that I would be in love, and second that I would have parted with my lover. I guess my misery was what really overwhelmed him. He hadn't expected to feel for me...I said that even though things with Harry were over, I still loved him and so perhaps we should separate. Larry said that this had made him realize that he still really loved me and wanted me and that it was the first time in years that he had seen me as a person.... A little later Larry carried me upstairs to bed. I laughed about it and quoted Elena in The Deer Park *about the attractiveness of unfaithful women, but for the first time in I can't remember how long, I found myself excited by him.*

From my journal—June 23, 1960

What is going to happen between Larry and me I don't know. He loves me now, really loves me I believe, and it's very appealing. I feel for him, cannot help but sympathize with his love, so much do I feel it like my own for Harry. He gets life from me as I got life from Harry. How between the two men I feel. I can understand and sympathize with both. I suddenly enjoy being with Larry now, I feel as if I can talk to him again. But I know I'll never be able to love him the way I need to love, and the way I'll probably go on loving Harry for the rest of my life. So part of me wants to run away, even if I never find love again. And another part feels that I can really do Larry some good now, even, finally, free him.

Underlying it all was my existential dilemma.

From my journal—July 4, 1960

I really do not know what shape my life should take now, what shape I would like it to take. Should I go off? Should I stay? Should I write? Should I study? Should I find a job? Should I be faithful? Should I be promiscuous? All these things pull at me, taunting me. To be oneself, to use oneself, this is the source of life. But to find oneself, my God, how hard, how often tenuous and elusive. For I know that one cannot be simply what one is. One is what one becomes.

What I really wanted was the freedom to pursue new experiences. But I was also caught up in Larry loving me again, after having for so long felt so little for anyone, himself included. He said to me, "I'd rather love you and get hurt, than not love you." Shades of my feelings for Harry. But I felt more sympathy for Larry than Harry had felt for me.

Larry went into therapy. His therapist told him that as long as we were living together, he should insist that I remain faithful to him. I agreed, but also felt that our marriage would therefore probably end. We went to Provincetown for a few lovely weeks, during which I was embroiled in the histrionics of Jillen and Jacques who were going through the breakup of their marriage. Mercifully, I felt involved in the world outside my life. Jacques had become a major photographer of the Kennedys, and Norman had done an interview with Kennedy for *Esquire*, so I felt for a while more interested in national affairs than in my own emotions.

But back in New York, I discovered that Harry hadn't yet left for Italy and was in a deep depression. Manny told me he was very worried. He had seen Harry get depressed before, but this time it seemed worse. I don't think I'd realized just how fragile Harry's purchase on life felt to him at that point. Not only had the results of the Knoedler show faded, but he'd realized that he was not going to clear very much from the works he had sold, and probably he was questioning his artistic vision. We talked on the phone, and I saw him a couple of times, much to Larry's fury. I ached at how little I could help him. Eventually, he came out of the depression, and we continued to discuss my going to Italy, but I became increasingly convinced that he didn't really want me to, and more and more aware of how little we knew or understood each other.

From my journal—September 21, 1960

I feel as if I've reached a new quietus. I love Harry. He loves me. But finally so what? If we don't move on our emotions, finally they must dissolve. . .Once again I feel as if it's really over, and in another way, I think that it may never be. What happened yesterday was not an ending, though once again we said goodbye (as Larry cracked, our goodbyes are becoming like

Sarah Bernhardt's farewell performances). Harry was his old self again—Harry on the phone, something to do with getting one of the big bronzes taken by the Met. Then, still in the midst of his "operating," he began to make love to me. I felt as if he were treating me like a casual lay and told him I didn't think he needed me for that. Thank God I did. He is so responsive. We talked.... . When we finally came together it was with the same urge to join that I always feel, the same delight at every small touch of him, the same unutterable feeling that he completes me and that nothing else exists. And knowing that it was the same for him. He said, "You are wonderful," and "You've never been so beautiful," which he always says and which I always feel at the moment is really true because I've never felt so beautiful. And then we were in a rush to leave, he had an important appointment. We talked gaily, almost casually, about my coming to Italy, and then we said goodbye.

Typically, a couple of days later my impatience resurfaced.

From my journal—September 23, 1960

Today I feel mad. . .I'm fed up with the whole goddam thing, I'm fed up with thinking about it, I'm fed up with living it. I'd just like to wash the whole goddam thing down the drain. It struck me just before how lonely I am with Harry...he seduces me with love into the feeling of joining, then breaks away and leaves me abandoned.

Going through the journal, I am struck now by how aware I was of how incompatible Harry and I were. I hadn't remembered it that way. What I remembered was how much I loved him, how alive he made

230

me feel, and how great the sex was. But in those early days of October, before he left, I wrote again and again about how skewed I thought his image of me was. And yet in my fascination with all the unusual parts of his life, I really didn't understand how alone he was, how deprived of any sense of support. He couldn't help but hate me for my family, couldn't help but want me to throw it all over and damn the consequences. At the same time, it was clear that if I did, he would take no responsibility.

Larry, for his part, was also getting fed up. He began challenging me to leave. Probably out of some deep sense of self-preservation, I felt incapable of moving.

At some point in October, Harry finally left for Italy. The last entry in my journal of 1960 is dated October 20.

During the following month, Norman enlisted, no, insisted on my helping him with his desire to run for mayor. I thought it was a terrible idea, which of course angered him. Indeed, he seemed to be angry with everyone. He was drinking too much, and as I learned later, taking drugs, and furious with his family, because we weren't the Kennedys and we couldn't seem to understand that he was going to save the world. On November 19 he held the party which was supposed to herald the announcement of his campaign. Instead, he stabbed Adele.

I spent the next couple of months consulting with lawyers, agonizing over what at the time seemed like the loss of my lodestar, my brother.

Harry called once, from Italy, and asked if there was any way he could help. I shrugged.

"What can you do?"

Larry, on the other hand, came through for me. He just backed me up completely when I rejected all the crazy things that people were telling me to do. At one point I said to him, "I feel like you and I are the only two sane people left in the world." I thought things would never be the same again, and in a way, they never were. But Adele survived,

Norman spent some weeks in Bellevue, she didn't bring charges, and by January of 1961, we were even going to parties again.

Sometime in January, Harry came back to New York. I don't know what brought him. Perhaps he came back for me. In any event, he asked me to go back to Italy with him—for that month we had talked about so endlessly the previous summer.

Now I'm rather astonished that I was able to do it. First, I convinced Larry to accept it. I think he felt that if I didn't go, we would never be whole again, and he probably hoped that a month of Harry would get me over him.

I asked Brigitte, Peter's beloved former nanny, who was working as an airline hostess for a small airline in New Jersey and staying with us on her days off, to come and take care of Peter for the month. Out of pure friendship, she managed to get herself free for the month. I told my mother that I was simply taking a month's vacation from my family. Battered as Mother must have been feeling then, she didn't ask too many questions. Since Harry wasn't offering to pay my way, I cashed in, at some loss, a stock my parents had given me a couple of years before. It was my only asset.

The trip began badly. On the crowded plane, Harry and I huddled together, eager to make love, but when we got to Paris and into our attic room in a Left Bank hotel, both of us exhausted, he started making phone calls. There was a countess to see and he had to go to the Louvre. I began to wonder what we were doing this for. On to Rome, and he fell asleep as soon as we reached the hotel.

We moved the next day into an apartment offered to Harry by a friend who was out of town. It was in an old tower overlooking the Forum. I knew that I should feel like I was having an extraordinary and privileged experience, but I was too preoccupied and confused because Harry started finding fault with me. Probably I reeked with the expectation of attention, not realizing that in Rome, as in Paris, he had to operate. He called everyone he knew, and we visited several people.

I still remember vividly a dinner in a Chinese restaurant, and a party we went to, both of them painful for me. Harry had at some point befriended Iris Tree, a member of the British cultural coterie of writers, painters, and actors. Except for Harry and myself, most of the eight people at the table were English. Next to me was a very shy man who was dubious about the Chinese food that was served. I tried to reassure him, then admitted that I hadn't caught his name.

"Fry," he said, "Christopher Fry."

Of course, I knew who Christopher Fry was. *The Lady's Not for Burning* had been a big success on Broadway. But I had neither seen the play nor read it. Idiotically, since I couldn't say anything about his work, I felt I couldn't let him know that I was aware of his reputation. My sense of social ineptness only grew worse when, after dinner, Harry and I moved on to a party, where he deposited me in a chair and said there were some people he had to talk to.

I must have sat alone for the better part of an hour, pondering for the first time in my life, the nature of identity. Since as yet I knew no Italian, there would be no way to have a conversation. And indeed, what could I talk about? Out of deference to Larry, I really didn't want to talk about New York or the people I knew, or even tell my name. I thought, without those things, who am I? I finally got up and sought Harry out, and offered to go home alone. He said he was ready to leave, but bawled me out the next day for having made the offer, that even if he hadn't wanted to leave he would have. Since I had been trying to be strong and brave while feeling utterly miserable, his take on it just made me want to cry.

It was a relief to leave Rome and take the train to Pietrasanta, the town in the north where he had a studio. He'd told me it was a nothing town, but across from the train station was a beautiful 12th-century

233

church. I had bought a little Olivetti typewriter in Rome, and I began again to keep my journal. I was also studying Italian, and pretty quickly found that I could go into a store and order groceries and function easily in restaurants, since the Italians, unlike the French, were always eager to understand you. But of course, underlying it all was a sense of displacement. I kept seesawing between depression and love.

There were good days. One morning Harry said to me that whether we stayed together two days or two years, he loved me now. For Ever. A couple he knew came by and induced us to join them for lunch at the trattoria.

From my journal—February 8, 1961

> *At lunch for the first time since we arrived I felt vivacious and open and witty with other people, and between Harry and myself there was the kind of tenderness which doesn't even need to touch. Perhaps that's why I felt so open, because so really secure.... Later we went to the hotel where we ran into the Professore again and Ricardo and another man and all had dinner together. Talked with everyone, speaking four languages, (three of which I really didn't know). Harry was proud of me. I knew it even if he hadn't told me so later. And hardly talking to each other, we were very much together, just the easy way I could lean against his shoulder for a few moments.... Later, made love. And we talked. For hours. A beautiful time. That almost excruciating mixture of sadness and happiness that I feel so much here. Harry talking about how for the first time he could even begin to think of the possibility of our living together.... But today I am missing Peter, missing Larry, really wanting to see them and to feel the accustomed structure of my life.*

From my journal—February 9, 1961

Another beautiful day today. Extraordinary light. Late in the afternoon, we went for a drive. Both of us less than cheerful. . .Both of us sad on the drive back in the dark along the sea. Harry asked me if I could stay another month. But today I've been missing Peter so, I couldn't even consider it. God, how I would like to pick him up at school or read him a story or just sit with him a while with my arm around his shoulders, see his grin and get a big buss and a mommy I love you. I think I even miss the crying and the mad-ons and all the hours when we ignore each other but know we're there.

I was thinking before that there is a part of myself I have with Larry that I miss here. And I don't know whether Harry could ever bring it out in me. With Harry, I'm all woman and only woman. Because that's all he wants, I suppose, and I am either too weak or too feminine to force the expression of a part of me that isn't wanted. But the writer in me feels stifled. I feel so uninspired, even muted. Somehow, I feel as if I've lost the power and the use of words.

Harry kept asking me to stay longer and I kept missing Peter. The most vivid memory I still have of that month is the cold day on which, casually looking for something to read, I found a copy of *Anna Karenina* in the bookcase. I had read it before, at least twice. This time I just cracked it open in the middle and found Anna in Italy with Vronsky, her lover, having left her son in Russia with his father. It was excruciating to read, but I couldn't stop. Never before or since have I so identified with a fictional character. It was so painful that I couldn't commit myself to the book by taking it to a cozy chair. Yet I couldn't put it back on the shelf. I just stood there for an hour, turning the pages, cold

235

and anguished. Through it all, however, there was one big difference. I knew I would never give up Peter.

Because I said I couldn't stay another month, Harry kept getting angry and depressed.

From my journal—February 13, 1961

Talked about my leaving. Harry said that if it stays this bad another few days it would be the only thing to do. . . It was all agonizing, for at the same time that we felt like absolute strangers, he might be touching me and his touch was the touch of my lover. Suddenly after one freshet sprung from my eyes, he had me in his arms and was telling me how I was all different again, how the change was in my eyes, in the way I felt, in the way I kissed him. I don't think I knew what the hell I was feeling by this time, I was so numb. But we were making love again...we had some coffee and sandwiches, and some more misunderstandings, and finally we crawled under the covers together and it was all right again. Made wonderful love.

During the next few days, Harry talked and talked—about his Wyoming years, about his abstract work which he felt was still some of his best, though he felt it used only one-tenth of him. "It's a world of refugees," he said, "which perhaps makes abstraction more relevant." But he felt the need to find another vision.

From my journal—February 18, 1961

Harry asked me yesterday if I couldn't stay another ten days... I feel mixed about it. I want to stay. Since it seems necessary to leave for good, I want to have those few more days with Harry, to have the pleasure of them, and the strength I think we may both get from them. I think it is irresponsible of me not to go back when I promised, and yet at the same time, I like the idea of being a little more irresponsible, of stealing a little more of what is sheerly my own desire and my own pleasure. I do terribly want to see Peter, but I have to remind myself that I will have a whole lifetime for Peter.

It's just hit me that one can't really love one's children until one loves a man. And yet, finally, one's love for a child is more necessary to live by. One may part with a man, and certainly one will part with one's child. I feel for the first time that I can give Peter sympathy and understanding and love and a sense of his own strength in a way that I can't give to anyone else.

How totally bifurcated were my feelings for Peter and for Harry! Later that same day I wrote:

Last night in bed. Beyond sex, beyond pleasure, beyond desire. The two of us coming with love. Joined, but not owned...times like that with Harry I feel unconscious of everything but the joy and the knowledge of joining...the incredible sweetness of him inside me and of me for him, and of the two of us leading each other a little further and a little further and a little further on.

From my journal—February 20, 1961

Nervous stomach. Am going to call Larry in an hour to discuss staying another week. Valentine from Peter this morning. How I ache. Harry said something last night about wishing I had Peter here and could stay. I keep going over the whole thing and the answer always comes out the same. I need my child, but I don't think Harry needs a child and I don't want him to feel responsible and I certainly don't want to be at the mercy of his responsibility. The truth is I'm afraid to stake my life on Harry.

From my journal—February 25, 1961

How complex and agonizing a week this last has been. Moments of intense joy and understanding. Others of abysmal weakness. Was supposed to have flown home today, but I'm still here.

When I called Larry to tell him that I wanted to stay another week, he said that Brigitte was leaving in a few days. I assured him that I'd get home before that, but he sounded remote and cold, which upset me, though I half hoped that the coldness was real.

Harry comforted me, said it was all right that I was leaving and the next time we got together, we would find each other more easily, it would be different, and maybe better.

A few days later, I flew home. And the journal ended.

It turned out that the coldness I'd heard in Larry's voice did have a cause. He had met someone during my month away, and he informed me that if I didn't renounce Harry, he was ready to separate. Indeed, he had met the lovely Libby who was much more on his wavelength than I. She would eventually become his second wife. Mostly, I was relieved. Larry moved out and I began to look for work because I knew that whatever child support we settled on, it would not be enough to live on. I thought Peter was too young for me to take on a full-time 9 to 5, so instead, I found a part-time job with the photographer, Jerry Cooke, figuring I could supplement it with freelance assignments. I contacted whomever I thought might help and got a temporary job writing book reports for a paperback reprint publisher. The pay was pitiful, but I could do it at home and on the subway, and every dollar counted.

I wrote long, loving, sexy letters to Harry, and occasionally got back some purple prose, along with excuses for his not writing more often. I suffered when too many weeks went by without a letter. At no point did he ask me to join him. He also made no promises. But he did come back to the States in June.

It's hard to remember much of what happened in the year that followed. At first, we saw a lot of each other. And always there was the intensity of life when I was with Harry. But we were each involved in getting divorced. I was also struggling financially. When the publishing job ended, I found another freelance gig, doing picture research for a documentary series. Late one day, after spending time in library picture collections and stimulated by the work I'd been doing, I went to Harry's studio. Some people were there when I arrived. When they left, Harry said to me, "It's amazing. When you walked in, the air, the very air changed. You made it glow." Though I was pleased, it didn't occur to me that what caused the glow was my interest and delight in the work I had been doing, nor did I realize then that to keep him wanting me, I needed to maintain a meaningful life of my own, despite his insistence on having me in thrall to him.

When we were alone, there was always the magic of his presence, and the intense sense of love and of connection. But in social situations, we both spent so much time with other people that I sometimes heard an expression of surprise when we left together. And despite his having complained when I was married that we could not socialize together, he never invited me to go with him to the parties of rich Texans and Westerners whom he was cultivating.

Norman once said to me that I had too much sense of self for a man like Harry.

Adeline, who really hit it off with Harry when she met him, sparring back and forth with him in great style, said afterward, "That's a man to have an affair with but not to marry."

And Mother, who from very few clues could make a devastatingly accurate prognosis for most relationships, knew from the moment I told her about it, that this one was not promising. When she finally met Harry, he managed to offend her. Afterward, she said, "He told me you're a very good cook. What kind of thing was that to say to me! He should have told me that I have a wonderful daughter." Poor Harry, he couldn't have cared less about my cooking, he just said what he thought a bourgeois mother would appreciate.

Gradually, I began to feel a change. I noticed that his execrable habit of always being late was becoming more pronounced, and sometimes he would not show up at all. One night when I expected Harry for dinner, Norman called and I invited him to join us. I looked forward to having them both over, but Harry never showed, nor did he call. We ate late, and Norman said grimly as he was leaving, "If you let a man treat you like that, he'll have no respect for you." I felt he was even angrier at me than he was with Harry.

Sometime in the spring of 1962, Larry and Libby went to Europe and it was agreed that Peter would spend the summer with them. To help make ends meet, I arranged to sublet my apartment. I assumed that I would move in with Harry, but as the time approached and he said nothing about it, I brought it up myself.

He said he couldn't do it because if we lived together all summer it would be too painful to go back to being alone again in the fall.

It amazes me now that I did not fault him for what a lame excuse that was, since if we wanted to continue living together, we certainly could have worked it out. As usual, I believed he meant what he said. It never occurred to me that he wanted to keep his studio open for someone else.

When and where did we finally call it quits? Maybe it was the day we were having lunch and I said, "I don't know if anyone can make you happy, Harry, but if I can't, perhaps we'd best forget the whole thing."

Facing the summer of 1962 completely alone, I was still sure that Harry and I loved each other and hoped that he would realize he could not live without me.

I sublet my apartment to several Australian law students. Before I moved, Harry called to find out where I was going. Norman and Lady Jeanne, his about-to-be third wife, were spending the month of June in Provincetown, and Jeanne had offered me the use of her apartment in the Carnegie Studios, a rather grand and uncomfortable place, which I would have to share with a gay friend of hers.

Harry thought it was a terrible idea for me to accept help from my family.

I got angry. "You have no right to tell me what to do."

"I have every right."

"Not if you're not willing to pick up the pieces."

He refused to see it my way. The implication was obvious. I wasn't being brave enough.

For the first time, I sensed a malevolence in him. He was like a child who smashes a toy he no longer wishes to play with. I thought, I'm willing to die for him, but I won't let him kill me.

Thus began my gypsy summer. The Australian boys helped me move in June. In July, I moved into my friend Barbara Solomon's apartment for two weeks while she was away. Finally, I managed to find a cheap sublet for the remaining time before I was to leave in late August for my Mexican divorce. The sublet was a minuscule one room, a quarter of a floor of a brownstone in an area near the UN that was being torn down for high rises. Even the corner newsstand disappeared. I knew no one in the neighborhood and most of my friends were out of town. Never before or after would I feel so isolated and alone.

When the telephone rang one evening and I heard his voice, I could not suppress a rush of elation. It was quickly squelched. He said he was calling to tell me that he was living with another woman.

"Why are you telling me this?"

"Because I didn't want you to hear it from someone else."

I was furious. "You think it's better doing it on the phone?"

"Let's meet," he said.

Painful as I knew it was likely to be, the thought of spending time with him was impossible to resist. I agreed.

All these decades later I cannot remember where we met or what we said to each other. Probably in a restaurant, and probably he insisted that he still loved me but did not feel our lives could ever mesh. Still, he wanted to keep me in his life. I didn't see how that was possible. I might have quoted Engels to him, that ultimately it was the actions and not the sentiments of men that made history. I understood that he could love me but not be able to accept the baggage that I carried—like Peter. But it hurt that after all, he did not love me as much as I thought I loved him.

I do remember vividly the end of that meeting. We were walking to a bus stop on First Avenue. Suddenly we were kissing. As always, I felt the magic, that we were flowing one into the other and that was the only thing that mattered. A passing car honked at us. We broke apart and continued to the bus stop. But when the bus came, he said, "Wait for the next one." The buses kept coming, and he kept holding me back. Finally, between buses, Harry decided it was time to say goodbye.

I watched him walk away. In my head, I silently cried out, "Oh Harry." I saw him stop, and I thought, I could will him back. But what's the use? He wouldn't stay.

He didn't turn around. He stood still for a minute, then walked on.

It was a long time before the next bus came. It was a perfect summer night. I looked at the beauty of the tree leaves lit by a street lamp, felt the poignancy of late summer, and thought, he has aborted my life's adventure. I also thought how typical of him to have left me standing there alone.

The future looked empty. Some women, I thought, would not have let him go. So I had to admit to myself that finally, my pride was greater than my love.

When I reached home I wrote him a letter in which I said, "All the time we were together I felt as if I were chasing you up a mountainside, dropping pieces of myself behind me as I ran. Now that it's over, I suspect I will go back down the mountain, picking up the pieces, and when I get to the bottom, I will probably never again go anywhere unless I can take all of myself with me."

Some months later I had a phone call from a woman whose affair with a painter friend of Harry's had also fallen apart. Claire was calling because having learned that her former lover was living with a much younger woman, she felt totally done in. She wanted company in her misery. She said, "Doesn't it bother you that Harry is marrying a twenty-year-old?"

I was shocked. Not because I felt diminished as Claire seemed to, but because I was disappointed in Harry. I had expected him to find someone who would be more than I was, and I didn't think a twenty-year-old could fill that bill. Other details Claire gave me increased my sense of disapproval. The young woman had a rich family and had promised Harry that though she wanted to paint, she wouldn't, at least for the next five years. So he was opting for connections and domination. I had thought him better than that.

On the other hand, I was ready to make a harsh judgment. It's only in retrospect that I can see how devoid of support he felt.

I saw Harry only once again, nearly three years later, on my thirty-eighth birthday. I've thought of it ever since as one of the more comic

243

days of my life.

Al, my boyfriend who would become my husband, had arranged a dinner party at one of our favorite restaurants, and I was meeting him beforehand at a book party for another friend. Earlier that day, a young editor, with whom I'd been carrying on a mild flirtation, had insisted on seeing me for lunch, so I'd invited him to have a drink with me at my home. He did the bartending, making us both gin and tonics. But as soon as I took the first sip of mine, I realized that he'd poured us almost pure gin. I continued to drink it anyway. Years before, I'd stopped drinking martinis after realizing that they turned me into Mr. Hyde. What was borne in upon me now was that it wasn't only martinis—it was the concentration of gin that made me nasty and aggressive. Very soon, I felt irritated with the young man. I said, not very nicely, "Why is it whenever I try to get a little under your surface you run away?"

He jumped up. "I have to get back to the office."

"You have plenty of time. Sit down."

He sat down, then looked at his watch and stood up again. "No, I really have to go," he said and left.

I was quite literally in a drunken fury, determined to get very angry with someone. Who could I diss?

Without another thought, I picked up the phone and dialed Harry's studio. It was probably his wife who answered. I gave my name and asked for him. He came to the phone.

Accusingly, I said, "It's my birthday. Why haven't you called me?"

There was a moment of stunned silence. Then he said, "Do you know my birthday?"

"Of course I do." I stated the date.

I don't remember what else I said, but it undoubtedly had a sharp, angry edge, and was so out of character that he may have become worried. Or curious. He said, "I'm coming over."

I said, "No, don't. I have to leave soon."

He said, "I'm coming," and hung up.

I suspect there was a large satisfied smirk on my face as I proceeded to dress for the evening. Applying cosmetics wore the gin off, and by the time Harry arrived, I was totally sober.

And no longer angry. He must have been bemused by the change. Our conversation was civil, even friendly. I can't remember what we talked about. Maybe it's because as we talked I just kept thinking that although I could remember how alive he'd made me feel, I didn't feel it anymore. Was I determined not to fall prey to his charisma? Or was it just gone? Finally, since I was taking a cab to my date, I offered to drop him off. Perhaps that day ended it for him too. At any rate, neither of us made any attempt to see each other again. But from then on, I was able to think of him without rancor, to think of him with gratitude for having given me a new dimension, a new intensity of feeling, and ultimately changing my life.

So why was it that his website had upset me so much? Whatever he was like now, what did it matter? It was only the past that had relevance to me. Or did all the disparities between what I had been told fifty years before and what was on the web somehow disfigure the past?

I felt I had to go back to the website and read it all, distasteful as it might be.

This time I took in the details. He'd married twice more and had five children. Though both marriages had ended in divorce, they'd lasted some years, and I was glad to know he had family. He'd continued to make his Western sculptures and paintings and had achieved some wealth, with many commissions and exhibitions, sales and awards. He'd also established his own foundry in Italy. He named all the well-known people with whom he'd had contact. He'd become a Republican, but voted for Obama. His epilepsy had continued and he'd had two brain operations in the late '90s. He said he'd gone into therapy because of uncontrollable rages. Was that why his marriages had ended? And was he suffering from brain damage rather than dementia? Had it not been for the cultish prose and the name-dropping, I would have felt nothing but sad. Like other old men that I'd known, he wanted to believe that he'd had some effect on the world.

I didn't realize the nutty lengths to which that desire led until I went back to the webpage and found another link called Writings. It briefly summarized his Mafia antecedents and horrifically abused childhood, and then went on to even crazier stuff in which he identified with a "Hairyblackhominid Satan Harry, who BECAUSE HE IS PSYCHOTICALLY WOMB ENVIOUS" killed Lucy 3 million years ago. Yes. He meant the fossil Lucy discovered in Africa by Johansen, and connecting this to the beginning of all racial violence in the world today, he felt personally responsible.

The megalomania, as well as the nuttiness, took my breath away. I remembered my momentary sense of his malevolence and realized that he'd known it himself. And he was making up an eon distant past for himself, as he had created his childhood and early life for those of us who knew him later.

How much of what he'd told me was just made up? I checked out the Norman Corwin program about the United Nations. It was narrated, not by Harry, but by Martin Gabel, and Harry's name was not even listed among the other people who had contributed.

During the war, documentaries had been made of both the Iwo Jima and Tarawa battles. The narrators were not named in the credits, but neither voice sounded like Harry's. Why did he think he had to make these stories up? It astounded me that someone so charismatic, so gifted as Harry, would create a phony past for himself. Did he never know who he was? Or did he feel that the past was not immutable, that he could treat it as creatively as he did the present, moving from moment to moment?

Perhaps our sense of connection had been so intense because it had been so unlikely. Stranger still that it had not totally disappeared. Despite fifty years of silence, there must have been some remnant thread between us. How else to explain why I Googled him that day?

Norman

Milly called the other day. Laughing a little, she said, "I just remembered how I met Norman. He was coming over with your mother and I was told that I was about to meet a genius. I was only five years old, and I didn't know what a genius was, but it sounded pretty impressive. Of course, he was only seven years old."

Suddenly I remembered that when Norman was seven and I was three, there were two events that had probably transformed our relationship for the rest of our lives.

Until that time Norman had frankly detested me. When he'd discovered upon my birth that I was not a playmate, but a baby, and furthermore he was no longer the only apple of his mother's eye, his dearest wish was to hit me and get away with it. I didn't help. I had only to see the threat in his eyes to shriek "Sto-pppp it," and my parents would come running. Norman told the story many times of the crucial event that changed the dynamic between us. Perhaps that's why I still have a vivid memory of it. Our mother had taken us to a gathering of kids where games and competitions were being held. My age group, the three-year-olds, were each given a flat dixie cup spoon and a pea, told to put the pea on the spoon and carry it to the other end of the room, maybe fifteen or twenty feet away. All the other toddlers kept dropping their peas. But I, somehow, walked all the way to the finish line without dropping mine. In other words, I won. Norman decided in that moment that I was someone to be proud of.

I think around the same time he realized how special he was. In the 1930s, the New York public school system gave the Stanford-Binet intelligence test to second graders, and Norman, at seven, scored higher than anyone at P.S.161 ever had before. Mother was told that his IQ was genius level. I'm sure she spread the word to everyone she knew, including Millie's family. Indeed, it became family legend. At some point in my childhood, she told me. I don't know if she actually told Norman, but he surely heard her boasting and realized that to her he was too special to be usurped by me.

The fact that I was physically more adept than Norman was of little consequence to anyone in the family, myself included. We never thought of physical dexterity as something to be cultivated. Physical energy got expended in the street—the boys played ball and the girls jumped rope. But what I loved most was reading. When I was in the third grade, one of my report cards came with a B in reading. Mother was outraged. She went to the teacher and said, "How can you give her a B when all she does is read?"

Books were our culture. I revered the notion of theater and music, but there was no money for Broadway or Carnegie Hall. Movies, much as we loved them, were just fun and games. Even after I started to play the piano and danced myself silly to any music I heard on the radio, reading was what I still loved most.

Norman began to recommend books to me when I was ten. First, there were the Edgar Rice Burroughs Mars novels, which grabbed me and informed my fantasy life for a year or more, and were also maybe the source of my lifelong fascination with space travel. Then came the romantic derring-do adventures of Raphael Sabatini and Jeffrey

Farnol. At twelve, I had graduated to Austen and Tolstoy and Chekhov. For my fifteenth birthday, Norman gave me two books—Melville's *Moby Dick* and *An Introduction to Psychoanalysis* by Sigmund Freud.

During our childhoods, Norman and I lived by the gender norms of the time. His friends were boys, mine were girls. I embroidered and played potsy, he played ball and built model airplanes. In the few memories I have of the things we did together, he was benign and protective, and sometimes inspiring—looking for an iced-over tennis court where we could skate (mostly we just got frozen feet), or taking me to the movies on Saturday afternoons—those four-hour sessions of two features, a serial, a cartoon, and the March of Time newsreel, sometimes stretching to five hours if we had come in the middle of a feature and stayed to see it to the end again. I have a particularly happy memory of his teaching me to do a belly flop as we sledded down a deserted street after a big snowstorm. When an occasional very slow car did show up, he would make sure I was safely off to the side. And he always included me in the Monopoly games he played with his friends. At fourteen, he got interested in girls and decided he wanted to learn to dance. So of course he got a book. I was his practice partner, and together we parsed out the diagrams for the foxtrot and the waltz. I learned all the steps, but I'm afraid he never did get the hang of ballroom dancing.

As we got older he became ever more interesting. In his teens, he was full of ideas, many iconoclastic. It was always exciting to be around him. Although I thought he was the most interesting person in my world, I was curiously smug about him. After all, he was only my brother, so I took him for granted. At the same time, I felt sure that nobody else had a brother like him.

And then, when I was twelve, he went off to college. While I was proud to have a brother at Harvard, I missed him immensely. My fantasies about Mars evaporated. Fueled by his stories of what he was doing and the people he was meeting, and also by the few movies I'd seen of college and campus life, I dreamed about his inviting me to a football game and a college dance where I would meet a wonderful boy.

Remarkably and wonderfully, this actually came to pass. In his senior year, when I was only fifteen, he induced Mother to let me come for the Princeton/Harvard football weekend and arranged for me to have a date. I fell in love, not only with the boy but with Cambridge. It was my senior year in high school and I knew then that I wanted to go to Radcliffe.

Norman had begun writing seriously at Harvard—story after story. This too inspired me, not that I thought of going into competition with him, but because him doing it made me think it was possible. He even gave me advice—write about what you know—advice he did not follow himself. His early stories were largely about people he didn't know and experiences he hadn't had. But I took his advice and at age thirteen, in bed for a week or so with a bout of flu, and having read whatever books were at hand, I decided to write my autobiography. As I remember, it was a collection of funny incidents in what at that point was my hardly hazardous life. Whatever. I sent it off to Norman. He sent it back, covered with comments and corrections, and with a note to my parents—"Mom, Dad, the kid can write."

How we reinforced each other! For a while, Norman used to joke about our Mutual Admiration Society. It couldn't have hurt that I believed his every idea. I was an acolyte. When at one point he began to advocate free love, I too began to spout support for the idea, even though, at fourteen, I had no intention of acting upon it.

He made everything seem more interesting. He expanded my sense of life's possibilities. I felt totally alive when he was around. And I think he loved having so much influence on me. Looking back, it seems to me now that he rather engineered my love affair with Jack Maher. Jack and I hardly knew each other. There had been only our date at Harvard, then a few hours in New York when he was on his way home, and the beginning of a correspondence. About to enter the Army, he wrote to Norman that he had fallen in love with me. Norman told me. I remember catching my breath. A boy loved me! What did Norman see? Delight in my eyes? Awe? Whatever it was, he jumped to the conclusion that I too was in love and said, "Shall I tell him?" Since I believed everything Norman said, I thought that I must be.

Was it his enthusiasm, his intensity, his conviction, about everything he chose to think or do, that wrapped an aura of special value around it? During the Christmas vacation of my freshman year at Radcliffe, Norman, who had graduated the previous May, was still home in Brooklyn Heights, waiting to be called into the Army, so we hung out together. He took me to Poor Richards Corner, a sad little piano bar in a small neighborhood hotel called the Franklin Arms. It was always empty, the pianist played romantic ballads, and it made me feel like I was experiencing *life*. He took me to visit his classmate George Tooker, who had a dingy studio in an old factory building on Middagh Street, just a few blocks from our home. I was speechless with awe at meeting a real-life painter. Even the neighborhood Chinese restaurant where we occasionally lunched for 30 cents, seemed special. And then one day there was the interesting conversation Norman and I had on the subway platform at the High Street station, as we waited for the A train to Manhattan. We were talking about writing and Norman said, "The problem I have is that I don't yet know how people turn out."

I was amazed. That he felt a lack in himself was surprising enough. But what most astonished (and educated) me was the notion that people change. Until that moment I had just assumed that we were all immutable.

Perhaps I did not learn it well enough. In the years that followed, I don't think I was sensitive to the ways in which life was changing him. Perhaps neither of us expected the other to change. I think maybe he kept expecting me to accept all of his ideas as gospel, and I, despite his charisma and his celebrity, thought that he would continue to be the "nice Jewish boy from Brooklyn," as he described himself in *The Armies of the Night*, the part of himself he most detested.

By the time *The Naked and the Dead* was published, and he became a celebrity, I was getting on with my own life. And I didn't want people glorifying me as Norman's sister, or demeaning me as *only being* his sister. It was many years before I realized and could accept that being Norman's sister was an ineluctable part of my persona.

My memories of the 1950s are cloudy now. The large events remain—jobs, getting married, having a son, getting not so married. There were lots of parties. Lots of drinking. For me, Norman was always there. Sometimes he lived nearby, sometimes not. We were both going through the fever and the ennui of being in our late twenties and early thirties. We assumed we were grown up, but at least for myself, I can say I wasn't very thoughtful. I still hadn't learned that people change. So no matter what trials Norman was experiencing, I still assumed that, given his extraordinary talent and the success he'd already had, he must be sure of himself. Failing to recognize the inner turmoil that his increasing volatility indicated, I instinctively insulated myself against the fallout. When his anger began to get directed at my good friends, like Adeline Naiman and Rhoda Wolf, I did not let it influence my own relationships with them.

During the couple of years in the late '50s that he and his second wife, Adele lived on Perry Street, around the corner from my home, I worked as his secretary, taking dictation and typing his letters. It was during this period that he wrote *Advertisements for Myself*. As he wrote each piece, he would give it to me to type, and for the first time, I dared to criticize him. After I had typed up his critique of all his contemporaries, entitled, "Some Quick and Expensive Comments on the Talent in the Room" I mutely handed it back to him, so appalled that I didn't know what to say.

"Well, what do you think?" Norman said.

What I *thought* was that one shouldn't treat one's fellow writers that way. What I *said* was, "You're not seriously thinking of publishing this, are you?"

"You're damn right I am."

"Norman," I said, "this is the sort of thing that shouldn't get published till after we're all dead and gone. Also, you could be sued for slander."

He was furious with me. For years after that, he used it as an excuse, whenever I criticized or questioned, to tell me I was always wrong. But he did, in fact, make some changes in the piece after I weighed in.

The problem was that he wasn't used to getting anything from me but validation, and it remained difficult for me not to give it to him. At one point he handed me some scribblings he had done, and they were so bad, I didn't know how to tell him. So I dropped off what I had typed and immediately left on a ski trip with my family. On the car trip, I told my husband, Larry, how I felt. He said, "You've got to tell Norman."

Skiing, I broke my leg. After we returned, Norman came over to commiserate, and to my horror, Larry said, "The reason Barbara broke her leg is because she didn't want to tell you that the piece she'd just typed for you wasn't up to snuff."

Norman nodded and said, "Yeah, I realized myself that it wasn't any good."

Even after this, he didn't like it when I criticized anything he wrote. When I gave him my critical notes on one of his books, he told me I was a terrible editor because I was mean (a couple of my criticisms may have been snide). At least that helped me recognize the need for some diplomacy when doing an edit.

I remained pretty dense about his inner demons and the effect drugs and alcohol were having on him. At the time, my own life was falling apart—as it seemed were the lives of almost everyone we knew. When Norman decided to run for mayor in 1960, I thought it was an absolutely terrible idea. Give up writing for politics? Absurd. I knew it was hopeless to argue him out of it, but I'm sure my skepticism was palpable. He felt he wasn't getting the support he needed from his family. His anger bewildered and worried me, but the angrier he became, the more impossible it was to reach him.

The buildup of that anger culminated, horribly, in the stabbing of Adele.

It happened at a party he organized to announce his candidacy for the mayoralty. It was one of the usual melees of friends and friends' friends and probably not-so-friendly friends and crashers, but none of the important people he had hoped to attract showed up. Larry and I left well after midnight and were asleep when the phone call came at 5 or 6 in the morning. I went to the hospital and found Norman sitting in a waiting area. Adele had been taken to surgery. I said, "Norman, you've flipped out." It seemed like the only possible explanation or excuse for what he had done and I expected him to agree with me. Instead, he got furious. And so we sat in silence for hours, not knowing if Adele would live or die. Those were certainly some of the worst hours of my life. I felt that any joy in life had ended. I could not imagine how we would go on.

The weeks that followed were grim. Norman was committed to Bellevue, and a lot of people, many of whom I hardly knew, were giving me advice. I remember one lawyer I saw said that I should get Norman committed to Dannemora, the prison for the criminally insane, and on the same day I read an editorial by Max Lerner, sounding off on the incident. I turned to Larry and said, "we may not know what it is best to do, but all these people who think they know, are just grinding their own axes. They're using it as an ego trip." We finally found a lawyer, Joseph Brill, who was calm and sympathetic (he acted as much like a therapist as a lawyer). To my relief, Norman accepted him.

Norman eventually got out of Bellevue. Adele recovered from her wound and didn't bring charges. Life went on. We partied, we laughed again. But much changed. Norman and Adele separated. And although Larry had been wonderful all through "The Trouble," I'd fallen in love with another man, and our marriage ended.

I didn't quite realize it at the time, but my relationship with Norman was different too. The love and the loyalty came back, but a certain intimacy was gone. We stopped talking about our feelings or what was going on in our lives. We never again discussed the stabbing. I think that for a while Norman felt that I had not been loyal, that in some way I had deserted or betrayed him. And I felt that in almost ruining his own life, he had somehow failed my belief in him.

All of which led to the worst fight we ever had.

It was the summer of 1962. I was in New York, working a couple of jobs. Peter was in Europe with his father. To save money, I'd sublet my apartment, expecting to move in with Harry for the next few months. Instead, we split up. So I moved from one borrowed dwelling to another until for the last month, I rented an inexpensive studio sublet near the UN, an area of the city, that at the time, was in the throes of high-rise construction. All the small businesses had closed. It was an urban desert. Worse, nearly all my friends were away. Even my boss was out of town. I spent my days alone, largely in silence.

Norman called from Provincetown one day. He needed bookcases for his new apartment in the Brooklyn Heights house he and Mother had bought and renovated. With his usual desire to make things interesting, he had designed a ceiling that sloped along one wall of the living room, and now he wanted bookshelves to line that wall. He asked me to find secondhand bookcases of varying heights to fill the space. That day. I knew it was Mission Impossible and told him I was working. He was so insistent, though, that I agreed to try. During my lunch hour, I went to a few thrift shops. None of them had any bookcases, let alone twenty linear feet in the required sizes.

Several weeks later, I went to visit Norman in the apartment and saw that there was now a handsome wall of bookshelves conforming to the irregular line of the ceiling. Norman immediately lit into me for having failed him. He had built them himself, he said, and it had cost him three weeks that he could have spent writing. For him to cast blame on me for this seemed nuts. He could easily have hired someone else to construct them, and while he resented the time it had taken, I rather suspect he enjoyed making them himself. Still, his anger kept escalating until finally he exploded and said he wanted nothing more to do with me. I burst into tears and left the house, thinking I had been disowned.

I knew, of course, it wasn't really about the bookcases. He felt I had failed him in some way a year earlier, during the months after he had stabbed Adele. Unfortunately, I didn't have any notion of how to talk to him about it.

I also didn't know that his marriage to Lady Jeanne was crumbling. For my part, I hadn't told him that Harry and I had broken up.

Several months went by in which we didn't speak to each other. I went to Mexico to get divorced and had the feeling that life as I had known it had ended and the future might be very bleak.

Sometime that fall Norman learned that Harry was gone from my life. He came to visit me and to apologize. He said that he hadn't realized what I was going through. After that, though we may have disagreed about things from time to time, we never again had a real quarrel.

In the years that followed, we both lucked out. Norman regained his talent and his brilliance. In the 1960s he wrote some of his best books. And living on my own, difficult as it sometimes was, I felt as if I had finally taken hold of my own life. While Norman's marriages kept ending, he also kept having more children, and I discovered in the summer of 1970 that one of the most enjoyable roles in life was that of aunt.

It happened in Maine. Peter and I were visiting during Norman's first summer there. I was due to leave when he had a phone call from Carol that she was pregnant. Norman felt he had to go to New York to see her and asked me to stay another few days with the kids. With only one child of my own, it seemed a bit daunting to care for another five, aged 4 to 13. I gulped but agreed.

It turned out to be a wonderful time, not only for me but for all of us. Since we knew no one else in Maine, it was a stretch to keep all my charges entertained, occupied and safe. We had two traumas—six-year-old Michael got his finger caught in the car door, and on one of our hikes, eight-year-old Kate got slashed across the face by a tree branch. But by the time I left, I felt that I was now a permanent fixture in their lives. I also had a moment of pure joy that I have never forgotten.

I had taken the kids to the Restaurant at Jordan Pond for their famous popovers. As we finished eating, they looked silently at one another and one of them then asked me if they could be excused. I had no idea of their intent but said yes. They all ran out to the lawn, which descended to the pond, and, throwing themselves on the grass, rolled down the hill. Six beautiful, laughing children. I felt as if I'd been transported to another time—maybe the years before the first World War. Glancing around the room, I saw that everyone else had on their faces the same beatific smile I imagined on my own.

Each summer after that, for as long as Norman went to Maine, I would join the family there for a week. If available, Peter would come too. I loved those times. We'd hike; we'd cook; we'd read; we'd eat. The hikes were always uphill. Danielle and Betsy would walk with me, asking so many questions that I'd get breathless with the combination of talking and climbing and beg them to stop. Norman, ever the teacher, instructed me in how to descend the cliff ladders without fear of falling—"three points of contact at all times." I was almost sorry when he gave up Maine and began again to spend whole summers in Provincetown again. But then Provincetown became even more of our family center. Al loved the friendly, unpretentious tennis club, and the visual delights that he began to photograph. After we retired, we spent whole summers there, never more than a short walk away from Norman's home, which we called The Big House. My memory of those summers is bathed in the glorious light of Provincetown on its best days. Even at the time, I knew how precious they were because they would not last forever. From the year in the 1980s when Norman first discovered he had a heart condition, I worried about his dying. I could not imagine my world without him.

So much of what we did together revolved around the family, and particularly around eating—my dinner table in the winters, Norman and Norris' huge table that filled the dining room of the Big House in the summers. Norman always sat me at his right at his table, and at mine, he would always take the seat to my left. Yet I don't remember our talking very much to each other at those meals. Mostly he held forth. When Mother was still alive, he delighted in provoking her, poking at her prejudices, and the two of them would spar with each other while the rest of us hooted with laughter. The more outrageous Mother got, and I think she did it in perfect awareness that she was playing her role, the more he would egg her on, until he'd announce to the rest of us, "She's like an old club fighter. She gets mad when you miss." It was one of his favorite refrains.

I still have a lovely memory of the unexpectedly delightful dinners we had in Provincetown in the aftermath of Hurricane Bob when the town lost electricity for most of a week. Since Al and I had an apartment with a gas stove, Norris brought over the food in her freezer and we cooked it all and ate by candlelight for the next few days.

Philosophically, by then, Norman and I had diverged somewhat. In the early '50s, after reading Simone de Beauvoir's *The Second Sex*, I had decided I was a feminist. Norman claimed he found the book unreadable, but that may have been because he never got beyond the early, somewhat turgid chapters, and so didn't grasp the significance of her concept that women experience themselves not only as subject but also as object—the Other. He always rather grumbled about my being a feminist. I'm not sure he realized how little I sympathized with the humorless ladies who beat up on him in the 1970s.

We also had very different intimations about what lies ahead and beyond. Contemplation of our infinitesimal place in the cosmos comforts me—that we can be so small and yet so complicated. Reading Lewis Thomas' *Lives of the Cell*, and thinking about what might lie beyond, I suddenly thought—perhaps this entire universe is simply a pimple on some God's ass. I am too aware of how contingent any intimation of this sort is, to take it seriously, but thinking it would amuse Norman as much as it did me, I one day presented the notion to him. To my shock, he was enormously offended. Ah, I thought, he wants to be more important than that. He often said that God was in danger of dying, and maybe we were here to save him.

Since so many of Norman's off-the-wall ideas had ultimately proved right, I never dismissed them out of hand. Consequently, I continued to ponder his take on God, eventually coming up with an even more disturbing notion than the idea of the pimple: perhaps we were actually a cancer, and God was trying to kill us off. But in the end, I didn't have the heart to present this idea to him. If he had taken it seriously, it would have made him very unhappy.

For a long time, he and I disagreed about whether fiction or fact more clearly illuminated the reality of our lives and times. But I finally came to agree with him that fiction might be the better light, since in years of research, trying to establish some facts about our mother, I had come to realize how impossible it was to know not only what happened a hundred years ago but to even agree about what happened yesterday.

There's one discussion I do regret we never had. Norman disliked television because he thought most of it (save perhaps *Charlie Rose*), allowed one only to speak in soundbites. Yet as he grew older, he grew so impatient with the slowness of other people's minds, that it became very hard to have a reflective conversation with him. I know others in the family felt the same way, and I'm sorry now that I never told him that he was forcing *us* to talk in soundbites.

Because I no longer subscribed to every word he said, Norman decided at one point that he no longer influenced me at all, and when he got wedded to a notion in this way, it was difficult to disabuse him of it. What finally did was an introduction that I wrote to an anthology of women writers that I published in 1967. There was one turn of phrase in it, which even as I wrote it, I thought, that's just the kind of thing Norman might say. My friend, Adeline Naiman, when she read it said, "You sound just like your brother." And Norman, when he read it, said with some delight, "I guess maybe I've had some influence on you, after all."

The truth is he never stopped teaching me—sometimes even inadvertently. I remember when Peter was still quite young, Norman and I were discussing Mother and for once he was complaining about her. I finally said, "Norman, one thing you've got to give her is that she really loves us."

"Yeah," he said, "and she never taught us how to deal with people who don't."

With an inner giggle, I thought, "In parenting, there's no way you can do everything right. So I might just as well relax."

That conversation also made clear to me one of the differences between us. Mother had always told me, "If they don't love you, it's their loss." That had been good enough for me. I would just walk away. But Norman expected and wanted everyone to love him.

I also have Norman to thank for my understanding of a basic existential tenet—that if you act stronger than you feel you often end up feeling as strong as you act. I was discussing with him a relationship that I found unsatisfactory. He made a suggestion as to what I might do, and I said, "Oh Norman, that's just not me." With some exasperation, he said, "Must you always be exactly who you are? Can't you sometimes act a little stronger than you feel?" At the moment, I felt somewhat put out, but I must have taken his criticism to heart, because the next time I felt mistreated, instead of pouting, I acted as if everything was just fine, and suddenly, it was.

I'm not sure why, perhaps it was a mixture of pride and caring, but once Norman became a "famous author" I was loathe to ask him for advice on my own writing. However, in the 1990s, when I wrote a memoir that some relatives and friends found interesting, I gave it to Norman to read. His reaction to the first draft was a gruff, "This is not professional. Work on it."

After the second draft, he said, "It's not there yet but it's getting better," picking out a couple of things as examples of what was wrong. By the third draft, he astonished me by saying, "This is getting good. I want to go over it with you." So we sat down one day and discussed it line by line. He had a lot of specific suggestions, most of which I couldn't use because even when I liked them, I felt they were in his voice, not mine. But he gave me one piece of general advice which flicked on the proverbial lightbulb. He said, "You can't make exposition go on too long. You have to intersperse it with narrative." Afterward, I said to myself, "Of course. Why didn't I think of that?" Going through the piece with that in mind, everything began to fall into place.

Somehow I've gotten the reputation for having done a lot of editing on Norman's books. I don't remember it that way. I did read most of them in manuscript, afterward giving him some specific notes as well as my reaction to the whole. One day, when we were discussing a new piece of writing, sitting in the bar in the Provincetown house, Norris stormed in and handed Norman a sheaf of papers. I don't remember what she said, but it was apparent that she'd discovered he'd been having an affair with Carole Mallory.

After she left the room, I asked him, "Why? Why did you do it?"

His answer was, "Life was getting too safe." Which was only one of the possible answers he might have given me. "Curiosity" might have been more accurate. "Greed" another. I can understand the curiosity.

My thought at the time was a common female reaction—How stupid men are.

I had met Mallory once and had immediately sensed that she could be bad news. While I was still at Simon & Schuster, Norman had sent her to me. She had a couple of unfinished manuscripts. I found them appalling. One was the beginning of a novel in which a woman masturbates in the back seat of a taxi for the benefit, or shock, of the driver. The other was a memoir of all the famous men she'd been to bed with. Since Norman wasn't in it, I guessed that he was trying to help her get it published in return for keeping him out of the book. But I couldn't help him. I didn't think that either book was publishable, and in any case, did not wish to be associated with them. It came as a shock to me to realize that our early efforts to bring sex out of the closet had simply fostered one more way to paint the world as mean and ugly. I didn't like what the culture was becoming. I was now a throwback to the past. I thought: I guess I'm now an old fuddy-duddy.

What I found hardest to understand was that Norman, already in his seventies, would jeopardize the wonderful family spirit that Norris had done so much to nurture. Ultimately, I think she couldn't give up either him or the family. She stayed, and I was immensely grateful that this woman that I—and all of us loved so much—remained in our lives.

While it was Norman who had made me realize that people change, I think he forgot it in relation to me. In one of our last conversations, I told him how disappointed I was when I reconnected with Jack Maher, my first love, after 60 years of silence. Norman said, "He really was the love of your life, wasn't he?"

I was startled to realize that Norman had a romantic notion that my life had been blighted because I had not married Jack.

My God, I thought, Norman doesn't know me at all. Astonished, I said, (again the soundbite thing), "Oh no. Al was."

Only later did I think of how and what I should have said, a reply that would have captured more accurately the nuances of love and of our lives.

It should have gone like this—

"No, not Jack. Al was."

A beat, and then,

"Or maybe, Harry was."

And after another pause,

"Or perhaps, Norman, you have been."

I don't think that would have surprised him. But I think he would have been pleased that I too knew how important he had been to me.

Acknowledgments

I must first thank my good friend, Mike Lennon, whose love of the written word infuses both the appreciation and the criticism with which he blesses one's work. He read all the memoirs and gave his kind attention to each.

It is a relief to realize that I can be genuinely grateful to my final editor, Peter Alson, since he is my son. That we both survived the process with love and respect intact is due to his forbearance, his writerly sense, and his excellent editorial skills. Since he has also mastered the process of publishing, his ability to turn my memoirs into an actual book doubles both my admiration and my thanks.

Many friends and much of my family have also cheered me on. Because the memoir "Spain, 1948" was published in the October 2000 issue of *The Hudson Review*, there were many who made complimentary and encouraging comments, too many to name, but I thank all of you who did. Especially appreciated was an extraordinary letter that Pearson Marx wrote me about the piece. David Michaelis and Tom Piazza had many suggestions, both editorial and where to publish.

My daughter-in-law, Alice O'Neill, read many of the memoirs, which then benefited from her dramatic sensibility and her intelligence. My good friends, Rhoda Wolf, Adeline Naiman, Susie Seligson, Chris Huneke, and Jillen Lowe read one or more of the memoirs in early stages, which helped me to improve them. Several of my nieces read some of the memoirs as I wrote them, and gave me valuable feedback. Susan Mailer always zeroed in on anything she thought invalid. Kate Mailer kept pressing me to publish. Betsy Mailer's extensive notes were sensitive, thoughtful, enthusiastic, and often surprising, making her a writer's dream reader. The interest of my cousin, Jim Rembar, in the history of the family that we share, spurred me into writing about what I had learned. I also thank Ike Williams, whose professional acumen combined with the interest he expressed made me think that people other than family and friends might enjoy what I have written.

My delighted thanks go to my niece, Danielle Mailer, for allowing me to use the painting she made for Al's 80th birthday for the cover of the book, and to Rachel Ake for her beautiful design. Finally, the good humor and caring companionship of my nephew, John Buffalo Mailer, has helped to keep me cheerful throughout these years, despite our increasingly worrisome world.